CLAREMONT

A HISTORY

CLAREMONT

A HISTORY

Geoffrey Bolton and
Jenny Gregory

University of Western Australia Press

First published in 1999 by
University of Western Australia Press
Nedlands, Western Australia 6907
for Claremont Town Council, Claremont

National Library of Australia
Cataloguing-in-Publication entry:
G. C. (Geoffrey Curgenven), 1931–   .
Claremont: a history.

Bibliography.
Includes index.
ISBN 1 876268 38 7.
ISBN 1 876268 39 5 (pbk).

1. Suburbs — Western Australia — Claremont — History.
2. Claremont (W.A.) — History. I. Gregory, Jenny (Jennifer Anne). II. Title.

994.11

Front cover: full image and detail from Edwin Summerhayes *View from Freshwater Bay*, watercolour and pencil, 25.2 × 35.5 cm
Collection, Art Gallery of Western Australia, presented by Mr G. Summerhayes 1976.

Back cover: William Habgood *Scene on Melville Water near Perth, Western Australia, 1842*, watercolour, 16 × 22.4 cm
Rex Nankivell Collection, NK6582, T1970, National Library of Australia.

Produced by Benchmark Publications Management, Melbourne
Edited by Allan Watson, Perth Editorial Service, Perth
Designed by Sandra Nobes, Tou-Can Design Pty Ltd, Melbourne
Typeset in 11½ pt Sabon by Lasertype, Perth
Printed by Frank Daniels Pty Ltd, Perth

Contents

Preface

THIS BOOK HAS been many years arriving. Not long after the Claremont Museum was established in 1975 I agreed to write a history of the suburb. An appointment to London and other distractions arose, and it is only in 1998, with the centenary of the Town of Claremont, that after years of guilty procrastination the manuscript has been completed.

In good postmodern fashion, there is no single authorial voice. During the delay Jenny Gregory was awarded her PhD by The University of Western Australia for a thesis entitled 'The manufacture of middle-class suburbia: the promontory of Claremont, Nedlands and Dalkeith within the City of Perth, Western Australia' (1989). Generously she agreed to my suggestion that much of the Claremont section of her thesis should be incorporated into this history on a basis of co-authorship. It is my belief that our somewhat different styles and approaches complement one another well, and result in the production of a more rounded history.

It must be acknowledged also that much of the early research for the project was undertaken by a team coordinated by Angela Chaney, its members being Val Prescott, Elizabeth Vinnicombe, Elizabeth Jones, Jane Gascoine and Joanna Sudlow, and that Juliet Ludbrook and Chester Andruskewicz acted as research assistants in the final stages and Geraldine Byrne for help and advice. Incorporated into this history are two eyewitness accounts of Claremont: one by Sir Paul Hasluck for the 1930s and the other by Professor George Seddon for the 1960s, and these are reproduced by courtesy of Mr Nicholas Hasluck and Professor Seddon respectively. We are also indebted to Brian Pope for advice and information on Claremont's nineteenth century postal services.

Sally-Anne Hasluck gave much of the original impetus to the project, some of which is based on her research while curator of the Claremont Museum. She has continued to encourage its progress with a decently critical eye, and her

Preface contribution is valued. Annie Smith did a fine job of word processing a somewhat messy manuscript, and we are grateful to her. It is also a pleasant duty to thank the Claremont Town Council for financial support and for good-humoured patience while awaiting this history, and to acknowledge the efficient and courteous help of Clare-Frances Swindells and the staff of the Claremont Museum.

Geoffrey Bolton

This has been a most agreeable collaboration, and I thank Geoffrey Bolton for the suggestion that I become involved in the project. Thanks are also due to colleagues in the Department of History at The University of Western Australia, especially Professor Tom Stannage, for their support and encouragement in the development of an earlier incarnation of part of this work as a doctoral thesis. At that time too the support of my husband and children was, as ever, inestimable. Debts of gratitude are also owed to staff of the Battye Library, to Helene Charlesworth for assistance with the illustrations, and to the people of Claremont who generously shared their memories with historians in the hope that future generations would come to understand a little of life in Claremont during the early twentieth century. We also thank University of Western Australia Press's expert team: editor Allan Watson, designer Sandra Nobes, typesetter Keith Feltham, with production managed by Janine Drakeford and assisted by Anthea Wu.

Jenny Gregory

Acknowledgements

The authors and publishers are grateful for permission from the following to include photographs and other illustrative material:

Battye Library—pages 23 (621P), 29 top (1869P), 50 (4387B/8), 58 (1805P [Thomson], 62159P [Burnside], 5484P [Edwards]), 61 (103c/61), 64 bottom (4975B/13), 66 (5549B/26), 69 (top 3024B/1, bottom 20393P), 72 top (20394P), 77 (1289P), 86 (3024B/2), 90 (3055/B31), 97 top left (4387B/57), 102 (388B/31), 104 (3395B/35), 113 top left (6347B/7), 114 centre left (5422P), 125 (78c/c34), 133 (4387B/42A), 134 (24194P).

Christ Church Grammar School Archives—page 156.

Claremont Museum—pages 22, 29 bottom, 30, 33, 35, 47, 48, 49, 51 bottom, 52, 53 bottom, 55, 56, 58 (Poole), 62, 63, 64 top, 71, 72 bottom, 74, 85, 87, 88 except top left, 89, 92, 95, 96, 97 top right and bottom left, 98, 99, 101, 103, 111, 113 except top left, 114 except centre left, 121, 123, 124, 131, 132, 142, 143 bottom, 144, 152, 153, 157 top, 159, 164, 165, 169, 171, 179, 180, 181, 197, 202.

National Library of Australia—page 7 and back cover.

Phototone Colonial Library—pages 107, 147.

Public Record Office, London—page 20 (9780/52).

Scotch College Archives—page 160.

Acknowledgements   West Australian Newspapers—pages 27, 34, 40, 51 top, 53 top, 88 top left, 93, 97 bottom right, 120, 122, 128, 143 top, 146, 148, 157 bottom, 170, 174, 175, 182, 195, 200.

The photograph of E. V. H. Keane on page 58 is taken from W. B. Kimberly, *History of West Australia: A Narrative of her Leading Men*, and those of A. B. Kidson and J. E. Richardson from Thiel & Co., *Twentieth Century Impressions of Western Australia*.

Several of the Battye Library photographs are from the A. Stirling Collection: 4387B/8, 1289P, 4387B/57, 6347B/7.

The following donors to the Claremont Museum are noted in respect of the illustrations indicated: Mr D. Abraham (page 114 bottom left); Mrs Chapman (page 63); Claremont Yacht Club (page 99); Cordin family (page 121 top); Mrs P. Cullen (page 96 left); F. G. Doepel (page 33); Mrs Flynn (page 113 bottom left); Mrs V. G. Forsyth (page 114 top left and top right); Miss E. Goode (page 49 top); Mrs J. Hopkins (page 47 right); Mrs A. Kidd (pages 30, 179); Mrs Knight (page 88 bottom left); Mrs Lefroy (pages 48 left, 52, 72 bottom, 113 centre left); Mrs F. Locke (page 53 bottom); Loreto Convent (page 159); W. and E. Lucas (pages 114 centre right, 132, 165, 171 top); Mr D. Middleton (page 143 bottom); Mrs O. Middleton (page 144); Mr R. Potter (page 131 top); Mr A. Prior (page 113 centre right); Mrs C. Quin (page 113 bottom right); Miss S. Rose (page 124); Royal Western Australian Historical Society (page 95); R. Sandover (page 48 right); Mr C. Shellabear (page 111); Mrs E. Smith (page 103).

Imperial to Metric

one inch = 2.54 centimetres
one foot: 12 inches = 30.5 centimetres
one yard: 3 feet = 0.91 metre
one mile: 1,760 yards = 1.61 kilometres
one perch: 30.25 square yards = 25.3 square metres
one acre = 0.41 hectare
one pint = 0.57 litre
one gallon: 8 pints = 4.55 litres
one ounce = 28.4 grams
one pound: 16 ounces = 0.45 kilogram
one ton = 1.02 tonnes

Monetary

one penny (1d) = 0.83 cents
one shilling (1s): 12 pence = 10 cents
one crown: 5 shillings = 50 cents
one pound (£1): 20 shillings = 2 dollars

In comparing monetary values it should be borne in mind that the currency has inflated forty- to fifty-fold over the past century. To write 'five shillings (50 cents)' would give a false impression. In the 1890s £1 was worth roughly $100 in today's money and the value of a penny was on the high side of 40 cents. By the 1920s and 1930s the equivalents would be about $75 and rather more than 30 cents.

Chapter I

The Mooro and the Colonial Agitator

JOHN BUTLER WAS the man who was given the whole of Peppermint Grove and fretted obsessively throughout his career in Western Australia because he could not have Claremont.

He was thirty-five years old when, in 1829, he left Liverpool to try his fortunes at the Swan River Colony. He claimed kinship with the Butlers who had been earls of Ormonde and great men in Ireland since the Norman times, and his high temper and aspiring imagination did not make the claim ridiculous. It was not surprising that he was enticed by the beguiling propaganda that followed Captain James Stirling's all-too-brief survey of the Swan in a calm and mild season at the end of summer in 1827. Stirling's colony was envisaged as a society free of the convict taint of New South Wales and Van Diemen's Land (Tasmania) and fit for the transplantation of a land-owning gentry of the traditional English stamp. It was calculated to appeal to those on the edge of gentility in the old country: substantial farmers and merchants and halfpay officers left over from the Napoleonic wars. With a wife, Ann, three young children and a bachelor brother, Archibald, John Butler was typical of those optimists who threw in their lot with Stirling.

Of these seekers after opportunity the Butlers were among the more prosperous. They came on his own brig, the *Skerne*, and their goods and possessions made up virtually the entire ship's cargo. This included a plentiful supply of farm implements and tools, casks of seed wheat and barley, two boxes of vines, a sufficiency of provisions (including twenty gallons of rum and twenty gallons of brandy, a nice anticipation of the colonial thirst) and a considerable quantity of household furniture, including three cases of books. Their livestock comprised six sheep, a cow, five pigs, four goats, twenty fowls and ten dogs. Two married couples and a single man came with them as potential farmhands.

Having arrived on 17 January 1830, John Butler wrote five days later to the Colonial Secretary, Peter Broun, and submitted an inventory of his possessions.[1] Until the passing of the 1831 Lands Act, which established a price for the purchase of Crown Land, a settler's entitlement to free land grants in Western Australia was based on the amount of capital and number of employees that the person introduced into the colony. The assessment of capital took into account the value of household goods as well as livestock and liquid assets. John Butler's assets were valued at £997, and after allowing an extra £203 for his family he was given entitlement to select a total of 16,000 acres (about 6,500 hectares).

Butler lost no time in following up this opportunity. The somewhat hectic scramble for land during 1829 had subsided a little, leaving some strategically placed unoccupied blocks at no great distance from Perth. On 11 February 1830 he made two applications. He asked for 3,000 acres on the south side of the river near the present Causeway, perceiving that there would soon be a need for a major road on the southern side of the river along the line of what we know as Canning Highway. He also requested a grant 'on Fresh Water Bay in the NNE bight to run back toward Captain Currie's House in Melville Water': in today's terms the southern part of Claremont and the adjacent portion of Dalkeith. This grant he desired 'for the purpose of immediately getting my Family into something like a Winter's habitation'.[2]

Fresh Water Bay (or as a later generation knew it, and it will be convenient to use this form from the start, Freshwater Bay) was an attractive site, even to the

---

KEY TO FACING MAP

1 A & B Beereegup: the place of banksias

2 Curveergaroup: unknown

3 Dyoondalup: the place of white sand where the *dyoondal* plant grows

4 Gabbee Derbal: body of estuary water

5 A & B Galbamaanup: the place of black water

6 Jenalup: the place where the feet make a track

7 Karbamunup: the hill that is haunted, as punishment by the Waugul, due to Nyungars breaking a food law

8 Kar-katta(up): the place of the sandbanks where crabs or spiders are located in Freshwater Bay

9 Katabberup: the high ground where the *byer* (zamia) grows

10 Mandyari: unknown

11 Mandyooranup: the place where young initiates visited, located near rocks at the upper entrance to Freshwater Bay near Point Resolution

12 Mandyooranup: a fishing spot and marketplace

13 Maningyup: the place of vegetables

14 A & B Minderup: the place for alleviating or causing sickness (hot springs)

15 A & B Nyeergardup: the place where fresh water flows from the top of the cliff (*nyeera* = above) through limestone to its base (*gardup* = below)

16 A & B Waugul Mia: the Waugul's home

17 *Compass directions*
Katta moornda (East—blackheads or the Black Hills)
Minung (South—type of vegetable)
Woordal (West—ocean)
Yabaru (North)

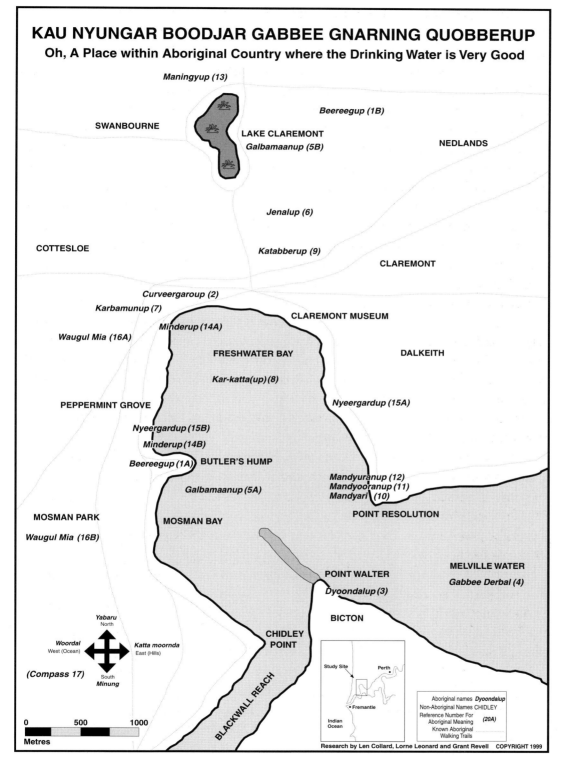

KAU NYUNGAR BOODJAR GABBEE GNARNING QUOBBERUP
Oh, A Place within Aboriginal Country where the Drinking Water is Very Good

Maningyup (13)

Beereegup (1B)

SWANBOURNE

LAKE CLAREMONT

Galbamaanup (5B)

NEDLANDS

Jenalup (6)

COTTESLOE

Katabberup (9)

CLAREMONT

Curveergaroup (2)

Karbamunup (7)

CLAREMONT MUSEUM

Minderup (14A)

Waugul Mia (16A)

FRESHWATER BAY

DALKEITH

Kar-katta(up) (8)

PEPPERMINT GROVE

Nyeergardup (15A)

Nyeergardup (15B)

Minderup (14B)

Beereegup (1A) BUTLER'S HUMP

Mandyuranup (12)
Mandyooranup (11)
Mandyari (10)

Galbamaanup (5A)

MOSMAN PARK

MOSMAN BAY

POINT RESOLUTION

Waugul Mia (16B)

MELVILLE WATER

Gabbee Derbal (4)

POINT WALTER

Dyoondalup (3)

BICTON

Yabaru
North

Woordal
West (Ocean)

Katta moornda
East (Hills)

CHIDLEY
POINT

(Compass 17)

South
Minung

BLACKWALL REACH

Study Site

Perth

Aboriginal names Dyoondalup
Non-Aboriginal Names CHIDLEY
Reference Number For
Aboriginal Meaning   (20A)
Known Aboriginal
Walking Trails

Indian
Ocean

Fremantle

0   500   1000

Metres

Research by Len Collard, Lorne Leonard and Grant Revell   COPYRIGHT 1999

Chart of Aboriginal place names, based on map prepared by Len Collard, Lorne Leonard and Grant Revell for Claremont Museum. Site positions are approximate, as names refer in some cases to large regions rather than specific points. (Note: in the Nyungar language, 'up' means 'the place of'.)

- 3 -

eye of a newcomer habituated to the gentle contours of English scenery. Aborigines knew it as a campsite of plentiful spring water, abundant fishing and the resort of a constantly changing skein of waterfowl—duck, teal, pelicans—to say nothing of numerous land birds in the forests of jarrah, marri and tuart that swept back along the gentle slopes surrounding it. They buried their dead there: a woman who was interred about the time when the Americans were signing their Declaration of Independence was to be uncovered in 1970 during excavations for the foundations of a multi-storey residential building, the likes of which neither Aborigines nor Americans could have envisaged in 1776. Vlamingh's men trudging through the bush in the January heat of 1697 had been delighted by the spectacle when they came on the western shore of the bay, and astonished by the black swans, which were so contrary to tradition and the laws of nature that there could be no other name for the river than the Swan. Other navigators had praised the attractiveness of the bay, last and most fatefully Captain Stirling in 1827.

In applying for the land at the head of Freshwater Bay, Butler was not merely responding to the charms of a pretty site. Judging from the large quantity of liquor he brought with him from England he probably had it in mind to turn innkeeper, and this must have strengthened his interest in securing land strategically sited on a main road leading out of Perth. For his purposes the head of Freshwater Bay would be a prime location because it was almost exactly half-way between Fremantle and Perth. Besides, while there were a number of possible routes for a road between the two towns, any route on the north side of the Swan would have to pass along the ridge immediately north of Freshwater Bay. Any detour further inland would bring the track to an obstacle in the form of a low-lying hollow densely covered with tea-tree and blackboy and inclined to be swampy in winter.

Part of Butler's strategy included taking up a block on the small permanent lagoon at the south end of the hollow. In later years this lagoon, with the rising of the watertable, would flood most of the hollow to form what we know as Lake Claremont. For more than a hundred years it was known as 'Butler's Swamp', the only memorial to the district's first pioneer. In Butler's own time and for the rest of the nineteenth century, there were only a couple of permanent waterholes in the hollow, though in the more remote past it had been the site of a lake larger than at present. To the eye of an early settler the spot promised a patch of fertility contrasting agreeably with much of the neighbouring sand-dune country.

It was not to be. Governor Stirling's officials granted the Butlers their other requests, so that Archibald entered into possession of 2,000 acres south of the river and John got his Eagle's Nest Farm, 972 acres in the neighbourhood of the current boundary between Victoria Park and South Perth. But he was not given the land at the head of Freshwater Bay. The Surveyor-General, John Septimus Roe, simply stated that 'the neighbourhood is not open for selection'.[3] A discerning judge of country, Roe probably anticipated Butler in seeing the potential of the Freshwater Bay site, and with Stirling's concurrence decided against alienating it from the public domain in case of future need. No specific reasons were given to Butler, but in compensation he was granted 250 acres on the west side of Freshwater Bay in the vicinity of a stubby peninsula known to the Nyungars as Beereegup. The white people called it Butler's Hump.

John Butler named his grant Prospect Place. Its frontages flanked the Perth–Fremantle road as well as the river, so it was a convenient site for an inn for the travelling public, and indeed at the end of April 1830 he was chosen from among several competing applicants for the grant of a licence. During the next twelve months he built a stone house—some accounts say of two storeys— 'rigged out with native mahogany' and known as the Bush Inn, or sometimes as the Halfway House. For the rest of the 1830s it was a landmark for travellers. But Butler was not content with it: his heart was set on the block at the head of Freshwater Bay, for which he already had a name picked out—Aston Bank. Beyond that he coveted the lagoon at Butler's Swamp. And he intended to keep trying for it all.

In December 1830 he wrote to Roe asking for an accurate survey of the boundaries of his property. In November 1831 he put in an application for ten acres at the lagoon, but without result. In March 1832 he made a fresh request for land at the head of Freshwater Bay, bearing from a spot on the shoreline that he called, perhaps with a flash of irony, Mokbeggar Point. In August he renewed his claims: 300 acres at Prospect Place, 320 acres at Aston Bank and twenty acres at the lagoon, which he now called Experiment Town—could he have already been using it as a nursery without waiting for the land grant? Once again he was disappointed. Prospect Place was already his, but the two other blocks were still reserved for government purposes. Perhaps the authorities had been casual about clarifying the situation to Butler, who by this time had worked up a powerful sense of grievance. In December he took his troubles to the Executive Council, alleging that he had not been allocated a quarter of the land to which he was entitled, and was again told that he would have no more in the Perth district.

Probably he was too touchy and quarrelsome to know contentment. He made a powerful foe in Major Irwin, who stood next to Stirling in seniority among the Colony's officials. The dispute arose over the proper charge for a flat-bottomed boat that Butler hired to Irwin early in 1831 for the purpose of freighting timber and limestone. This not only gave rise to two years of desultory litigation but also made Butler a persistent critic of the use that Irwin and other officials made of the labour of soldiers of the 63rd Regiment. Privates were paid only one shilling and sixpence daily, and this put their employers at a great advantage over settlers who had to hire labourers on the open market at five shillings a day. In April 1831 Butler addressed a letter of complaint about this practice to the Secretary of State for Colonies in London, Viscount Goderich, who of course took no notice of it.[4]

Butler's love of a lawsuit had no end. He sued one Alfred Waylen over a petty debt, and went to law with the Colonial Engineer, Henry Reveley, over another trifling dispute. He had a running feud with Adam Armstrong, who lived at Dalkeith, on the other side of Freshwater Bay. He accused Armstrong of stealing his pigs and sued him for the loss of a rudder from a hired boat—despite Armstrong's plea that the mishap occurred during the rescue of three men from drowning. As if he had not problems enough of his own, he set up as an agent to appear before the courts on behalf of other litigants, and won one or two cases but lost more.

He covered himself with ridicule in May 1833 when, ignoring a great deal of advice, he insisted on suing the urbane and well-connected Judge-Advocate, W. H. Mackie, for £2,000 for saying he was 'beastly drunk' when he called at Mackie's house one evening. The evidence of respectable eye-witnesses soon showed that Mr Mackie's language was not unreasonable, for if Butler was not drunk he was at best incoherently angry. Once more he lost his case, and the *Perth Gazette* reported it for all to read. Undeterred, Butler continued to frequent the law courts, concluding the year 1833 by bringing a charge of libel against the *Perth Gazette* and yet again coming off unsuccessfully.[5]

It was surprising that Butler had so much time and energy for litigation, as he was kept busy enough with his property. As an innkeeper he must have been regarded as providing a useful public service, for in June 1832 and again in 1834 he was exempted from the payment of licence duty. There was certainly need of assistance to passing travellers, such as the postman on his way to Fremantle who found an exhausted sheep that had strayed from a drover's flock near Butler's Swamp and carried it two and a half kilometres to the Bush Inn—for which trouble he received two shillings.

Despite occasional travellers Prospect Place was a somewhat isolated out-post, and so it became a main point of contact between the settlers and the local Aborigines. Before the coming of white settlement, Butler's property had formed part of the traditional country of the Mooro, who occupied the region between the north bank of the Swan and the sea, stretching north to a point not far short of Lake Joondalup. According to an estimate of 1837, the Mooro numbered only about twenty-eight, but this must be an underestimate: Jane Currie's diary of

1831 records about forty of the same group camped at Matilda Bay alone.[6] Larger parties were seen in the neighbourhood of the Bush Inn during the first few years of white settlement. This was not surprising. The freshwater springs that gave their name to the bay made for an attractive campsite, and the Swan estuary environment, with its plentiful game and fish, must have been as desirable a habitat to Aborigines as it was to their white supplanters. Lacking European concepts of private property, the Mooro continued to range the country around Freshwater Bay after Butler's arrival, prepared if possible to co-exist amicably with the white newcomers but not at all unwilling to help themselves to the pigs, sheep and other introduced animals that competed with the native fauna on which their livelihoods depended.

South of the river, Archibald Butler had to contend with the more formidable presence of Midgegooroo of the Beeliar and his son Yagan, and the spearing of his servant Anyon Entwhistle in August 1831 was one of the first major acts of Aboriginal hostility. Despite his brother's unhappy experience, John Butler evidently favoured moderation and conciliation. He was aware that his conduct would probably influence the attitude of the Mooro towards travellers on the Perth–Fremantle Road, and in October 1831 Governor Stirling officially approved his attempts to maintain friendly relations.

Butler did not reckon with the traditional Aboriginal summertime custom of burning off the country to flush out game and regenerate new growth. When on 17 February 1832 some of the Mooro fired the stubble around the Bush Inn he assumed they meant to destroy and plunder his property. 'However,' he informed Stirling, 'by the great exertion of a few steady men that I have on the place, we succeeded in turning the course of the fire around the enclosure', and a providential sea breeze did the rest. 'The Natives still continue about,' he added, 'and by their manoeuvres are evidently meditating some hostile act, having twice broken into my people's cottage.'[7] He requested the protection of soldiers, but Stirling replied that help could be given only if there were grounds for fearing a premeditated attack by the Aborigines. This was no great use, and provoked an angry retort from Butler, reinforcing his low opinion of the military. He was stung into protest again on 25 May when a large party of Mooro chased away three of his men and speared three pigs—the last survivors of a herd of thirty whose loss Butler blamed on the Aborigines with some help from his neighbours. This time a small patrol visited Prospect Place and went away again without encountering any Aborigines.

Yet in December the Mooro were back again, showing in Butler's opinion their accustomed confidence and a friendly disposition. When they had stayed three weeks Butler wrote to the authorities asking for rations to distribute to them, as his own stock was running somewhat low; but by this time relations between the white authorities and the Aborigines were turning sour, and the Colonial Secretary refused the request as he thought no good would come of it. In January a party in the neighbourhood of Armstrong's property fired on a group of Aborigines without provocation, and a few days later Butler renewed his application for rations, pointing out that the Mooro were flocking to his place because they knew they would not be molested there.[8]

It was an uneasy summer for the outlying settlers around Perth, with Archibald Butler's property ablaze with summer fires and John Monger seriously thinking of quitting his holding at the lake that bore his name. Within a few weeks the tensions south of the Swan would lead to the execution of Midgegooroo and the murder of Yagan. Yet despite his exposed isolation, despite his combative temper towards his fellow whites, John Butler contrived to keep the peace with the Mooro. Their leader, Yellowgonga, though a greatly respected warrior, was described as 'most distinguished for a humane peaceable disposition', and this no doubt accounted for the absence of open conflict in the neighbourhood of Freshwater Bay.

In July 1833 he wrote that the Aborigines were frequently about his house, and since it was imprudent to treat them harshly they were a great tax on his resources. At the end of the year he was requesting the authorities for a boat to remove a sick Aborigine, and when the sick man's companions left Prospect Place they presented Butler with a large heap of firewood. So far so good, but at the end of February there was a fracas:

> On Sunday last several natives were assembled in the neighbourhood of the Bush Inn, the half way house between this and Fremantle, and offered some molestation to Mr Butler's son by setting their dogs at the goats and other stock he was tending in the bush. The boy hurried home for assistance, when Mr Butler and one of the soldiers stationed at his house went out and overtook the natives. They were told to stand aside in order to admit Mr Butler's shooting the dogs, which had been set upon, and worried the cattle; this they appeared reluctant to do, and on the soldier endeavouring to enforce it, his gun was nearly wrested from him, and a spear placed at his breast. The injury he received, however, was but trifling. Mr Butler was prevented from offering any resistance—had it been the desire of the natives to have committed a violent assault—the ball which he had put into his gun being too large, and having stuck halfway. So much for this eventful history, which has been magnified by report into a dreadful and alarming encounter with the natives.[9]

It was to be Butler's last major adventure with the Mooro. Before long their traditional way of life would be too disrupted for them to have the spirit for such a reaction. But it would be John Butler who was the first to go.

Archibald Butler quit the Swan River Colony in August 1833, but John still had energy to fight his battles, and in the same month he exchanged a crossfire of correspondence with the Colonial Secretary renewing his claim for the land at the head of Freshwater Bay in recognition of his substantial improvements to his property. After another refusal his tone was reproachful: 'It appears to be the determination of the Local Government to oppress such settlers as they may judge to be obnoxious to them'. And he complained that settlers were kept in the dark about their rights of land selection. Undoubtedly Butler was an outsider among the snug inner circle of Stirling's advisers. Roe, Irwin, Reveley, Broun—he quarrelled with them all, and in their eyes he was 'the Colonial Agitator', a crank and a troublemaker in a community which to this day has seldom taken kindly to cranks and troublemakers. His Irish background may have told against him; his impulsive and undignified pugnacity certainly did.

And he was running short of funds. In March 1834 he made an expedition fifty-five kilometres north of Perth to search for cattle pasture, but failed to find any attractive country and was forced to make the most of his dwindling current assets. Although during 1834 he went on pressing his requests for Aston Bank and Butler's Swamp, trying for the last time when Stirling returned from a two-year absence in England, even Butler could see that the game was up. Towards the end of the year he began to put his affairs in order and to plan a move away from Freshwater Bay. In January 1835, the *Perth Gazette* carried an advertisement:

TO BE LET

The Bush Inn at Freshwater Bay, and 300 acres of good sheep pasture land, with two Lime Kilns, good Stone Quarry, and excellent fishing. Six acres of land on the Property are in tillage—and vegetables may be grown during the dry season on part of the land which abounds in freshwater springs.

Also
Cattle and Sheep will be taken on ley at the 'Eagle's Nest Farm' on the Flats near Perth, where there is the richest pasturage.
Apply to the Proprietor, Mr John Butler, or to W. N. Clark, Solicitor.[10]

Shortly afterwards, Butler leased Prospect Place and the Bush Inn to Thomas Bailey, a survivor from Thomas Peel's ill-starred venture who had been farming land at Matilda Bay on the present site of The University of Western Australia.[11]

Butler's move to Eagle's Nest Farm failed to restore his fortunes. He might have chosen to move to the Avon Valley, where he had an undeveloped holding of about 6,000 acres, but he had apparently had enough of the Swan River Colony. In October 1835 he sailed for Sydney on the *Zebra*, leaving his wife to sell up much of their remaining possessions. Duly advertised in May 1836, these included a great variety of useful tools, a well-bred young horse, a Devonshire bull, a small flock of goats and a few pigs that had somehow survived. In September Ann Butler and the children sailed on the *Truelove* to join her husband. When he died in October 1841 at the early age of forty-seven, the family were living in Macquarie Place in Sydney, where his widow was subsequently reduced to taking boarders and advertising genteel apartments to let.

Butler's failure meant that the land that would later become Claremont remained largely undisturbed bush during the 1830s and 1840s. It was too far from Perth or Fremantle to attract much attention from timber-getters and its soil was thought too sandy for successful farming except for the pockets of black-soil tea-tree country to the east and south of Butler's Swamp. Interspersed with poorer patches of scrubby country there were significant stands of jarrah (then known as Swan River mahogany), marri, tuart and a profusion of banksia. In the spring the sandy soil was covered with spider orchids and other wildflowers, and in summer groups of Mooro that had dispersed into hunting parties during the winter had been in the custom of coming together in larger groups. Although they were sorely harassed during the first years of colonial settlement—their leader, Yellowgonga, was probably speared in a payback killing in 1837, and official policy favoured trying to settle the remnant of his people in semi-permanent camps—some of these traditions seem to have survived until the very end of the nineteenth century, well after the process of suburbanization had begun in Claremont.

Freshwater Bay before the coming of the settlers had been a country of plenty for the Mooro. Catomore has listed its advantages:

> The abundant freshwater springs on the northern and western sides of the bay would have been camp sites for groups engaged in harvesting crabs and swans and spearing tailer and herring in the river shallows in summer and autumn. The surrounding bush had abundant Banksia and Marri trees from which nectar laden flowers could be picked in autumn for flavouring water at festive group gatherings. The bush also had snakes, goannas, brush turkey, and birds of various kinds, all of which were harvested as a source of protein (including eggs). Decayed trees and blackboy stumps in the bush also yielded bardi (moth or beetle larvae), a favourite food.[12]

Much of this could have been said of any part of the south-west coastal plain, but the future site of Claremont was specially favoured. It had a river. And at Butler's Swamp it had an unfailing source of paperbark for shelter and reed rhizomes, a carbohydrate staple that was ground and made into damper.

The Mooro carried the map of this country in their minds, but little of their knowledge survived to be passed on to the settlers. It is noteworthy, though it should not be surprising, that modern Claremont's major thoroughfares—Stirling Highway, Princess Road, Gugeri Street, Victoria Avenue—follow closely the tracks used by the Mooro. While this is partly due to geography—a modern engineer no less than an Aborigine on foot will follow the routes dictated by the terrain—it also reminds us how much the first generations of settlers relied on Aboriginal practical knowledge in coming to terms with the country. We do not know nearly enough about the locations of special importance to the Mooro. One was Katabberup, the place of plentiful zamia nuts, dominated by a huge old tuart. This was a landmark for meetings and corroborees, just as it became a landmark for the settlers marking out the first Perth–Fremantle Road, which was the ancestor of Stirling Highway.[13]

Daisy Bates recorded a story of Karbamunup, the hill where the modern Stirling Highway leaves Claremont and takes a south-westerly curve before descending into Cottesloe. The legend says that some children disobeyed the food laws, and the Waugal living in the hill became so angry that it came out and ate all the men, women and children living in the vicinity except one pregnant woman. There was a peculiarly shaped stone near the foreshore which was supposed to be this woman, and both stone and hill were forbidden ground. No spears could be sharpened by night in this locality, nor must green wood be burnt or meat cut up or broken in the wrong way. Within recent times, wrote Daisy Bates in 1912, an Aborigine named Bimba broke a crow's wing in the wrong manner, and that same evening his dog's back was broken. Still more recently some North-West Aborigines, unaware or uncaring about the story, held a corroboree on Karbamunup Hill, and two of them were killed by the Waugal.[14] Such were the stories passed down among the surviving Mooro as they continued to walk the as yet unalienated land between Butler's Swamp and Freshwater Bay or, as they would have said, between Galbamaanup and Minderup.

Meanwhile the years dawdled quietly in the backwater of the Swan River Colony. Travellers from Fremantle to Perth, unless they chose to go the whole way by river, were ferried across the water at Preston Point. From the disembarkation point, somewhere near the present border separating North Fremantle and Mosman Park, a ride of three kilometres along the coastal sandhills and a similar distance through gently undulating country with a thick covering of jarrah and redgum brought one to the Bush Inn, where Bailey now ran a well-regarded hostelry. Passing along the line of what are now Palmerston and View Streets, the route followed the ridge through Claremont before diverging through the current localities of Karrakatta and Shenton Park and the north-west corner of Kings Park to enter the town centre by way of Mount Street.

As the track through the jarrah was tediously sandy, and as Bailey's was the only inn along the road, its custom was steady, though modest, until 1838. In that year, following an unpleasant mishap in which that prominent citizen Lionel Samson took a tumble from his horse while negotiating the Perth–Fremantle road, it was decided to alter the route. In consequence the section of the road between Leighton Beach and the present site of Claremont shifted a few hundred metres west and north, leaving the Bush Inn out of the main traffic. Bailey went off to Mahogany Creek in 1838 making over his lease to an elderly tailor named Robert Powis, who appears to have let the inn licence lapse within a year.

Powis and his family settled in contentedly. Governor Stirling, having nursed the colony through to survival and made in the process a tidy profit through his land speculations, left for England in 1838. In his place came the sober and methodical bachelor John Hutt, under whose guidance the economy of Western Australia kindled into modest growth. Along the Swan the flat-bottomed boats

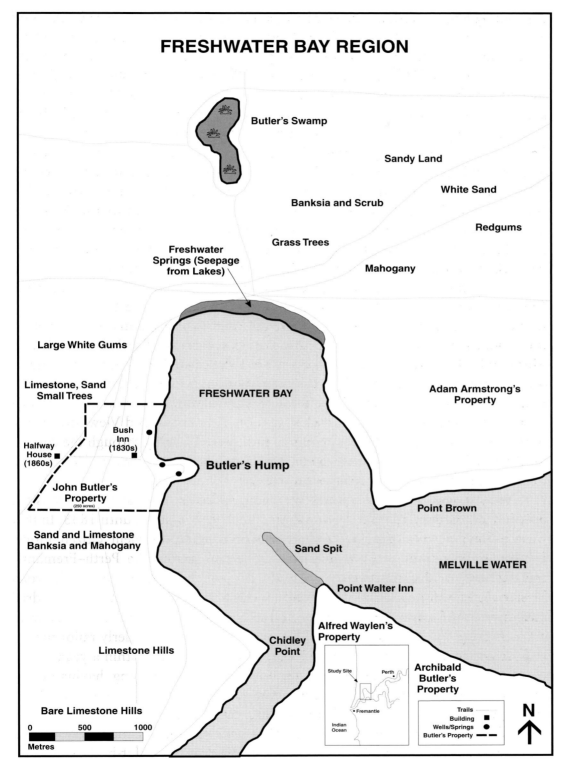

FRESHWATER BAY REGION

Butler's Swamp

Sandy Land

White Sand

Banksia and Scrub

Redgums

Grass Trees

Freshwater Springs (Seepage from Lakes)

Mahogany

Large White Gums

Limestone, Sand Small Trees

FRESHWATER BAY

Adam Armstrong's Property

Bush Inn (1830s)

Halfway House (1860s)

Butler's Hump

John Butler's Property (250 acres)

Point Brown

Sand and Limestone Banksia and Mahogany

Sand Spit

MELVILLE WATER

Point Walter Inn

Chidley Point

Alfred Waylen's Property

Limestone Hills

Archibald Butler's Property

Study Site

Perth

Bare Limestone Hills

Fremantle

Indian Ocean

Trails
Building ■
Wells/Springs ●
Butler's Property

0   500   1000
Metres

N

Freshwater Bay region, mid nineteenth century. The Bush Inn of the 1830s is Butler's original establishment; the Halfway House of the 1860s (now the Albion Hotel) was a completely distinct enterprise run by the Briggs family. Map prepared by Lorne Leonard and Grant Revell, 1999.

sometimes carried cargoes of wool bales bound for the export market, and among the taverns of Fremantle free-spending whaling crews bore witness to the prosperity of Western Australia's first offshore industry.

The leading citizens of Perth set up a bank and, when that was absorbed by a Sydney-based competitor, founded another and triumphantly drove their rival out of business. The law courts where John Butler so often argued in vain were now housed in a handsome little Georgian building, and there was talk — resulting in action in 1840 — of building a causeway across the islands at the eastern end of Perth Water, thus providing a direct route to what was once John Butler's Eagle's Nest Farm. In St George's Terrace, where the easterlies stirred the dust in summer and the winter rains turned the footpaths to slop, they planted young cape lilac trees to give an ampler shade than the native eucalypts.

Robert Powis sought no part in public life. His great hobby was the cultivation of his aloe. How he obtained it one can only conjecture, but by cherishing it sedulously and building a shelter to 'preserve the blossom from the frequent and powerful winds which prevail in this quarter' he produced a plant forty feet high which came to bloom in the summer of 1842. Such a blossom, he was sure, was 'one of the grandest sights that this Colony can, or perhaps ever will again produce', and he threw his garden open for those members of the public who could afford a shilling admittance. It must have been a simple, placid community whose citizens would travel miles through the summer to Freshwater Bay to watch the aloe bloom.[15]

His easygoing existence was shattered in June 1847 by the unexpected arrival in Fremantle of Ann Butler and her daughter, returning to Australia after a trip to England. Without troubling to visit the property, she advertised Prospect Place for rent. Several weeks passed without a tenant offering, and in September she determined to make a visit, having heard that Powis was in possession and 'wasting the place and furniture'. There was no meeting of minds. According to Ann Butler, Powis was very abusive and doubled his fists at her. Surprisingly, she took no further action for over two years.

Powis feared ejection so little that in 1848 he managed to scrounge the means to acquire a flat-bottomed boat and set up his two sons in business cutting and delivering banksia firewood. In February 1850 he unwisely wrote to Ann Butler advising her that he intended to vacate the property in May and asking her to present his two sons with some of the furniture. She refused. Some time later an Aboriginal woman informed her that Powis was conveying a large boatload of articles from Freshwater Bay to Perth. Finding the old Bush Inn at Prospect Place stripped bare, she went with a constable to Powis's new residence and discovered her missing property there. Court proceedings followed. Powis was found guilty of theft, but in consideration of his being an old colonist he was awarded the light sentence of six months' hard labour.[16]

Little good came to Ann Butler from her victory. She remained in Perth a few more years, at times apparently accompanied by one of her sons. In 1849 her daughter married Horace Samson, a member of the Fremantle merchant family and himself a government draughtsman with some claims to fame as a water-colour painter and designer of some of Western Australia's first postage stamps. In 1854 he moved to a similar post in Victoria, where both his wife and his mother-in-law joined him. Ann Butler lived on until 1886, holding on to Prospect Place as an absentee owner. By the time she died the first news of gold was arousing Western Australia, Perth was shortly to experience its first boom and property values were beginning to stir out of their long stagnation. But the Samsons were too old and too long out of Western Australia to pay much attention to their inheritance. The lawyer George Leake persuaded them to sell the estate to a syndicate comprising himself, Alexander Forrest and the surveyor Charles Crossland, and in 1891 they subdivided the area into what was designed from its beginnings to be the prestige suburb of Peppermint Grove.[17]

This development had some importance for Claremont. As a planned precinct, Peppermint Grove competed, on the whole successfully, for the hallmark of acceptability as the most affluent of the western suburbs. Claremont, having previously aspired to that eminence, became a more varied community. But it was possible for Peppermint Grove to grow in this way only through the accident of having remained locked up throughout Ann Butler's long life. Had John Butler gained his heart's desire of obtaining the future site of Claremont as well as Peppermint Grove, the whole neighbourhood of Freshwater Bay would have been preserved until the nineties in one great parcel, and the shape of the later development of the area might well have been considerably different.

Chapter II

Pensioner Settlement

FOR AN OLD colonist such as Robert Powis, the experience of going to prison might not necessarily have seemed a crushing disgrace. Many resorted to odd expedients during the makeshift early years of Western Australia in order to make a living, and a number of old colonists fell foul of the law only to recover eventually and win respectability for their families.

The sting of imprisonment in 1850 lay in the fact that for the first time Western Australia's convict population was being increased by the transportation of wrongdoers from the British Isles. Consequently all the social distinctions of earlier years were swallowed up in the great gulf between 'bond' and 'free', and Powis was on the wrong side. He had the misfortune to be sentenced within weeks of the arrival of the first shipload from England on the *Scindian*, which anchored on 2 June 1850, exactly twenty-one years after the colony's establishment as a community free of the convict taint. This proud boast was now to be abandoned, thanks to a happy coincidence between the clamour of the Fremantle merchants and the Avon Valley landowners for a cheaper and less independent work force and the need of the British authorities for a home for the convict outcasts recently rejected by the other Australian colonies. For the Freshwater Bay district, however, the coming of convict transportation marked the beginnings of growth.

Convicts required guards, and the British Government had plenty of old soldiers. It was now thirty-five years since Waterloo, and—still under the command of the aged Duke of Wellington—the British Army was stagnating. One means of providing for deserving veterans was to establish them on small allotments in various suitable British colonies, where they might be called on to act as a reserve force for police duties. Pensioners, as these semi-retired soldiers were called, had already been established in Van Diemen's Land before 1850. When the need arose for convict guards in Western Australia, there was no difficulty in recruiting a company of fifty-four veterans who, in return for their pay during the voyage of the *Scindian* and free passages for their wives and families, were willing to volunteer for service. They were to be the first of nearly 1,200 pensioner guards who came out before convict transportation was discontinued in 1868.

At first it was intended that after their arrival in Western Australia the pensioners would be paid at a daily rate only while actively engaged on guard duty, or if required to defend the community against foreign foes or local disturbances of the peace. Otherwise they would be free to seek employment for wages:

> It being considered more advantageous for the Pensioners and their families that they should supply the demand for labour, than attempt settling on land of their own, no grant of land has been promised them, but if they acquire money to purchase it in the interior, there will be no objection to their settling there, even though the distance should prevent them from serving as enrolled Pensioners.[1]

Second thoughts were more generous. The British Government was prepared to recommend that the pensioners be established in village settlements with ten-acre blocks on which they could maintain themselves and their families.

The British Government intended that these village settlements should be close to either Perth or Fremantle, and thus—as so often—fixed upon a plan without considering the inconvenience for the men on the spot. As Governor Charles Fitzgerald pointed out, politeness almost concealing his exasperation, the Western Australian Government had no land in that vicinity:

> The country in and about Fremantle, for miles around, consists of nothing but barren ranges of sandhills or rocky eminences, with a scanty herbage, giving little promise that it would make to the husbandman any return for his labour.
>
> In the neighbourhood of Perth the possessions of the Crown are equally worthless. Situated in South Perth, on the opposite side of the river, are a few vacant allotments, thickly wooded, consisting of sand and swamp, these have been declined as hopeless to clear, much less to cultivate.[2]

Nevertheless on 5 July 1850, five weeks after the arrival of the *Scindian*, Fitzgerald visited the pensioner guards' camp and informed them that he would give each of them ten acres. They would hold it on a nominal lease for seven years, and then it would become their own if they worked it properly. Each man would have an advance of £10 to begin with, and the convicts would clear their land.

Fitzgerald had no idea how these promises would be put into effect. On 18 July he was still thinking of purchasing two absentee-owned properties on the south side of Melville Water, one of them the 2,000 acres belonging to Archibald Butler, who was believed to be living in London. But at some point within the next few days — and it is surprising that it had taken so long for the idea to occur to anybody — attention fell on the Crown reserves at the head of Freshwater Bay for which John Butler had contended so persistently and unsuccessfully. Perhaps Ann Butler's lawsuit against Robert Powis had brought it to mind, for John Septimus Roe was still Surveyor-General. At any rate by 24 July the Controller-General of the convict establishment, Captain E. G. Y. Henderson, was recommending Freshwater Bay as the only locality suitable for the purpose.

Henderson was spurred by a petition from the pensioners themselves. Their spokesman was Andrew Gordon, a corporal of the 40th Regiment with a clerk's skills and a ready instinct for plucking at his readers' sympathies. He wrote:

Honourable Sir,
Your humble petitioners most humbly shew that they are most anxious to accept of the boon or grant of land of 10 acres offered to them by the Government... Your petitioners likewise shew that they are men who fought, bled, and conquered — also, who gained honours for their Queen and country, in various parts of the world, at the same time undergoing vicissitudes and privations of a long-contested campaign, consequently, from the nature of the above-mentioned trials...their health and strength cannot be equal to that of other men who have not been exposed to such hardships.

Your petitioners also shew that their sole object in coming to this colony was in the hope of bettering their conditions, and, if possible, to make themselves and families a permanent home. Fortune, however, is a fickle goddess, and cannot be relied on; the slender thread of life may be cut away before the expiration of seven years, and it would be heartrending to all of your petitioners to consider at their last moments that their long-cherished (wives and children) hopes had been frustrated, knowing that they were going to leave their families without a home, and probably in no better condition than when they first entered the colony; therefore it is particularly on that account your petitioners memorialize your Excellency, hoping you would be so kind as to allow the land to become their own property after the expiration of two years, instead of seven, which has already been spoken of...

Should your Excellency deem it expedient to comply with petitioners' requests, they will always endeavour to gain your esteem by following good example, which is so well calculated to inspire them with industrious pursuits. May God grant you never to know sorrow, but long to live in health, prosperity, and glory, surrounded and supported by a grateful and admiring people, is the humble prayer of your Excellency's

Most dutiful and most devoted servant,

(Signed) A. Gordon

On behalf of Pensioners[3]

This eloquence had its effect. On Henderson's recommendation it was decided that, if a pensioner's widow and family remained on their land, it would become theirs at the end of seven years as if the grantee were still alive.

In the end pensioner settlements were established both at Mill Point in South Perth and at Freshwater Bay. The South Perth settlement soon failed because of the unsuitable nature of the country. At Freshwater Bay, Roe reported the completion of survey by the end of August 1850. Doubtless it was at this time that the survey line that was to become the axis of the district was plotted north from the head of Freshwater Bay along the line of today's Bay View Terrace and Davies Road. The area of good soil around Butler's Swamp was divided into eighteen lots of 9.5 acres each. Today this area is bounded by Davies Road on the east, Shenton Road on the south and Servetus Street on the west. In addition twenty half-acre lots were marked out along the shore of Freshwater Bay between the present intersections of Victoria Avenue with Bay View Terrace and Bay Road, the lower end of Chester Road representing the halfway mark. Each pensioner was to have one of the half-acre lots on the waterfront as a residential block and one of the larger allotments at Butler's Swamp for cultivation.

The half-acre lots were allocated as follows, numbering from west to east with Lot 1 at the Bay View Terrace end:

1. Andrew Gordon, Corporal, 40th Regiment
2. Michael Stokes, Private, East India Company Artillery
3. Robert Lindsay, Private, 2nd Queens Regiment
4. Moses O'Keefe, Private, 44th Regiment
5. Henry Herbert, Private, Royal African Corps
6. John Kingdon, Private, 43rd Regiment

Plan showing pensioners' lots at Butler's Swamp and on Freshwater Bay, 1851.

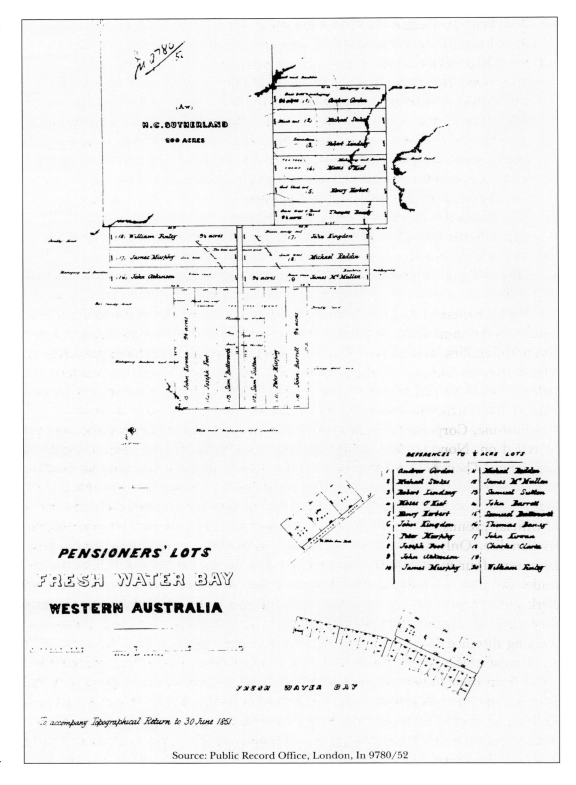

7. Peter Murphy, Private, 31st Regiment
8. Joseph Foot, Private, 76th Regiment
9. John Atkinson, Private, 2nd Dragoon Guards
10. James Murphy, Private, 19th Regiment
11. Michael Reddin, Sergeant, 61st Regiment
12. Thomas McMullen, Private, Royal Artillery
13. Samuel Sutton, Private, Royal Marines
14. John Barrett, Private, 61st Regiment
15. Samuel Butterworth, Acting Corporal, Royal Artillery
16. Thomas Bandy, Private, 98th Regiment
17. James Rourke, Private, 27th Regiment
18. Charles Clark, Private, 40th Regiment
19. Not Allocated
20. William Finlay, Private, 97th Regiment

Each of these men also drew one of the lots at Butler's Swamp, though not always in the same order. All were between forty and fifty years of age, married and with families, and all were pensioner guards from the *Scindian* except Bandy, who arrived in October on the *Hashemy*. So chance threw together nineteen old redcoats who, from fighting Queen Victoria's wars on three continents, would pioneer the district that became known as Claremont.

Fortune, Corporal Gordon had written, was a fickle goddess and could not be relied on. None of the nineteen pioneers of Freshwater Bay was to make an easy living. They had no capital to tide them over the lengthy period while their blocks were cleared and brought into production, and Governor Fitzgerald's hint that the clearing would be undertaken by convicts was somehow lost in the limbo of official promises. Few of the old soldiers had prior experience of farming in civilian life. Only four were described as farm labourers; three were general labourers, four were semi-skilled (two porters, a groom and a cook), three had trades (a tailor, a painter and a shoemaker), and two had white-collar skills (a clerk and a teacher). The pensioners had to earn enough for subsistence while they developed their blocks, whereas their holdings were beyond convenient walking distance to daily employment in Fremantle or Perth. By the autumn of 1851 most of the Freshwater Bay settlers were spending more than half the week away from their homes because of work. Some volunteered for spells of guard duty. Others sent their wives into the town to work as washerwomen for two shillings or half-a-crown an hour while they remained at home clearing their blocks, but their willingness to live on a woman's earnings was seen as a mark of indolence by those in authority.[4]

Pensioner guard
cottage, Victoria
Avenue, 1890s.

Because of their poverty, few of the pensioners could build substantially. The majority, wrote one observer, 'were compelled to shelter themselves in a very indifferent manner'. The biggest cottage along Pensioners Terrace (now Victoria Avenue) belonged to Henry Herbert. Here on occasional Sundays an Anglican clergyman used the house for Divine Service, and here in 1851 with the aid of a £10 subsidy his wife, Anne, established a small school for the neighbourhood's children, having had some experience as a regimental schoolteacher when her husband served in the Royal Africa Corps. But on the whole Freshwater Bay's early progress was disappointing. Governor Fitzgerald decided to allocate no more blocks there, but instead to settle pensioner guards who arrived later on one-acre lots at North Fremantle, where they had easier access to job opportunities.

Captain John Bruce, the officer in charge of the pensioner guards, was anxious that the Freshwater Bay settlement should not fail, and looked after his men with what Fitzgerald described as 'an almost fatherly care'. He found that because of the high cost of provisions many of the men were spending all their time cutting firewood for a living. This should have earned them between three and four shillings a day, but the market for firewood was controlled by two contractors who supplied the government establishments at Fremantle. These contractors claimed to be short of ready money and paid the woodcutters with provisions at their own valuation, so that the pensioners were almost always working to pay off debts. With mingled feelings, Bruce noted that the two contractors were ticket-of-leave men. No doubt it was good to see ex-convicts reforming to become little capitalists capable of operating a truck system, but Bruce wrote, 'It is with deep regret that I see the pensioners of Freshwater Bay surpassed by them in intelligence and enterprise'.[5]

Captain John Bruce, officer in charge of pensioner guards.

Hoping to improve the prospects for the woodcutters, Bruce grubstaked three of them for £30 to purchase a large flat-bottomed boat, with the aid of which they built up a promising business freighting limestone from Point Resolution at the east end of Freshwater Bay to Fremantle. Unfortunately their main customer was an innkeeper who allowed them credit against their earnings. One of the partners took to standing drinks for all his mates, and when the other two found out that his hospitality was being debited to the joint account they quarrelled and broke up the partnership. The boat was sold and it was only after a lapse of time that Bruce got his money back. Nor did he succeed any better with a proposal that the pensioners should be allowed to fence two acres of their properties for cultivation on condition of surrendering four unimproved acres to be made available for selection by other pensioners. In vain he exhorted them to grow vegetables for the highly priced Fremantle market, and pointed out how James Gallop, although at least two miles more remote from Fremantle, made £200 a year or more by the sale of produce from his property, which in former years had been Adam Armstrong's 'Dalkeith'. The Freshwater Bay settlers, he complained, simply lacked initiative.

Bruce may have been a little harsh. Most of the Freshwater Bay settlers had so little margin for investment that fencing was out of the question and the improvement of unfenced properties full of hazards. Gallop brought to the improvement of 'Dalkeith' capital and experience accumulated over half a lifetime in the colony. All the same, Bruce might have been right when he argued that men with years of service in the army were less likely to develop good business habits than the better class of ex-convict. In any case, he said, 'the elite of the pensioners, as regards education and good sense, are employed in situations of trust in the convict establishment, police force, and commissariat department...'[6] —rather a damning comment on the poor old Freshwater Bay settlers.

Freshwater Bay could not be expected to thrive until communications improved. For freight the river remained the main highway for many years, though its sandbanks and shoals were often an impediment and the journey was slow. The main road from Fremantle to Perth was still deplorable, a mere sand track through thick bush for most of its length. When the convicts came, one of their first tasks was to be its improvement, and in 1852 work began on the section now known as Mounts Bay Road. A convict depot was established at Point Resolution, at first under canvas, until in 1862 a substantial limestone building was erected as quarters. Confusingly, this location was also sometimes known as Freshwater Bay. Today all that survives is a pair of aged but still prolific olive trees.

In the July and August of 1853 the authorities in charge of the convict system were confronted by a minor crisis. Two convict ships, the *Robert Small* and the *Phoebe Dunbar* arrived at Fremantle almost simultaneously. Disease was rife on both, and the prison accommodation in Fremantle was strained to the utmost, so the decision was taken to set up a number of temporary out-stations. Freshwater Bay was an obvious site, as guards could sometimes be drawn from among the pensioners settled in the district, and the convicts could be put to work on the Perth–Fremantle road. It would not even be necessary to accommodate them under canvas. A wooden depot capable of accommodating eighty men in hammocks could easily be provided: it had been budgeted for Albany, but Albany was a long way distant and the need at Fremantle was urgent. It may have been built of local jarrah, but had possibly been prefabricated and brought from England; we cannot be certain. So it was that in September 1853 a convict depot was established at Freshwater Bay.

The depot, with its well, was situated near the modern site of the Claremont Police Station on Stirling Highway. A track meandering south-east through the bush emerged at the Freshwater Bay foreshore at the east end of the pensioner allotments. None of the present streets in Claremont would appear to follow its route, although Goldsworthy Road was sometimes considered as replacing it. This meant that the district now had three possible centres of gravity: the convict depot on the Perth–Fremantle road, the farms at Butler's Swamp and the pensioner allotments on the foreshore. The pattern of growth would depend on whether the river continued to be the main artery of commerce or whether the upgrading of the road between the colony's two main towns would divert traffic to the neighbourhood of the depot.

It took a considerable time for the road to be improved. Convict gangs were at work in the Freshwater Bay district consistently during the 1850s and 1860s quarrying stone for road metal and felling timber for wooden blocks. One account states that much of the area now occupied by Karrakatta Cemetery was cleared of timber for road-building purposes. By 1857 about seven kilometres of the highway were metalled from North Fremantle towards the Freshwater Bay district. At this point the number of men available had fallen off to the extent that there were seldom more than twenty convicts at the Freshwater Bay depot. On the other hand an increasing need was felt for an invalid depot for ticket-of-leave men, some of whom fell victim to the prevailing curse of ophthalmia ('sandy blight') while others succumbed to various forms of psychiatric illness, often as a consequence of drink.

In 1855, the Controller-General Henderson, wrote:

> The immediate proximity of Freshwater Bay Station to headquarters, and its being sufficiently removed from towns to prevent a too frequent access, might perhaps recommend it as peculiarly eligible for the purpose. Upon the question of its relative salubrity the principal medical officer can best pronounce.[7]

The medical report was evidently favourable, and from 1857 to 1859 Freshwater Bay became an invalid depot. After being disused for a period, it reverted in 1861 to its old status as quarters for road gangs. An outcamp was formed in 1858 at Sutherland Bay (now Matilda Bay, near the current site of The University of Western Australia) for hard cases who had been re-convicted.

The convict depot at Freshwater Bay must not be depicted as a felons' hell, ruled by the lash and curbed by the leg-iron. Time and again the prison authorities commented with almost bemused wonder at the lack of trouble and the good behaviour characterising the Freshwater Bay convicts. 'The men', reported Superintendent Thomas Dixon in 1856, 'have worked on the road peaceably; and although no armed guards have been placed over them, either day or night, no attempts to escape have been made.'[8] This good conduct does not seem to have been the result of inspiring leadership. The first warden in charge of the depot was reprimanded for an undignified altercation with a subordinate and removed from his post in October 1853—but he was back in a few months, for good staff were scarce. For day-to-day supervision reliance had to be placed on 'trusties' selected from among the convicts themselves, and Henry Johnston, Frederick Judd and Joshua Ratcliff earned themselves early tickets-of-leave by the fidelity with which they carried out their duties. Ratcliff had been sentenced to transportation for life for murdering a policeman, and it may be that his rehabilitation came more easily in the 1850s than it would have in the late twentieth century.

Religion does not seem to have been the clue to the convicts' good behaviour. An Anglican clergyman visited the depot whenever possible on Sundays; Bishop Salvado, on behalf of the Roman Catholics, gained permission to send a chaplain among the out-stations in 1854, but five years later his colleagues were requesting financial help because it had not been possible to man such outposts. Most effective of all seems to have been the Congregational layman Henry Trigg, who ministered regularly during the later 1850s to the Freshwater Bay depot.

Those who could read had access to a library, but the authorities were often worried because the convicts preferred light fiction to works of more improving character. In other respects their rehabilitation seemed to depend on a strict respect for routine, from the first bell in the morning—which summoned the convicts to rise immediately, fold their bedding neatly and wash properly—to the evening grace after supper. Their meals were utterly predictable: ten ounces of bread, one ounce of treacle if available and a pint of sugared tea for breakfast; fourteen ounces of meat, twelve ounces of potatoes and four ounces of bread for midday dinner; supper as for breakfast, but with a little less bread. Balance was achieved in their diets by the substitution of lime juice for tea sometimes during the summer and two rations weekly of vegetable soup.

And yet this routine produced few outbreaks of indiscipline: between 1854 and 1861 only three cases of wrongdoing have been found. On a fine spring day in 1854 two ticket-of-leave men from Freshwater Bay went into Fremantle and helped themselves to a lifeboat to cross the river. Apparently they had no intention of escaping, but their unauthorised cruise landed them back in the main gaol at Fremantle. In 1859 two convicts were punished for spreading scandalous reports about a third. There was a more serious incident in 1861, when seven miscreants killed and barbecued a heifer valued at £3, the property of Sergeant Crowdy, but they were caught and, after a good deal of bureaucratic correspondence, the Government agreed to refund the Sergeant for his cow.[9] It was all very low level crime, and against it must be set the performance of the convict gang at Matilda Bay, which hurried to the rescue of one of their warders when he was buried in an accidental landslide—and these were the hardened offenders who were serving time for second convictions. Those who find high drama and the origins of social tension in aspects of our convict past will find little to satisfy them in the Freshwater Bay depot. But of course the mere presence of so many transported felons was in itself a cause of deep uneasiness to the respectable families of Western Australia.

Under the somewhat parsimonious Governor Kennedy, progress on the construction of the Perth–Fremantle road slowed. From 1853 to 1865 there was a regular mail service, with the mailman from Perth and the mailman from Fremantle exchanging their loads under the shade of the Halfway Tree, a little to the east of the convict depot at a spot known to the Nyungar as Katabberup. A big old tuart that could be identified two kilometres away, the Halfway Tree was a grand landmark, thirty metres high and a metre and a half in diameter. This revived a service that had run for a few years in the late 1830s, since when it had been found easier to transport the mail by river. The quality of the road was still so poor in places that the Perth mailman was said to remove his boots and wear

Contracts for Fresh Meat.

THE Assistant Commissary General will receive sealed Tenders (*in triplicate*) until 12 o'Clock, on Thursday, the 15th January next, for the supply of such quantities of

Fresh Meat (Beef or Mutton).

as may be demanded during the period from 1st April 1852 to 31st March 1853, inclusively, for the use of Her Majesty's Troops, Pensioners on duty, Her Majesty's Ships or Vessels, or hired Transports, or Convict Ships, or other Government or hired Vessels, also the

CONVICT ESTABLISHMENT and HIRING DEPOTS at FREMANTLE, NORTH FREMANTLE, FRESH WATER BAY, MOUNT ELIZA, and PERTH.

All deliveries are to be made at the expense of the Contractor.

Proposals may be made, either for the whole of the Services collectively, or for any one or more Services or Stations separately.

The Tenders are to be marked on the envelope "*Tender for Fresh Meat,*" and they must state the prices in Sterling, in words at length, per 100 pounds Avoirdupoise, and be accompanied by a letter, signed by two persons of known property, engaging to become bound with the party tendering, for the due performance of the Contract, in the several Sums stated against each Service respectively, or the several amounts in the aggregate, provided one party supplies the whole, namely, £1700 : if for the Supply of Her Majesty's Troops, Pensioners on duty, Her Majesty's Ships or Vessels, or hired Transports, or Convict Ships, or other Government or hired Vessels ; if for Perth and Mount Eliza £400; if for Fremantle £800; if for North Fremantle £100; if for Freshwater Bay £100.

Payment will be made monthly, upon production of Receipts from the proper Officers for the quantities delivered, in Specie or in Bills at thirty days' sight, on the Right Honorable the Lords Commissioners of Her Majesty's Treasury, at Par, at the option of the Assistant Commissary General.

The conditions of Contract may be seen on application at the Commissariat Offices at Perth and Fremantle, and at the Offices of the Resident Magistrates throughout the colony.

The attention of Parties tendering is directed to the Form of Tender hereunto annexed, in which all Tenders must be must be made, or they will not be attended to.

Contracts for Flour.

NOTICE is hereby given, that the Assistant Commissary General will Sealed Tenders (*in triplicate*) at his Office, at Perth, until 12 o'clock on THURSDAY the 15th JANUARY next, for the supply of such quantities of

20 and 12 per Cent. FLOUR

of unquestionable quality and warranted to keep sweet and good for four months after delivery, as may be required for Her Majesty's Service in this Colony, during the period from 1st April, 1852, to the 31st March, 1853.

ESTIMATED QUANTITIES.
Number of Sacks of 200lb each :—

	20 ℔ C.	12 ℔ C.	
Fremantle	700	1230	
North Fremantle	70	200	
Freshwater Bay	35	100	
Perth and Mount Eliza	300	200	NOTE.—It is, however, to be distinctly understood that such number of Sacks as may be required at each Station, whether in excess or short of these quantities, will only be delivered or received.
Guildford	100	200	
Toodyay	100	200	
York	100	200	
Bunbury	100	200	
King George's Sound	230	430	

The Flour is to be delivered into the Commissariat Magazines at the Stations above mentioned, subject to the above stipulations, in three portions, viz. on the

1st April, 1852,
1st August, 1852
and 1st December, 1852

them around his neck rather than risk damaging such a valuable item of working-man's apparel on the rough road.

The arrival of Governor Hampton in 1862 gave a new impetus to road-making. Hampton was a martinet of the old school with a Van Diemen's Land background, but he was a considerable builder and the Perth–Fremantle road stood high on his list of priorities. Rebuilt in limestone in 1863, the Freshwater Bay depot was capable of accommodating road parties of up to forty men; beside it stood a small two-room house for warder's quarters. At the same time another party was sent to Point Resolution for quarrying, and presumably some of this stone was carted by teams to the labourers on the Perth–Fremantle road. The sections of the road that had not been metalled were paved with circular wooden blocks, known as 'Hampton cheeses', and given a limestone topping.

In 1868 the postal service was upgraded to a four-wheeled, two-horse mail van which took passengers. This might have suggested the need for liquid refreshments at the halfway stage between Fremantle and Perth, but a pub would not be encouraged near the convict depot and it was left to an enterprising old Indian army soldier named Briggs to set up what was described as 'a very small sort of Irish "Sheebeen"' at a point where the present Cottesloe Shopping Centre was to develop, not far from John Butler's original Bush Inn. Briggs's colonial beer was famed for 'a headache in every glass', but a young English migrant travelling on the mail van noted that 'everybody had to go in for his six penny worth of headache'.[10]

With a greatly improved road link, the future was assured for the pensioner guards who still held their land grants in the district, and despite Captain Bruce's misgivings most of them hung on to their holdings with surprising tenacity. Of the original grantees, Foot and Kingdon died before the end of 1852 and John Barrett became totally blind, later moving to South Australia. Four others—Bandy, Butterworth, Reddin and Rourke—abandoned their holdings, some to go to more promising situations. Contrary to Bruce's expectations, the men of education did least well. John Kirwan, steward and clerk to the Convict Establishment, applied in February 1851 for the blocks abandoned by Rourke and Butterworth. He was a sergeant who won high praise from the magistrates in 1852 for his activity and intelligence in tracking down an escaped convict, and by 1853 he was prospering enough to engage ticket-of-leave men on his property—the first of the pensioner guards to become an employer. Then at the end of the year he made off for South Australia and forfeited his land. Probably he would have done better for his family by staying in Western Australia, as he ended his days running a modest 'eating house' in a small country town and his sons remained labourers. Andrew Gordon, who so movingly argued for the right of old soldiers to provide for their wives and families, went off to New South Wales in 1857 leaving his own wife and family to government charity. Eventually nearly one-third of the pensioner guards managed one way or another to 'go East'.

Eleven of the original nineteen at Freshwater Bay—Atkinson, Clark, Finlay, Herbert, Lindsay, McMullen, the two Murphys, O'Keefe, Stokes and Sutton—stuck it out for seven years until they received the freehold of their properties. Within a few years five of them had sold their holdings, three immediately purchasing land in other districts. Perhaps they persevered at Freshwater Bay simply in order to secure freehold land so that they could sell it and thus raise the capital to buy property elsewhere.

It is significant that a few more pensioner guards joined those who remained. Charles Tranailles, who earned his good conduct medal as a private in the 29th Regiment serving in the Punjab, exchanged his North Fremantle holding for a Freshwater Bay block in 1855. Later comers included Bernard Kain, also a private in the 29th and later a warder at Fremantle Prison, and Edward Osmond, a private in the Royal Marines. William Smith, formerly a private in the 50th Regiment, arrived with his wife and daughter in 1859 and was granted a block at Butler's Swamp, but did not stay. By the mid-1860s he was living at Dongara, where his wife died. He then drifted to the Victorian goldfields and was killed there by a Sikh.

Thomas Bishop of the Royal Canadian Rifles took his discharge in 1862 and settled on a block on the west side of Butler's Swamp, but later moved to the barracks at Perth. Last of all was Samuel Efford, a grey-haired, sallow-complexioned private in the Royal Artillery whose twenty-three years of service included no fewer than five badges for exemplary conduct. He arrived by the *Dalhousie* in 1863 and for many years was compounder of medicines for the inmates of Fremantle Prison. He took up one of the blocks on Butler's Swamp in 1867, and his descendants remain in the district to this day. Together with the stayers from the original settlement, these newcomers ensured Freshwater Bay's future as a community of small property owners.

None of their colleagues apparently sought to share their opportunities, and they were not joined by any ex-convicts. Unlike such rural communities as York and Toodyay, Freshwater Bay was not to be one of those districts where families with long memories discriminated between the neighbours who paid their own fares and those who came out less fortunately. Even among the pensioners who took out the titles to their land, several appear to have left the district during the 1860s. Moses O'Keefe, for instance, went to Albany and joined the police. William Finlay lived to see his son become Mayor of Albany, only to be pre-deceased by him. Samuel Efford finished up as a lighthouse keeper, as did his son

Samuel Sutton, a former private in the Royal Marines, held his blocks of land at Freshwater Bay and Butler's Swamp until his death in 1891, when they passed to his children.

Samuel Efford with his two sons. His descendants still live in the district.

Ann Atkinson arrived in 1850 on the *Scindian*, the first convict ship to come to the colony, with her husband, John, a former private in the 2nd Dragoon Guards, and their three children. She bore another four children in the colony.

after him. Thomas McMullen added one of his neighbour's blocks to his own and thus became the largest landholder at Butler's Swamp. His family made their residence there; so did John Atkinson and his wife, who were noted for their excellent garden with its orchard of vines and fig trees. Some at least of the pensioner guards found rewards for their endurance.

Looking to the future, the pensioner guards bemoaned the lack of educational opportunity for their children. The subsidy for Mrs Herbert's school promised in 1851 failed to continue, and for several years nothing was available. Anne Herbert appears to have been a strong-minded woman, and she continued pressing for the reinstatement of the former arrangement. Possibly she was motivated as much as anything by the desire to use her skills as a teacher to supplement the family income. In 1858 the settlers again sent up a request for a schoolhouse, but authority was not given for its construction until late in 1861 after pressure from Anglican Bishop Mathew Hale, who required a building for church services. A site was found at the eastern end of the pensioner allotments on the foreshore, near the intersection of Pensioners Terrace and the track to the convict depot. Along that sandy track convicts marched from the depot to work on the building of the schoolhouse, and when it was completed they walked the same road on occasional Sundays to hear a clergyman preach a sermon and say matins in the traditional Anglican form used in the village churches they had attended as blameless small boys. Services were usually taken by the Bishop himself or by the Colonial Secretary, Frederick Barlee, while Henry Trigg, who had designed the building, continued his ministrations.[11]

The Freshwater Bay settlers were older men with conservative values. Accustomed to obeying orders, practical and resourceful if a little lacking in enterprise, they were mostly industrious and sober characters who aimed to provide their families with a comfortable living and a means of support after their deaths. A number contributed to a benefit society to assist their families in times of sickness or bereavement. In the face of considerable hardship they followed the yeoman ideal of pre-industrial England by coupling industry, sobriety and thrift with modest ambition. Appreciative that on the whole Western Australia provided more attractive opportunities than the workhouses of old England, the pensioner guards may well have contributed to the strength of conservative traditions in Western Australia. In Freshwater Bay they provided the district with an image of social respectability that helped to wipe out the odium of convict origins. This would be built on in the last decade of the nineteenth century, when Claremont became the residence of civil servants, white-collar workers, and—on the original pensioner lots overlooking the river—families of power and wealth.

In February 1862 the school was opened with Anne Herbert in charge. Over the years of its existence, the number of students on the roll ranged from twelve to sixteen. Attendance was not as good as at the average Western Australian school at that time, and it might be guessed that children were often kept at home to make themselves useful on their parents' properties, though as the average age of the pupils in 1868 was only 6.7 years perhaps the explanation lies elsewhere. Under Anne Herbert the school simply provided a decent basic grounding for unambitious country kids. An Inspector's report for 1870 commented, 'the reading and writing were fairly done. The arithmetic, a failure. Mrs Herbert tells me that the attendance of the older children is very irregular.'[12] In 1876 the school was described to the Central Board of Education as 'a fair specimen of an old fashioned Dame School. Without any pretensions to a high standard Mrs Herbert still imparts a good useful education as far as it goes.'[13] By this time she was probably over sixty years old and, although she taught intermittently until 1879, her retirement on a well-deserved pension followed soon afterwards.

Mrs Herbert's pupils might easily have found the routine of the schoolroom wearisome, for they grew up in a pleasant bush environment. There was always the river, with its plentiful fish and any number of wise old Aborigines who could tell the colonial lads where the best spots for bream or tailor might be found. Most of the children could ride as soon as they could walk, girls as well as boys. When John Atkinson's daughters were over eighty they would still be able to boast themselves fit enough to ride, having spent hours in the saddle in their young days at Freshwater Bay. Their brother Bob Atkinson had a great mate called Tom Briggs, son of the publican at the Halfway House. Young Briggs went to Mrs Herbert's school, where he prided himself on his skill in arithmetic and accounting. When he grew to be a mature man he wrote down his reminiscences, entitling them without false modesty 'Life and Experiences of a Successful West Australian'. He was at his best when he called back to memory the vanished landscape of his boyhood:

> The whole of the area…was teeming with game such as the large bronze-wing pigeons, blue pigeons, king parrots, and kangaroo, while the swamps were full of wild duck. At times we would get an odd turkey straying about the hills round Cottesloe.[14]

When he and Bob Atkinson were tired of bagging game with their muzzle-loading guns, they sometimes trapped live birds to sell as souvenirs to the captains of passing sailing ships.

Even when Tom Briggs and Bob Atkinson were small boys the omens of change were there for those who could discern them. In 1862, a year of great rain and tempests, a particularly wild storm did considerable damage to much of the tall timber in the Freshwater Bay district, after which people began to comment on the losses that were already evident from the activities of timbercutters and roadmakers. It would not be long before nearly all the original jarrah was cut out of the district. In 1867 the eight-year-old Tom Briggs parleyed himself into earning half a crown by taking a goat from a Freshwater Bay property to a purchaser in the town of Perth. His pride in walking the whole distance there and back was fed not only by the cash profit but also by the opportunity of witnessing the laying of the foundation stone of Perth's new Town Hall. This also was a portent of Perth's growth in size and civic dignity, offering a hint that even the ending of convict transportation in 1868 would not mark the end of progress and development in Western Australia. Unfortunately Briggs does not tell us whether as a boy he ever dreamed that within his own lifetime the whole tract between Perth and Fremantle would become a continuous stretch of suburbia, with Freshwater Bay in the centre of it.

Perhaps some far-seeing individuals already cherished that vision, for very gradually investors were being attracted to the vacant land near Freshwater Bay. Melbourne financiers were flush with investment funds after the golden decade of the 1850s, and the unsuccessful attempt to found a pastoral settlement at Camden Harbour in 1864 drew their attention to the potential of the North-West, and possibly also to growth opportunities in the neighbourhood of Perth. In March 1864 Archibald Munro, formerly a sapper in the Royal Engineers, took up twenty acres at the head of Freshwater Bay along the west side of the pensioner allotments, his eastern boundary corresponding to the present line of Bay View Terrace. More significantly for the future, in January 1867 James Morrison, a Melbourne investor, was granted Location 702 on the north side of the Perth–Fremantle road. This covered the area now bounded by Stirling Highway, Stirling Road, Shenton Road and Parry Street. Among their other business interests, the Morrisons were dealers in livestock, and it may be that they needed the block as a holding paddock halfway between the port and Perth. Morrison's son, also James Morrison, came over to Western Australia in the following year. He met and courted Clara De Burgh, daughter of a landowner in the Guildford district, married her in 1869, and settled in Western Australia to administer the family's properties. It would be his initiative that led eventually to the development of Claremont.

All this lay in the future. Although convict transportation ceased in 1868, many men were still serving out their sentences, and the road gangs labouring on the Perth–Fremantle highway continued to be a feature of the Freshwater Bay district until well into the 1870s. The sons of the pensioner guards growing into manhood could see few opportunities if they stayed at home. One or two, such as Bob Atkinson and Tom Briggs, might turn a few pounds at limeburning, but the best prospects were to be found in the bush or the North-West, and gradually they scattered. The Atkinsons were the last to go. Described as hard pioneering stock, they were a close-knit family, tenacious of their land, who made money breeding and training horses and gradually bought out most of the other pensioner families. They were down-to-earth, comfortable people, all of them with the skill to play a musical instrument. One of the Misses Atkinson became a local piano teacher and the last of the sisters left the neighbourhood only in the 1950s. But their homestead is marked only by the palm trees that surrounded it, and these have mostly been overtaken by the rising waters of Lake Claremont.

None of the homes in which the pensioner families grew up were substantial enough to survive to the modern day. The convict depot on the Perth–Fremantle road was already in a dilapidated condition and in need of a new roof when in 1880 it was allocated to the Anglican Church and its grounds set aside as a public reserve. After the church moved out in 1893 the depot survived into the twentieth century, a number of large iron rings on its walls testifying to its origins. For a while, a local identity named Tom Cooper lived there, but as early as 1907 local residents were complaining about its unsightly appearance, and in 1930 the remnant was destroyed by fire, though the foundations were left.[15]

Oil painting, 1910, by Alexander Doepel of a convict house, thought to be the warder's quarters at the convict depot located in the government reserve now known as Claremont Park. Doepel taught art in several local schools.

Pensioner guard
cottage, Butler's
Swamp, 1950s.

While the convict depot succumbed to neglect, the Halfway Tree met its end through official vandalism. Until the 1890s it remained a landmark, serving as the turning-point for the gentry of Perth on their Sunday afternoon drives with carriage and pair, while 'young men and maidens in less pretentious vehicles allowed the old horse to jog around the Mount and on through the forest over the block road to the Halfway Tree where a halt would be called to rest the horse and incidentally permit of a ramble through the flower-laden bush'.[16] Often it was the

The Halfway Tree
where mailmen on
horseback met to
exchange mail,
c. 1930.

spot for picnics. As the district became built up, a row of seats was provided around the butt of the tuart. These were allowed to fall into disrepair, and in 1907 the Claremont Council pruned the tree considerably because of the risk from falling limbs. When the tramline was extended along the main road in the 1920s, space was provided for the overhead powerlines by lopping the tree so drastically that it died. In February 1933 the dead stump was uprooted by the tramway authorities. Within another five years the trams were gone, and only a mailbox remained as a reminder of the Halfway Tree.

One link with the convict era survived: Anne Herbert's schoolhouse was used for church services throughout the 1870s, Parson Brown riding from Perth on a hired horse. In 1869 there were over thirty parishioners, although average attendances were lower. It was a long journey for families living near Butler's Swamp. When Anne Herbert retired in 1879 the church services were transferred to the old depot, while the school was, after a time, used as a lodging house known to the genial young bachelors who inhabited it as 'The 'Appy 'Ome'. Later it was altered to become a residence for one of the police officers stationed at Claremont and at that time the mistaken belief arose that, having been built by convicts, it must be the original convict depot. Finally the building became the Claremont Museum, and as such it has achieved recognition as a valued link with the district's origins. In 1983, in a pleasant commemorative gesture, the small reserve on its east side was named 'Mrs Herbert's Park'.

School and church building, Victoria Avenue, now Claremont Museum, 1892.

Chapter III

The Coming of the Gentry

IT SHOWED CONSIDERABLE foresight in James Morrison to make his investment in what was still a bush settlement at the edge of a very isolated small town. None could foretell how long Perth would languish in the doldrums after the ending of convict transportation, and perhaps only a young man with resources behind him could have afforded to play a waiting game. Yet if Western Australia were to develop at all it was certain that a position midway on the road between Perth and Fremantle must in time command a strategic position in any future suburban growth.

After 1871 the future site of Claremont also had a north–south axis, as in that year a road was marked out running parallel to the coast. It was intended to traverse the hollow of Butler's Swamp and head north towards those remote beaches where one or two families such as the Hamersleys had summer cottages. This line would eventually become Stirling Road and part of the modern West Coast Highway. The lines of communication met together between Butler's Swamp and Freshwater Bay.

Until the 1870s the road and the river were the only links between the settlers of Freshwater Bay and the outside world, and it was the road that received more care and attention. Local property owners competed for tenders to provide crushed stone for road-mending, but the actual navvying was still undertaken by convict parties. Their supervisor, a warder named Patrick Reilly, liked the neighbourhood well enough to apply in February 1873 for a grant of twenty acres. Responsibility for the highway was exercised from 1871 by the Perth Roads Board, and at a meeting on Boxing Day 1872 the chairman was able to inform the members, that 'the Fremantle Road was never in such good condition and he trusted that the Board would endeavour to keep it so'.[1]

In the eyes of progressive thinkers at that time, even the best of roads fell short of that symbol of nineteenth century technology—the railway with its steam trains. Sydney and Melbourne had enjoyed local services since the 1850s, but even by the end of the convict period the population of Perth and its environs was not nearly big enough to provide viable passenger traffic. It was improbable that a private investor would be attracted and unlikely that the colony's new Legislative Council would be allowed by the London authorities to borrow the necessary capital. By the early 1870s, however, lines were being constructed for the carting of timber to the coast, and plans were maturing for a line that would bring the copper and lead mined at Northampton to the port at Geraldton. The Avon Valley farmers, vexed at the trouble and expense of freighting their produce by dray across the Darling Scarp, clamoured for a railway to Fremantle. Any such line would, of course, necessarily pass through Perth and thus open up suburban land for development by astute real estate dealers. The examples of Melbourne and Sydney and of the modern cities of Britain and North America suggested that the railway would be the key factor determining the pattern of Perth's future growth.

The choice of route was by no means a foregone conclusion. A line running inland from Fremantle would need to bridge the Swan at some point if it were to pass close to the centre of Perth before climbing the Darling Scarp, but there were half-a-dozen theories about how this would best be accomplished. Two main schools of thought emerged. Some, mainly Fremantle merchants with a care for their port's independent access to the inland, argued for a line running south of the river. This would bridge the Canning and then either cross the Swan at the Narrows—like the modern Kwinana Freeway—or if, as seemed probable, this was too much for the engineering resources of the time the line could continue inland and a branch from Perth might be built across the Causeway to feed into it. On the other hand, the Swan could be bridged at North Fremantle and in that case the line could enter Perth from the west and require no further bridges until it reached Guildford. Although the route south of the river might possess a slight advantage in terms of access to good agricultural land, the interests of Perth and the convenience of engineering favoured a northern route. Any such line must pass a little to the north of the Perth–Fremantle Road, along the ridge between Butler's Swamp and Freshwater Bay, galvanizing the scattered settlements of that district into change and bringing profit to investors shrewd enough to secure land before the boom.

So it was that after decades of comparative neglect the Freshwater Bay district began in the early 1870s to attract the discreet attention of speculators.[2]

Morrison, with his family experience of Melbourne's expansion, was the first, although one may wonder why in May 1868 James Gallop decided to take up an extra block of 124 acres of back country at the western end of his 'Dalkeith' estate. Then from 1873, as talk of the railway grew more insistent, the pace quickened.

In 1875 the big money started to arrive—or what passed for big money in the Western Australia of those days. In April 1875 George Shenton purchased a hundred acres, and in November another forty. Thirty-three years old, Shenton was already respected as a canny merchant and speculator building up his family business. He was also proprietor of the Crawley estate, with its elegant homestead on the shores of Matilda Bay halfway between Freshwater Bay and Perth. He was a member of the Legislative Council, and in the same year that he began buying land in the Freshwater Bay district he also became for the first time chairman of the Perth City Council—clearly a man whose position gave him influence, if only benign influence, over the districts where he chose to invest.

In September 1875 Ignatius Boladeras, a Perth storekeeper who had come out as a layman in 1849 with Don Rosendo Salvado's Spanish Benedictines, and had shown something of the good bishop's discerning eye for real estate, took up forty acres athwart the Perth–Fremantle Road near the Halfway Tree, and in October added another forty acres. He paid ten shillings an acre. About the same time a hundred acres were purchased for £50 by Frederick Henry Stirling, colonial-born son of the proprietor of Perth's major newspaper, the *Inquirer*. This was to begin his family's long and prominent connection with the district.

Between September and November 1875 the Fremantle merchant Robert Habgood and his artistic brother-in-law John de Mansfield Absolon took up two blocks, totalling 143 acres, in what is now the central business district of Claremont, and in September also James Morrison was stimulated to add a further seventy-two acres to his holding. Senior officials recently arrived from England had their attention drawn to this promising locality. In February 1876 J. C. H. James, scion of minor gentry, six months after coming to the position of Commissioner of Land Titles purchased 17.5 acres to the west of the pensioner allotments overlooking the river. His block lay immediately to the south of Archibald Munro's land on the Perth–Fremantle Road. Later in that same year, when Munro died, he bought that estate and added it to his own, thus creating a splendid holding between the Perth–Fremantle Road and the head of Freshwater Bay. Two years later he sold his property to the newly arrived Colonial Secretary, Roger Tuckfield Goldsworthy, who planned a villa he intended to call 'Lucknow' in recollection of the days when, as an eighteen-year-old volunteer captain, he had ridden with Havelock's cavalry in the Indian Mutiny. Lieutenant Colonel James

Skinner, whose regiment was stationed in Western Australia and who had married one of the belles of Perth, in July 1876 acquired twenty acres to the west of 'Lucknow'.

Thus, a number of influential men of capital had a modest stake in ensuring that the Perth–Fremantle railway followed the northern route, which would necessarily traverse the Freshwater Bay district. Smaller investors began to follow, beginning with Samuel Sutton, one of the original pensioner guards and more thrifty than most of his colleagues, who applied for the land now bounded by Chester, Agett and Bay Roads.

It was July 1877 before the railway question came before the Legislative Council. W. E. Marmion, one of the members for Fremantle, sharply attacked the northern route. He said it would serve 'a barren inhospitable country, possessing few inhabitants—a number of limestone ridges, with no timber at all and no firewood, and no good country to open up'.[3] The southern route, he claimed, would tap the farming country along the Canning. But Shenton spoke up for the northern route, and so did two of the most respected and weighty members of the legislature—Luke Leake, the member for Perth, and his brother-in-law James Lee Steere. Goldsworthy did not speak, but he must have thought of his piece of land at Freshwater Bay as the debate went back and forth. The clinching argument came from the Director of Public Works, J. H. Thomas, who pointed out the cost and difficulty of building a bridge over the Narrows. That settled the matter for most members. They voted strongly in favour of the northern route. Authority having been won from London, Governor Ord turned the first sod of the new railway development as part of the colony's fiftieth anniversary celebrations in 1879, and by 1881 the line was ready to operate.

Morrison did not wait until then. Having given the authorities a piece of land for railway purposes, no doubt hoping that a station would follow, he made ready to market his estate to the public. Considering that 'Butler's Swamp' lacked class, he cast around for a new name and hit upon 'Claremont'. Perhaps he was complimenting his wife, whose name was Clara, but the name also sounded aristocratic since it belonged to a minor royal palace in Surrey that Queen Victoria had made over to her youngest and favourite son, Prince Leopold. On 25 August 1880, a large advertisement in the *Inquirer* launched Claremont with admirable bravado.

This set the tone for Claremont. It was to be home for the professional classes and the respectable bourgeoisie, householders who could afford to commute several kilometres each day from the centre of Perth or Fremantle, but who were not quite at the standard of George Shenton at Crawley or of the patricians and pastoralists who cut a fine figure on Adelaide Terrace and would

TOWNSITE OF CLAREMONT, 68 ACRES, SITUATED midway between Perth and Fremantle, at the junction of the North Road with the Main Road between Perth and Fremantle.

Fine elevated position, commanding magnificent views of the surrounding country and sea. Passenger vans constantly passing. Eastern Railway passes through the Estate. Opposite the Colonial Secretary's property, Lucknow, at Freshwater Bay.

Claremont is now being laid out in Building Sites, which will be offered for sale by public auction on a day to be named in September, when gentlemen engaged in business, wishing to have the pleasures of a country life after their day's work is over, will have a chance of buying, at a low rate, a Suburban Villa Site in a healthy, rural, but centrally-situated locality— a locality likely (in course of time) to become to the residents of Perth and Fremantle what South Yarra is to Melbourne, or Kensington to London.

Terms will be very liberal, and the upset price, if any, moderate.

For full particulars, apply to
JAMES MORRISON,
Stock and Station Agent.
August 25, 1880.
West Australian, copy.

before long be edging up Mount Street, taking advantage of the city views. Claremont was meant for prosperous solid citizens, men who expected value for their money but who, like good Australians, enjoyed the outdoor recreations of the river and the cricket pitch and wanted space in which their children could grow up. Like South Yarra, like Kensington, Claremont would be a good address.

Some practical problems remained. It was essential to have a railway station, easy of access to existing residents as well as potential buyers. Local opinion favoured a site where the railway line came close to the main road and the head of Freshwater Bay, but during the spring of 1880 the impression gained ground that another site would be chosen at the point where the line intersected Stirling Road. Half-a-dozen of the Butler's Swamp selectors, among them the McMullens and Samuel Efford, entrusted a petition in November 1880 to the trusty hand of George Shenton:

> We the undersigned residents of Butler's Swamp, hearing of the proposed site for a Railway Station here; would be thankful if you would use your influence on our behalf to propose that the situation of the said station be removed about four hundred yards up the line towards Perth. In getting to the present site, it is very awkward for us with our hay and other produce, whereas if removed as above proposed and where we believe it was first intended to have the station it would be much nearer and avoid a hill that leads to the present site.[4]

The official response was chilling:

> Government has never proposed a station at Butler's Swamp, no site fixed or land reserved for the purpose; a station at present is out of the question as it would not pay working expenses. Mr Morrison gave us a piece of land and it was accepted on the distinct understanding that Government made no pledge that a station would ever be erected at Butler's Swamp or that if erected it would be placed on any particular spot.

Shenton must nevertheless have persisted, as in 1881 a platform was provided and trains began to stop at Butler's Swamp. One more step was required, and this was reported by the *Herald* in May 1883:

> We also notice a suggestion we recently made as to the desirability of giving the station midway between Perth and Fremantle a more euphonious name than Butler's Swamp has been acted upon and that station is now known as Claremont, the name of Mr Morrison's property adjacent to the station. We have no doubt that in the course of time Mr Morrison will have the satisfaction of seeing a flourishing town spring up on his numerous building sites in this locality.[5]

It was not surprising that the *Herald* interested itself in the matter since, as was the case with the *Inquirer*, it was owned by the Stirling family, whose investment in Claremont was substantial. They and their neighbours could now travel to central Perth for a shilling first class and sixpence second class. The

Government Gazette, in proclaiming these fares, also advised that corpses would be carried at a cost of a shilling a mile provided 'a medical certificate is produced...setting forth that death was not caused by any contagious or infectious disease'. Within a very few years passenger traffic had grown to the extent that more than a platform was required. In April 1886 Philip Reilly's tender was accepted to construct the present railway station and stationmaster's residence for £1,669 13s 8d, and the site was shifted a few hundred metres east in deference to local pressure.

The railway brought moments of drama into the life of the quiet Claremont community. On the last Friday evening of 1884, a first class carriage was derailed a short distance from Claremont Station and the guard, William Lindsay, was killed. The *Inquirer* carried a graphic report:

> To the horror of all poor Lindsay's body was found lying in the rear of the train, cut literally to pieces. The limbs were severed from the trunk which was smashed into pulp and the lower part of the face had been cut away from the head. Death must of course have been instantaneous. Strange to say the poor fellow's watch was picked up quite uninjured and going.[6]

In 1886 Mary Anne Langoulant was killed while crossing the line. Sixty years old and deaf, she failed to hear the approaching train. Despite the tragedies, the railway was much appreciated by a generation for whom a twenty-minute train ride to Perth or Fremantle marked a great advance on a ten-kilometre ride taking more than an hour over a dusty limestone road. A mailbox was provided at the station and no fewer than six posts were dispatched daily to Perth.

The street paralleling the railway line was named Gugeri Street after a Swiss-born vigneron who had invested in the district. As early as 1883 a modest general store and post office was operating in this street near the original railway siding under the management of Samuel Efford's daughter, Margaret McMullen. Around the time the new station was built in 1886, the shop moved with it to a site on the western corner of Gugeri Street and Humble Street (now Bay View Terrace), and Margaret McMullen remarried, handing the business over to her daughter Elizabeth Ann. When she married in her turn in 1888, she passed the post office over to her aunt, confusingly also named Elizabeth Ann, who was married to stationmaster Thompson, but the store was taken over by an enterprising railway porter, Edward Massey, a young married man five years out of London. A section of his store was used as the post office, and in 1893 he himself took over as postmaster. On the other side of Massey's store a hotel was planned by one Thomas Walker, but it seems never to have opened.

From Massey's corner in Gugeri Street a track ran across the Perth–Fremantle Road a little to the west of the old convict depot and ended at the old pensioner allotments fronting the river. This was at first known as Humble Street in honour of George Bland Humble, Town Clerk of Fremantle, and the track along the river to Mrs Herbert's school was known as Pensioner Row (later Terrace). But Humble Street and Pensioner Row were not grand enough names for the founders of Claremont, and later they were rechristened Bay View Terrace and Victoria Avenue respectively.

It was now clear that the heart of Claremont would lie between the railway station and the Perth–Fremantle Road, and it was here that the real estate salesmen concentrated their efforts. James Morrison gradually unloaded his holdings for a tidy profit. The Fremantle merchant Elias Solomon carved up ten acres along the railway on Barnfield Road. Ignatius Boladeras judged it timely to divest himself of Section 621, which was bisected by the Perth–Fremantle Road. In October 1883 he put the southern half—approximately nineteen acres—on the market. Except for three acres sold to Edward Connor, proprietor of the Horse and Groom Hotel in East Perth, this land was acquired by Peter Gugeri in 1885. He commissioned the explorer-surveyor Alexander Forrest and his partner W. H. Angove to carve up the U-shaped piece of land into fifty-six lots varying in size from a quarter-acre to a half-acre. Edward Courthope, the auctioneer commissioned by Forrest & Angove, waxed eloquent in advertising these 'magnificent building sites on the main road at the well known Halfway Tree':

> This Estate is close to the Claremont Railway Station, and overlooking the delightful PARK-LIKE SCENERY of the Government Reserve (which alone intervenes between it and FRESHWATER Bay) enjoys the most CHARMING VIEWS OF THE RIVER SWAN.

Until they were built out, he might have added; but he did not rely on romantic rhetoric alone:

> It is well known that purchasers of Claremont blocks have found themselves in the position of being able to resell their lots at up to 100 PER CENT ADVANCE on the Auction price. The present Estate affords unusual attractions to both Investors and Speculators, as well as those who wish to build themselves a home easily accessible from either Perth or Fremantle.[7]

After a month's intensive advertising, the estate was auctioned on the evening of Thursday, 27 October 1885. Only ten lots were sold, and it took two years to unload the remainder. However the social composition of the eventual buyers of the estate is instructive. Few ultimately built on the land, which covered an area bounded by the Perth–Fremantle Road, Goldsworthy Road, Thomson Road and the reserve that would become Claremont Park. Most were investors, some buying as many as six lots. Of the twenty-two buyers, four were gentlemen or wealthy merchants, thirteen were middle-class white-collar workers, four were artisans and one was a semi-skilled worker. Among the well-to-do buyers were the Stirling brothers, proprietors of three metropolitan newspapers, and Thomas Molloy, then part way up the ladder in his climb from baker to Mayor of Perth and papal knight. The white-collar workers ranged from accountants to small businessmen, including a jeweller, a tobacconist and a surprisingly affluent shop assistant.

It would be tempting to speculate on how far Alexander Forrest, with his reputation as a successful explorer, his kinship with John Forrest (who was Commissioner for Crown Lands), his political ambitions, and his growing reputation as a bold and shrewd investor, was responsible for networking among his connections in Perth so that the blocks were seen as a good proposition. Certainly he was impressed with Claremont's potential. In December 1885 he secured a grant of a hundred acres east of Bay Road adjoining the Perth–Fremantle Road, and immediately sold it to Sydney investors attracted by the relative cheapness of Perth land. Swan Location 907, running east from Freshwater Bay, was created in 1886 and granted to the Western Australian Synod of the Anglican Church, but they left it undeveloped for a decade.

One of Alexander Forrest's old associates thought that he was missing out on the opportunities offered at Claremont. Tommy Dower was a Nyungar who probably had ancestral roots in the Claremont area as a grandson of Yellowgonga, the Mooro leader of the 1830s. He himself had been a significant member of Forrest's six-man expedition that opened up the valuable Kimberley district in 1879, but had missed out when the Legislative Council voted rewards to Forrest's party for their discoveries. He was now senior spokesman for the remnant of the Aboriginal communities around Perth, and in 1886 he applied for ten acres at Claremont—the same area as the pensioner lots—as a freehold reserve for the Nyungar community. The Stirling brothers gave him qualified support in the *Inquirer*. They noted Dower's intention to 'build him a house and plant him ground', and commented: 'provided that Tommy be restricted from selling the grant, it is to be hoped that his application will prove successful'. But nothing came of it, and a fortnight later a correspondent to the *Inquirer* found Tommy Dower and his group camping not far from the Swan. Dower was reported as saying:

That white man take all blackfellows' country, and that blackfellow no place sit down. That white man build houses, fence land, run cattle, sheep, horse on blackfellows country. But poor blackfellows, no horse, no kangaroo or emu left. That plenty blackfellow die, and no notice taken of him by white man.[8]

Despite a recession in 1888 the press continued to advertise real estate in the Claremont area. Some of the subdivisions had enticing names long forgotten: Swan Hill, Sunning Hill. But the prime specimen of advertisers' rhetoric may be found in an 1889 effort by Wesley Maley & Co., in which the copywriter went to town with a series of monstrous puns on the names of local families such as the Langoulants and the Weedons:

EVERY MAN HIS OWN LANDLORD
Claremont   Claremont   Claremont

Claremont is the only suburb approachable from the City by River, Road and Rail.

What Richmond is to Melbourne, Claremont must be to Perth, when this Colony's railway circuit is complete. But Claremont has this advantage over Richmond — it is situated mid-way between the principal city and port of the largest colony of Australasia and Richmond isn't.

A few years ago land at Richmond could be purchased at £10 an acre, now it is over £100 per foot. At next Saturday night's sale Claremont will be sold at less than a shilling a foot on terms within reach of everyone.

The water at Claremont is so good that it runs the Publicans clean off the field.

Barristers, Bankers and Butchers all believe in Claremont.

The people of Claremont are remarkable for their vigour and longevity. Some of the oldest people in the Colony reside at Claremont and its Cemetery is still empty.

There are no rates at Claremont and the money you spend in City and Port rates would pay for railway season tickets for all the family.

If you want to qualify your sons for seats in the new Parliament — the Upper or Lower House — buy them a block at Claremont.

The happiest of homes are at Claremont and birds in their little nests agree in that charming suburb.

You can weed-on and weed-on at Claremont, but the vegetation still grows at a galloping rate.

Sensible people long and long to live at Claremont.

Man's field of labour is Claremont.

John Bull is always in Claremont.

Claremont produces the best grapes and all other fruits and vegetables.

Claremont has its Church and its School — in fact, all the advantages of city life without disadvantages.

Claremont already possesses some of the best houses in the Colony.

Finally, if you want to make a competence for yourself and your family, attend the Mechanics' Institute next Saturday night and buy a block at CLAREMONT.[9]

Barristers, bankers and butchers were all attracted to Claremont, as well as a number of middle-ranking civil servants who would rise to seniority during the 1890s gold-rush boom. One of the first was Alpin Thomson, a middle-aged Englishman who may have formed a liking for Mediterranean climate and scenery through growing up in the south of France, where his father was a vice-consul. He arrived in Perth in 1879 to marry Eliza Egan, step-daughter of the Colonial Secretary, Roger Goldsworthy, and secured a good public service job as accountant to the Department of Works and Railways. In 1881 Goldsworthy left Western Australia for a career as a colonial governor, his last post being at the Falkland Islands. He had not completed his villa on the fine block at the head of Freshwater Bay, but passed it on to Thomson, who settled there two years later with his wife and two children and built a house which now forms the nucleus of Bethesda Hospital.

Thomson progressed steadily, and when his department was divided in 1891 he became Under-Secretary for Railways, which position he held throughout the strenuous decade of the gold rushes until his retirement in 1901. As a founding father of Claremont he contributed the discreet and respectable style of an English-bred public servant, concerned that his community should be well-served by churches and schools. In 1889 he was elected to the Perth Roads Board.

Alpin Thomson's influence was doubtless useful in securing the completion of the Claremont railway station close to his estate. Then he purchased Patrick Reilly's next-door block (Location 616: Reilly had retired to York and died in 1886), consolidated it with his own holdings and subdivided the estate into four riverfront sections, long blocks extending to the Perth–Fremantle Road. Their size ensured that he would have congenial neighbours of his own class, as well as increase his accessible capital. During 1885 and 1886 a mood of optimism prevailed because of the construction of the Albany railway, the discovery of the Kimberley goldfield and good credit for Western Australia on the London money market; and despite a slump in 1888 the land market was only marginally affected, speculation in Claremont continuing unabated. But where most investors were content to take their profit by subdividing into small suburban blocks, Alpin Thomson intended that his part of Claremont would become its dress circle, with suitable occupants. His plans had fateful consequences for the layout of Claremont's streets, since it was now impossible to construct a secondary road paralleling the Perth–Fremantle Road to the south in the way that Princess Road serves to divert traffic flow from the modern Stirling Highway. Motorists delayed in Claremont's congested peak-hour traffic have no reason to bless Alpin Thomson's memory. Also, despite public protest, he closed the track that ran across his land connecting the pensioner allotments with the main road and Butler's Swamp.[10] It was only years later that the creation of Queenslea Drive restored this line of access.

To the west of Alpin Thomson's property lay another large block, Lot 700. Its original owner, Colonel Skinner, had been recalled to England in 1878 and it came into the hands of the prominent lawyer and politician Stephen Henry Parker. In 1884 he sold it to Francis Bird, who had made his money as partner in a Darling Scarp timber mill, had served briefly as Colonial Architect and was now setting up in private practice. He was to design most of the big houses overlooking the bay, beginning with his own, before he decided to move to Albany in 1889. When he sold the estate to John Elliott Richardson, Roebourne pastoralist and future Legislative Councillor, the house became known as 'Corry Lynn'.

The first section of Alpin Thomson's estate to be sold, the most westerly of the blocks, was purchased by Robert Burnside, son of the Chief Justice of Ceylon. A dashing, forthright young man with a colourful turn of phrase, Burnside was practising at that time as a solicitor but would later rise to become Crown Solicitor

BELOW LEFT: The second 'Lucknow', built for Alpin Thomson on the cliff top, the first having been on the foreshore. It was part of Bethesda Hospital for many years. Mrs Thomson, in the white dress, was born during the siege of Lucknow in India, hence the name.

BELOW RIGHT: 'Corry Lynn', built by architect Francis Bird and later owned by John Richardson, Roebourne pastoralist, and then T. J. Briggs.

ABOVE LEFT: 'Craig Muir', built by Francis Bird for Judge Robert Burnside. It is now part of Methodist Ladies College.

ABOVE RIGHT: 'Knutsford', built for Barrington Wood, first Mayor of Fremantle, and later owned by Mr and Mrs Alfred Sandover for many years. It is now part of Christ Church Grammar School.

and, in 1902, a judge of the Supreme Court. He asked Bird to design his house, 'Craig Muir', which still stands in the grounds of Methodist Ladies College. Possibly to finance the building of his home, Burnside divided his property in February 1888, selling the eastern portion to John Maxwell Ferguson, a wealthy merchant who was shortly to remarry at fifty and start a second family. He is best remembered as a founder of the Swan Brewery and a generous patron of the infant Scotch College, but he also had extensive timber interests and from 1903 was briefly MLA for North Fremantle. In 1896 Ferguson built a magnificent two-storey verandahed stone house, 'Dalnabrek', on this site. Today it is the boarding house 'Walters' in the grounds of Christ Church Grammar School.

The second section of Alpin Thomson's estate was sold in October 1888 to Charles Macklin, newly arrived from Victoria and also a solicitor. Following Burnside's example, he bisected his block and sold the eastern half to Frederick Bennion, who had come from New Zealand in 1885 to manage an insurance company. The third section, adjacent to Alpin Thomson's own property, was sold in July 1889 to Barrington Wood. He was a land agent and merchant who had been Fremantle's first mayor—between 1883 and 1885—and who would enter Parliament in 1894, serving briefly as Sir John Forrest's Commissioner for Railways and thus as Alpin Thomson's ministerial head. In the mid-1890s Wood sold his house, 'Knutsford', to the rising Hay Street merchant Alfred Sandover, who lived there many years before the property was acquired by Christ Church Grammar School. Thus the head of Freshwater Bay west of Bay View Terrace would be dominated by the homes of the affluent and influential. The dominant ethos is caught by a granddaughter's description of Alfred and Rosalind Sandover, Australian-born but English-minded:

They were both well read, steeped in English tradition through family background, and here, though bush almost surrounded them and in early days to visit friends at night meant following roads or tracks swinging a hurricane lantern, they built a home and family life with all the happiness and also tradition of an English home.[11]

Alfred and Rosalind Sandover, *c.* 1900.

To the east, however, the original pensioner allotments were little changed in the late 1880s. On one of them an orchard still survived, and there was as yet no settlement beyond the modest house of a Mr Blythe near the foot of Bay Road. Few strangers passed by. Francis Bird's children, playing on the river shore one day, were surprised to see a young man wading along the shallow waters parallel with the beach. When they told their parents it turned out that he was Tom Hughes, a notorious escapee and admirer of Ned Kelly, who in 1887 was the talk of Perth after he shot and wounded a policeman.[12]

Another well-to-do element chose to establish their homes on the high, northern side of the Perth–Fremantle Road, a shorter walk to the railway station. Among them was Alpin Thomson's departmental colleague, a gentlemanly young architect named George Temple Poole, who did not mind if gossips whispered that Lord Palmerston was his grandfather, but whose claim to fame was the series of handsome public buildings that he designed for Perth and many country centres between 1885 and 1900. These include the Treasury buildings, the Cathedral Avenue wing of the Department of Land Administration, the Royal Mint, the Old Observatory (now the National Trust headquarters) and the original Museum. In Claremont his work is represented by the stationmaster's house of 1886, the Claremont Demonstration School, the post office building and the old police station, designed in 1896. A striking figure with waxed moustache and eyeglass, he established himself on the north side of the Perth–Fremantle Road at the corner of what is now Albert Street. Here he built 'Wingfield', a house in two-storey English villa style with an attic on top.[13]

George Temple Poole, Government Architect 1885–1900 and resident of Claremont.

Second to none in civic pride and energetic drive, at times verging on self-importance, was the colonial-born Horace George Stirling.[14] His brother had taken up land in the district as early as 1874, but it was Horace who built a fine house with tennis court and stables on the highway, a little to the east of Bay View Terrace overlooking the old convict depot and the government reserve that would later become Claremont Park.

The Stirling family's stable of successful newspapers had started as far back as 1840 with the establishment of the weekly *Inquirer* and had gone on to prosper

after the acquisition of the Fremantle-based *Herald* and the establishment of the *Daily News* in 1882. Horace Stirling was both managing editor and a prolific columnist under the pen-name of 'Hugh Kalyptus'. It was no doubt he who penned some of the favourable propaganda about Claremont that appeared from time to time in the *Daily News*: 'A few years since,' he wrote, Claremont 'had the appearance of a barren waste, [it] today contains some of the first residences in the colony'.[15] In 1894, taking advantage of the boom conditions of the gold rush, the Stirlings sold out to Arthur Lovekin. Now a man of independent means, Horace was able to devote his considerable energies to the affairs of Claremont. He shared with English-born neighbours such as Alpin Thomson and George Temple Poole decided views about the canons of good taste and discreet affluence that should characterize the appearance and amenities of their local community.

Such individuals played an active role in local affairs for many years, emulating their gentry forebears by providing leadership in the community and thus mirroring the traditions of rural England. They and their families appear to have lived in a manner not dissimilar to the gentry of late nineteenth century England. We can gain some idea of their lifestyle from a sworn valuer's description of Burnside's home, 'Craig Muir', when it was purchased by Methodist Ladies' College after his death in 1929:

> The improvements comprise a very old two storeyed stone residence, comprising originally Drawing Room (25' x 25'), Dining Room (16' x 13'7"), 2 pantries, kitchen (14'9" x 13'10"), servery (9' x 8') on ground floor and bedroom (20'8" x 15'7"), bedroom (16' x 14'6"), small room, bathroom, bedroom (14'6" x 15') and linen press on the first floor. Of recent years an addition to the ground floor has been made of billiard room (20' x 27'7"), hall (16'6" x 6'7"), sitting room (14'6" x 11') with lavatory off this.
>
> There are two storeyed stone out buildings (formerly stables and loft)... Attached to this is an open brick wood yard. There are eight fowl runs with...roosting pens. On the river is a galvanized iron boat shed and a small private jetty also...[16]

It was a large house set in extensive grounds which in spring were covered with jonquils and lilies: a home for entertaining as well as for pleasure and retreat. As a prominent lawyer with a wide range of interests, including yachting and the turf—he was at one time president of the Western Australian Turf Club and commodore of the Royal Perth Yacht Club—Burnside and his wife, Mary, would have been required by social custom and obligation to entertain guests regularly at both a formal and informal level. They apparently enjoyed the obligation. Their elegant drawing room and more intimate dining room suggest a gracious and urbane style of living. Since they had only one child, the size of their home and accommodation indicates the possibility of weekend house parties, including river excursions on Burnside's yacht, *Genesta*.

During the week, however, the village of Claremont was largely the province of women. Even men like Burnside used the train to commute to the city each day, and the rhythm of daily life must have revolved around the affairs of its women, as it had in Gaskell's *Cranford*. Although few of Claremont's women were spinsters or widows, the needs of husbands and children would not have precluded the card parties, the church and charity activities, that provided a focus for the women of Cranford. All would have occasioned the same pre-occupation with the network of relationships that formed a major part of daily life in the small world of the village.

Within this network was the relationship between mistress and maid. Families such as the Burnsides required servants to maintain their lifestyle. While servants' quarters are not mentioned in the description of 'Craig Muir', it is likely that a housekeeper or nursemaid lived in the main house, while other servants were drawn from the local community. A photograph of the Burnside family outside the house confirms this notion. Standing to one side of the family group is a most respectable figure, soberly dressed with her hair drawn back severely into a bun. She is thought to be Mrs Efford, the housekeeper, daughter-in-law of an original Freshwater Bay pensioner guard.

Inquirer, 16 November 1887.

Lazy days on the river. Judge Burnside and crew on his yacht, *Genesta*.

Afternoon tea at 'Craig Muir', Judge Burnside's home. Thought to be (L–R) Mrs Sharkey, Mrs Burnside, Judge Burnside (in cap), Mr St John Briggs (brother-in-law of Mrs Sharkey) in cane lounge chair and housekeeper Kitty Efford.

Even in the late 1880s the social image of Claremont, although in transition, remained that of country estate and rural village. It was still an organic whole, with a working class that in many cases derived income from farming small acreages of land and by serving the needs of a numerically small upper class, who overlooked them in both a physical and symbolic sense from their homes on the clifftops. The population of Claremont during the 1880s is hard to guess, as in official returns it is simply classified as part of the Perth Roads Board district. In the early 1880s there were probably between ten and fifteen families. The Government reopened Mrs Herbert's school under a new teacher in 1883, but closed it two years later as there were only twelve pupils on the roll, four of whom came from Perth or Fremantle 'merely to keep the school going on behalf of the teacher'.

The coming of the new post office and railway station meant that numbers increased during the later 1880s. The volume of mail handled by the Claremont post office almost doubled in 1887, and the school was reopened in the old convict depot as a 'classified' government school with twenty-one pupils in 1889.[17] In 1888 a general store was opened on the Perth–Fremantle Road by Fred Koeppe, who married Horace Stirling's sister. He later moved his thriving business to the corner of Bay View Terrace and competed with Massey for leadership among the town's storekeepers. Population increase was the result of the growing availability of real estate, and these subdivisions, as we shall see, attracted a different class of person to Claremont. For the leading families, symbolic representations of an ordered village community became increasingly important.

Respectability meant better churches. By March 1892 the Anglicans in Claremont were sure that the old convict depot would no longer serve their needs, although Alpin Thomson helped by making 'Lucknow' available for services. In March 1892 a meeting was called with the Dean of Perth, Frederick Goldsmith, in the chair and half-a-dozen substantial citizens attending. Dean

CLAREMONT POST OFFICE.

Sir,—Sometime back the residents of Claremont sent in a requisition to the Postmaster General asking for the removal of the Post Office from Butler's Swamp to the railway station, for the greater convenience of residents there, as very often it was days before they received their letters.

Through the medium of your valuable paper I would wish to call the attention of the Postmaster General to the boon all the residents would derive by the mails being shifted from Butler's Swamp to the Railway station, and left in charge of the station-master's wife, where a room could be set apart for them, and the mails, I feel sure, would not then be neglected.—Yours, &c.,
ALPHA.

Inquirer, 4 January 1888.

The first shop in Claremont was opened by the Koeppe family in 1888. It was situated on Perth–Fremantle Road (renamed Stirling Highway in 1931) between Leura Avenue and Mary Street.

Goldsmith commented that their present building was in a hollow but a church should be on a hill. To this Alpin Thomson responded by promising to donate a prime site of half an acre on the Perth–Fremantle Road opposite the intersection of Stirling Road. The Church's fifty-acre block at the east end of Pensioner Terrace was too far from the centre of population and Alpin Thomson's offer was gladly accepted. As architect they commissioned young Talbot Hobbs, still struggling to establish himself and occasionally working as carpenter on his father-in-law's building projects. No doubt he was aware of the responsibility that went with accepting a job under the eye of the suave and experienced Temple Poole, a member of the planning committee.

Hobbs designed a church capable of seating 120 with provision for expansion. As a man who would later become a military hero and gain a reputation as a stickler for proper form and discipline, it is significant that he chose to use a design influenced by the Gothic revival movement in British architecture. Now substantially enlarged and altered, the church was then akin to the archetypal village church of England and thus symbolized nostalgia for an ordered and idyllic rural past. Temple Poole probably encouraged this: when he designed the police station and quarters on the western outskirts of Claremont in 1896 he drew on an even older vernacular influence then emerging in Britain as part of the Arts and Crafts Movement in architecture, and used it as a symbol of order.[18]

Unfortunately, as so often happens, a great gulf opened between the architect's brief, calling for a church costing between £400 and £450, and the tenders submitted by Perth's builders and contractors, which ranged from £725 to £1,269. In a boom year, when almost every month brought news of a fresh gold discovery, labour and materials were in short supply and the committee had to make the best of it. They accepted the tender of Boundy and Locke for £810 5s 3d and decided to go without a church porch for the time being. Horace Stirling bought the old block with the convict depot for £150 and the National Bank, although in deep trouble because of the breaking of the Melbourne land boom, was prepared to lend £500 at the substantial rate of 7 per cent interest. Alpin Thomson allowed the contractors to quarry the limestone from the cliffs overlooking the river on his block, and this meant a further useful saving.

So it was that on a beautiful spring afternoon, 10 September 1892, Governor Sir William Robinson laid the foundation stone in the presence of Sir John and Lady Forrest and many other wellwishers who had come by train from Perth for the occasion. There was a choir headed by Dean Goldsmith, the scaffolding was decorated with bunting, and in a marquee with trestle tables and white tablecloths a lavish display of refreshments, much of it the home cooking of Claremont ladies, awaited the visitors.

Christ Church, built 1892.

There was an equally great occasion on the Sunday after the following Easter (10 April 1893) when, only a few months before his death, Bishop Parry consecrated the church, exhorting the people to profit by the increased opportunities for public worship. His hopes seemed justified, judging by an attendance of 250 people at a fundraising musical social and tea in May. At the suggestion of the parish secretary, a promising young civil servant named Martin Jull, the name of Christ Church was adopted.[19]

During that summer, when the builders' drays were hauling up the limestone from the riverside and the shinglers worked up a thirst as they fitted the roof for Christ Church, they would have seen busier traffic on the Perth–Fremantle Road than ever before. For in September 1892, a few days after the laying of the foundation stone, Arthur Bayley and his mate Bill Ford rode into Southern Cross with news of a magnificent discovery of gold at a place called Coolgardie. The excitement that had mounted with the earlier Yilgarn and Murchison discoveries now boiled over. Sailors deserted their ships in Fremantle, shopkeepers rubbed their hands in the expectation of profit, and in Melbourne and Adelaide, in Ballarat and Charters Towers, and eventually in England, hundreds of young men determined to seek their fortunes in Western Australia.

The children of James King, first Mayor of Claremont, on Stirling Highway near Christ Church. Mabel King is sitting side-saddle on the pony.

After sixty years of somnolence Perth and its surroundings were to experience a sudden spurt of growth. In this pattern of growth Claremont had already staked its claim to be regarded as a home for a comfortable upper middle class: the civil servants, the rising young professionals and businessmen, the affluent semi-retired pastoralists. Profiting from its strategic situation midway between the capital and its port, Claremont now entered upon its glad, confident morning.

Chapter IV

Constable Huxtable's Village

In April 1893 Claremont became the centre of a new roads board carved from the western suburbs of the old Perth Roads Board. Its boundaries were the north shore of the Swan River from North Fremantle to Sir George Shenton's Crawley House, now the site of The University of Western Australia, north along Ferdinand Street (now Winthrop Avenue) to Aberdare Road, thence along Alfred Road and to the coast. It included the modern districts of Mosman Park, Cottesloe, Swanbourne, Peppermint Grove, Dalkeith, Nedlands, Hollywood and Karrakatta as well as Claremont itself.

Polling for councillors took place on 17 May 1893 at the old school house. Of the seven elected to the first Claremont Roads Board, four were residents of Claremont proper: Alpin Thomson, who became Chairman, R. B. Burnside, George Temple Poole and John Elliott Richardson, first of a number of affluent pastoralists who, having prospered in the North-West or the Kimberleys, sought the comfort of a cooler environment with never-failing broad vistas of water. It must have seemed that the affluent citizens of Claremont were in a position to set their stamp on the growing locality. Already, however, the pattern of subdivision was beginning to challenge the image of the ordered village community. In their eagerness to find buyers for their land, Claremont's developers would produce a more diverse and unpredictable social mix, which was bound to challenge the village ideal.

With the discovery of gold at Coolgardie in 1892 and Kalgoorlie in 1893, Western Australia boomed. A swarm of migrants arrived, mainly from Victoria and South Australia, which were in the grip of the worst economic depression for half a century. The estimated population of the Perth metropolitan area went from 20,000 to 80,000 between 1891 and 1901, while that of Claremont grew even faster over the same period—from 250 to 2,500. This growth could occur only if the original concept of upper middle-class housing sited on spacious blocks gave way to more intensive subdivision, with smaller lots divided by short narrow streets.

There was improvement in demand for land in some of the mid-1880s subdivisions, which had at first sold slowly, but activity was keenest among what were known as the Melville Suburban Lots. These lots followed a model initiated by the Government at the original subdivision of Subiaco in 1883. Blocks ranging in size from three-quarters of an acre to five acres were released to attract small investors who would later carve them into smaller lots, thus minimising government expenditure but also ensuring that the investors of Perth would continue to make profits. Fifty-three such lots were released in 1889 in the area covered by the Claremont Roads Board. These were riverfront blocks in what would later become the 'Millionaires' Row' precinct of Dalkeith between Beatrice Road and Jutland Parade (then Hardman Street), but in the 1890s they were too far from shopping and transport to seem attractive. It probably did not help that the streets in the subdivision were given such everyday names as Smith, Jones and

Members of the first Claremont Roads Board, 1893. A. F. Thomson (Chairman), G. T. Poole, R. B. Burnside, Geo Edwards, E. V. H. Keane, A. B. Kidson, J. E. Richardson

Brown. River views were nevertheless sought after, and when ten one-acre sub-urban lots were released on Freshwater Bay immediately to the south of the old pensioner lots they were soon taken. They were among the few that were purchased by the well-to-do as home sites, probably because congenial upper-class neighbours were already building on the original pensioner lots.

Demand was strongest in the area west of Bay Road. Thirty-four further suburban lots were created from a large battle-axe-shaped section of land running from the Perth–Fremantle Road just to the east and south of Swan Location 621 (the old Boladeras block). One who did well from this release was the architect Edward Dean Smith, who had come to Western Australia from the eastern colonies in 1887 and later went into partnership with Talbot Hobbs. He bought the area bounded by Goldsworthy Road, Princess Road, Dunbar Street and Hammond Road, subdivided it into forty-two lots of 25 perches and found purchasers for nearly all of them through private sale within nine months. This enabled him to settle in Claremont on one of the old pensioner lots overlooking the river. Frederick Denbigh, a Perth draftsman, purchased two acres of the old Section 621 (bounded by the Perth–Fremantle Road, Bernard Street and John Street) and in 1895 subdivided them into fourteen lots varying in size from 27 to 36 perches. As in Smith's subdivision, these blocks were somewhat smaller than the conventional quarter-acre and considerably smaller than the sections of Location 621 subdivided in 1885, but most were sold without newspaper advertisement within a few weeks. Perth's upper middle class were prominent among the buyers, and many tended to acquire more than one lot. With Claremont now providing more amenities, perhaps the land would have sold even if the blocks had been larger. One purchaser not motivated by profit was George Randell, a veteran politician, who bought three neighbouring lots on the Perth–Fremantle Road and donated them as a site for a Congregational Mission Hall.[1]

The Congregational Hall provided a focus for those of the respectable classes who wanted an alternative to the Anglican Christ Church, and its architecture similarly reflected the values of its supporters. The hall was designed by young Henry Trigg, Perth's first locally trained architect and already notable as designer of Trinity Church in Perth. (He was, incidentally, the nephew of Horace Stirling: Perth in those years *was* a small town.) Trigg chose a style known as American Romanesque, which had been popularized in the United States by the eminent architect H. H. Richardson. As with the Christ Church design, the architectural sources were medieval, but they were from a different school. Although the hall is a diminutive version of this style, some of its architectural elements—particularly the use of rough stone, the heavy cylindrical piers, the round-headed arches and the tower—were time-honoured symbols of power and stability.

This symbolism was reinforced by social practices. When the foundation stone was laid in November 1895, the ceremony was performed by Mary Richardson, wife of John Elliott Richardson, pastoralist, Legislative Councillor and member of the Roads Board from its inception. This was appropriate, as she was 'a wonderful help to the church in every way over many years', but it was noteworthy that during the ceremony a young working-class woman held a sunshade over Mrs Richardson's head to protect her from the spring heat. When the hall was completed, seats for church services were allotted to members and adherents, who were expected to contribute a fixed amount to the church. By 1898 members of the congregation were rebelling against this practice as incompatible with the dissenting tradition of equality before God, a reflection of the fact that by this time Claremont was becoming a much more socially complex district.[2]

In 1896 a number of new investors entered into subdivision only to find that the market was saturated for the time being. The Catholic Church acquired acreage on the north side of Perth–Fremantle Road, but apart from marking its presence in the street names (Mary Street, Notre Dame Street) made little progress in marketing the land. George Frederick Gallop, merchant son of James Gallop of Dalkeith, bought the hundred acres of Location 1029 east of Bay Road and adjoining the Perth–Fremantle Road from the Sydney absentees who had held it for ten years, and had it subdivided into quarter-acre lots. Despite extensive advertising as the Prinsep Vale estate and the provision of free trains to the auction in October 1896 and free refreshments, lots sold very slowly. Indeed fewer than half had been sold by 1905. In 1896 also, the Anglican Church made a tardy move into the speculative land stakes with its Glebe estate. This too was subdivided into quarter-acre lots, its streets named after influential members of the clergy (Bishop Riley, Dean Goldsmith, Archdeacon Watkins—and Alice Street after Mrs Riley) intersected by streets named for prominent members of the St George's Cathedral vestry (Parker, Loton, Stone, Sherwood, Hackett). Despite this respectable ambience, advertising by the land agent, B. C. Wood, was low key and sales were slow.[3]

Even Horace Stirling's local knowledge failed to make him a lucky investor. Having visited Melbourne at the height of its land boom in 1888, he was no doubt impressed by the profits to be made from speculation. In partnership with 'Tombo' Cooper, a dapper young civil servant with the Lands Department, he acquired several suburban lots, including the area bounded by Goldsworthy, Princess, Caxton and Agett Roads, part of the deceased estate of the pensioner guard Samuel Sutton. Raising a mortgage of £500 on this property, they subdivided it into thirty-eight lots, nearly all of them no more than 16 perches in extent. This subdivision was marketed as the Bayview Estate in October 1896,

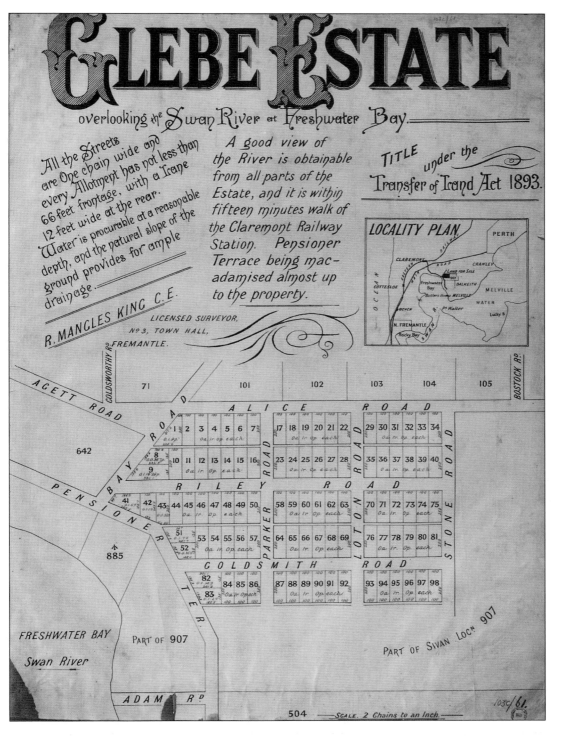

Real estate poster
advertising the Glebe
Estate, subdivided by
the Anglican Church
in 1896.

with an asking price of £35 for each lot. Although they were still being advertised at the same price in 1899, only half had been sold by the turn of the century.[4]

The customers for such modest properties were not among the wealthy and powerful of Perth society but, although they did not have the fine views and attractive settings enjoyed by the owners of waterfront properties, they lived within a short walk of the river and all its amenities. Thus they could share the pleasures of the local lifestyle in a way less accessible to the residents of such rising working-class suburbs as Subiaco, North Perth and Leederville. They used the same local tradespeople as the 'silvertails' and would in time barrack for the same sporting teams.

Inadvertently Stirling and his fellow developers had ensured that for most of the next hundred years Claremont would include a broad range of social classes in the make-up of its community. No longer could it be seen as exclusively a precinct for the prosperous. In this, Claremont contrasted with its neighbour Peppermint Grove, where subdivision was carried out under a master plan initiated by one group of investors, and all the blocks were large enough to attract the well-to-do. Claremont never quite lost sight of its village origins, as a distinct community halfway between Fremantle and Perth, but it was to abandon the

Watercolour panorama of Freshwater Bay, c. 1896, using considerable artistic licence to show in one sweep the Osborne Hotel, the Indian Ocean and the homes at the head of the bay. Artist unknown.

backward-looking hierarchical model that Alpin Thomson and his peers had brought from rural England. Instead it would become home to energetic newcomers from eastern Australia with prior experience of suburban life in Melbourne or Adelaide and knowledge of Australian models for suburbs like Claremont.

Among the most divisive issues between the older residents of Claremont and the newcomers was the provision of a hotel. Since the first abortive attempt in 1887, the old residents had successfully resisted hotels as lowering the tone of the suburb. In 1894 Edward Massey, the pioneer storekeeper on the corner of Gugeri Street and Bay View Terrace, and a respected citizen whose premises were often used for significant public meetings, tried to apply for a hotel licence. He was strenuously opposed by a group of ratepayers led by Horace Stirling, and the plan was rejected. In the same year, however, a bigger investor appeared who could not be resisted.

James Grave was a Melbourne man who, having followed his fortunes on the New Zealand goldfields in the 1870s, arrived in Perth as a thirty-year-old in 1878, married and fathered a large family, and throve as merchant. He became a close associate of Harry Anstey, the fortunate English new chum whose party found payable gold in the Yilgarn. Although they enjoyed mixed fortunes on the goldfields, Grave and Anstey did well as part of a syndicate that subdivided

Osborne Hotel from the driveway off Stirling Highway, *c*. 1895.

The Osborne steps
and jetty.

Afternoon tea at the
Osborne Hotel, 1895.

most of Bassendean.[5] Anstey also took up property on the west side of Freshwater Bay—Anstey Street and Bindaring Parade commemorate him and his country estate—and he transferred the northern portion, adjoining the Perth–Fremantle Road, to Grave. In 1894 the latter set about building Perth's finest resort hotel on the commanding heights overlooking the river.

This was to be no mere pub, nor even the kind of respectable watering-hole contemplated by Edward Massey, but a palatial establishment where weary pastoralists and men who had done well on the goldfields could relax with their families or other companions. Grave planned to name his palace 'Osborne', after Queen Victoria's residence on the Isle of Wight, though he may also have been paying a compliment to a wealthy Perth businesswoman, Mrs William Osborne, who presented the grounds with a substantial iron gate. The extensive hotel would be surmounted by a tower and turrets and surrounded by landscaped gardens, with a flight of steps to the water's edge so that parties could enjoy a river cruise from Perth on their way to enjoy the delights of Osborne. To cater for those arriving by road, Osborne Parade was laid out. The Roads Board was uneasy about the scheme, but it went through. Several nearby residents, such as the Richardsons and the Burnsides, were pleased to have their properties connected to the Osborne's waterworks. Besides, the interests backing Grave were too powerful to resist. On 21 December 1894 the Osborne was launched with a fine dinner attended by Sir John Forrest and many other notables. The following morning the *West Australian* carried an advertisement in which a dozen prominent businessmen headed by Alexander Forrest sought investors for a public company to acquire the establishment. In the upshot Grave continued to be the main shareholder and controller of the enterprise.[6]

For several years the Osborne Hotel was a landmark. In 1897 W. B. Kimberly, Western Australia's first significant historian, described it to his readers in high-flown prose:

> As one stands on that precipitous eminence at Osborne which looks down on the broad Swiss-like expanse of Freshwater Bay and which reveals to the eye a perfect panorama of picturesque landscape he may well appraise the excellent taste of the designer and owner, Mr Grave, who has rendered an Eden in the Golden West. Magical works of art blend harmoniously with the pliable resources of nature's handiwork.[7]

With 'refreshing air, bright waters and indolence and ease and pleasantry, pleasure of every conceivable kind, there is no place left in this fair land to compare with Osborne' claimed the *Western Mail* in its Christmas issue for

At the bar, Osborne
Hotel

1898.[8] But Grave was not content simply with affording Claremont a monument of late-Victorian elegance. Moving with the times, he planned an up-to-date water supply and that modern marvel, electric light—in both of which Perth was lamentably deficient. His first attempts to put down a private bore and construct water mains drew fire from the Roads Board, who questioned his authority. It was thus not remarkable that Grave, although a man who claimed he had neither time for nor interest in running for public office, became one of those who would challenge the 'ancient colonists' who tended to dominate the Roads Board.

It was natural that this body should be the arena in which the newcomers challenged the dominance of the old hands, as its activities touched on everybody's day-to-day comfort. Roads, of course, were its main concern. Immediately on its formation in 1893 the Roads Board arranged for the purchase of a roller and two draughthorses from the Public Works Department. Unfortunately they bolted and got away 'to join the brumbies in the Dalkeith bush',[9] and the teamster had to be paid for a month of idleness before a replacement was found. Soon the main roads in central Claremont were covered with blue metal, their potholes filled and their surface secured by watering and rolling. It took much longer to extend such amenities to the streets in the new subdivisions, where few ratepayers were yet in residence. As an old man Dudley Napier, whose parents

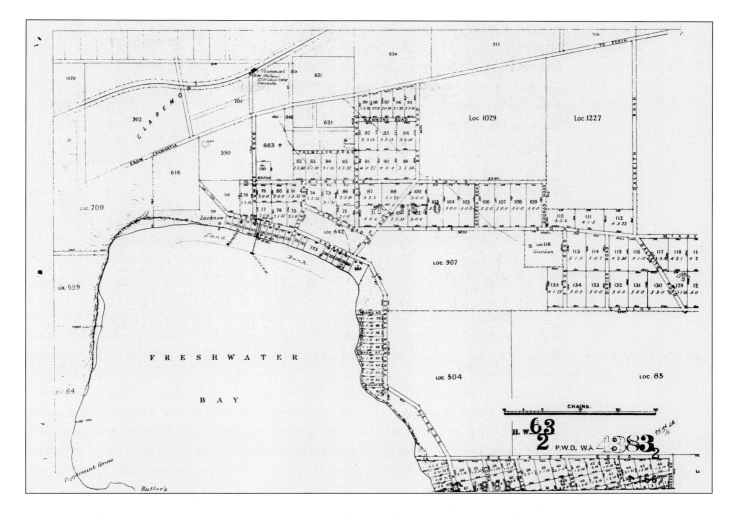

arrived at the Glebe estate in 1897, remembered that the road was only built to the first block, 'and the rest was just grey sand and bush; and I rather feel sorry sometimes for our parents when they had to lug us up through that grey sand. There was no water, light, power where we lived—nothing.'[10] Fortunately for the Napiers, a neighbour with a well allowed them to pipe water to their house. Householders living under such conditions were soon active in pressing the Roads Board for improvements.

The maintenance of the Perth–Fremantle Road was among the Board's heaviest and most financially demanding responsibilities. Under the hugely increased traffic resulting from the gold-rush boom, the highway deteriorated to the extent that the Roads Board was moved to authorize notices warning travellers that they used it at their own risk. Even Alfred Sandover's light four-wheeled carriage, known as a phaeton and drawn by a pair of fast-stepping

Public Works Department map of Claremont, 1896, showing subdivisions.

- 67 -

horses, would take more than an hour to go from Claremont to Perth.[11] At one or two particularly rough sections of the road cabmen would steer their horses through the scrub on the verge, even at the risk of hitting a stump. Hazards along the road included straying cattle, stumps left where trees on the verge had been felled without authorization and—most serious of all—camels. Afghan teamsters driving their beasts from the port at Fremantle were long remembered as an exotic feature of those years. At the March 1895 meeting of the Roads Board J. E. Richardson complained that camels were causing considerable panic and distress to other travellers on the road. As one historian puts it:

> The Board was not sure whether it had authority to deal with camels— cats, goats, pigeons, chimney-sweeps, condensers, bathing machines and public baths yes, but the Local Government Act did not appear to cover camels.[12]

Sir John Forrest's Government assured them that they did in fact possess the power, and camels were restricted to travelling the Perth–Fremantle Road between midnight and 5 a.m. For at least another year or two they were still sometimes found at large during daylight—and still frightening the horses of other road-users —probably because the road was poorly lit at night. When the Roads Board erected a water tank and troughs at the Humble Road (Bay View Terrace) inter-section it was necessary to provide a lantern by night, and the foreman earned an extra shilling a day for lighting and extinguishing it. The road as a whole remained ill-lit for some years. In the winter of 1897 a young man named McNamara, out driving at night with his girlfriend, was fatally injured when his gig collided with a cab without lights. But in other respects the road had improved sufficiently for daring young reinsmen to earn charges of furious driving. In August 1897 a bicycle race from North Fremantle to Claremont and back attracted fourteen competitors, but the Claremont policeman was able to report that they 'did no damage and did not interfere with any traffic on the roads'.[13]

The other transport artery, the railway line, was upgraded in 1897 by the duplication of the line. The Perth–Fremantle service now offered a train every hour—three times an hour at rush periods—the journey to either terminus taking twenty-two minutes in 1898. (In 1998 it took fifteen minutes, though only nine for the rush-hour express.)

Claremont's other main street was still struggling to establish its character as late as 1894, the year it was renamed Bay View Terrace. At the Gugeri Street end it began convincingly enough: there Massey's store and bakery, by now an established landmark, was balanced by a permanent post office opened in 1896.

Bay View Terrace, 1898, from the railway platform. The 'vote for' signs on Massey's General Store and Bakery relate to the first municipal elections.

Claremont Post Office, 1896, designed by George Temple Poole. He also designed the railway station opposite.

It was like many post offices of its day in being situated close to the railway station, and Temple Poole ensured that its architecture was worthy of Claremont. The first full-time postmistress, Susan Commerford, was a Geraldton-born young woman with telegraphic skills who enjoyed a job opportunity that would be denied women of the next generation.

The nucleus of store, post office and railway station turned the scale in ensuring that Bay View Terrace would become Claremont's major shopping centre; otherwise the Perth–Fremantle Road might have become a ribbon development of shops and businesses similar to Albany Highway in Victoria Park, which would have made for serious traffic congestion in the future. (And there was no wide alternative artery in Claremont that could have carried through traffic in the way that Shepparton Road supplemented Albany Highway in Victoria Park.)

The visitors who strolled south from the station down Bay View Terrace would have found few shops a hundred years ago. Old inhabitants remembered little more than a newsagent and tobacconist, a butcher and a hardware store. Halfway down the block, where Diver Street (now St Quentin Avenue) met it on the western side, Wing Hai's Chinese laundry was early on the scene. Its proprietors were frequently in trouble with the Roads Board for allowing soapy water to discharge into the gutters, and the pigtailed Chinese were sometimes harassed by the local small boys. Dudley Napier recollected that:

> … the thing to do was to go along there and spit on the ground, then put your hat over it and run around it—that was supposed to incite the Chinese. They would come out waving an iron, and we would run like the very devil. Why we did it, and why it incited them we don't know yet.[14]

Middle-class Claremont householders nevertheless patronized the laundry, and it remained in business until well after World War I. A second laundry appeared in the district in 1899, this one located on the Perth–Fremantle Road.

South of the highway lay the government reserve, still housing the decaying remnants of the old convict depot, and beyond was the State School, then a one-roomed limestone building erected in 1893. At this point Bay View Terrace still had a countrified look. Opposite the school was a little vineyard where children could buy a penny bunch of grapes, as well as the forge of a blacksmith named Wightman who could be persuaded to make iron hoops for the younger boys and girls. Beyond the vineyard was the block where David Forrest, pastoralist brother of Sir John and Alexander, built himself a wide-verandahed house which he named 'Minderoo' after the family's sheep station on the Ashburton. This

The home of land and estate agent Harry Blake, 1898, on the south-east corner of Bay View Terrace and Stirling Highway.

cheek-by-jowl combination of opulent residences and modest small businesses was not unusual in the overgrown country town that was Perth a hundred years ago: Sir John Forrest's own dwelling, 'The Bungalow' in Hay Street, was a spacious colonial residence well suited for a powerful premier, but its back yard in Murray Street was neighboured by very humble cottages, some of them brothels. Claremont was far too respectable for such establishments, but its social character was becoming rather mixed.

Claremont a hundred years ago comes to life in the unlikely pages of the police records, specifically the day-to-day occurrence book from September 1896 to December 1897 kept by the first officer posted to the Claremont police station, Constable Ernest Huxtable.[15] A mature man in his early forties, he had served five years with the British cavalry in India before coming to Western Australia, and was considered responsible enough to look after a district extending from Crawley in the east to Cottesloe and Buckland Hill. He patrolled this area on his horse, Hector, keeping strict accounts of his mileage, and performing an impressive variety of duties. He collected data for the statistical register, shot sick dogs and horses if their owners requested a merciful euthanasia, kept order at election meetings, prosecuted those who illegally killed wildlife and dealt with petty offences ranging from illegal firewood cutting on Crown Land and the larceny of chickens from fowlyards to the theft of a dinghy and fishing rod

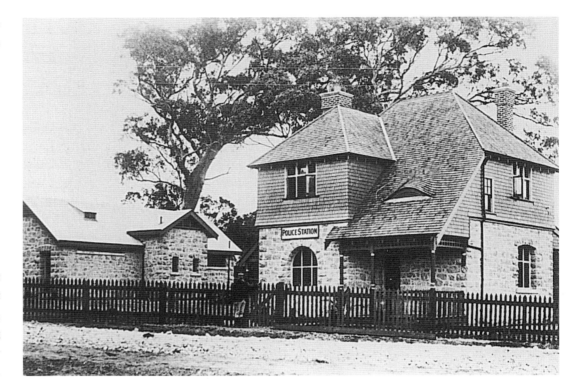

The Claremont Police Station, on Claremont Hill, Stirling Highway, 1895. This building also was designed by George Temple Poole.

Claremont Museum building as it was *c.* 1892. On the left is Constable Huxtable mounted on his horse, Hector.

belonging to the Attorney General, Septimus Burt. He interviewed suspected wife-deserters from elsewhere in Australia, and even—nearly thirty years after the end of convict transportation—took the particulars of one or two elderly ticket-of-leave men who were still required to report their movements to the authorities.

Claremont in 1897 was still a semi-rural community, and indeed thirty-two men and one woman made their living by farming. Forty-six hectares were under crop in the Roads Board district and about 840 hectares used for grazing; there were even 4.5 hectares of vineyards, mostly growing table grapes but with at least one small wine producer. Farm produce included modest amounts of butter, pork, ham and bacon and over 2,400 kilograms of honey from 113 beehives—wild-flowers were still plentiful.

Huxtable reported bushfires in Peppermint Grove in 1896 and on Gallop's Dalkeith property in the following year. Stray stock were a constant problem. The bull from Hamilton's dairy kept breaking loose in the winter of 1897, and there was trouble after it gored a horse belonging to Councillor Richardson. In August the trains were delayed when a cow wandered on to the line and was killed. Uncontrolled dogs worried cows, and when caught in the act were shot. There were even episodes of that classic Australian drama, children lost in the bush. In November 1896 Joseph Langsford's two boys, aged four and six, were missing all day but turned up safely in the evening at a friend's house in Mounts Bay Road. Some months later two slightly older girls, Esther and Ann Cleak, wandered away from their home in Grant Street, Cottesloe. Having slept all night under a large gum tree, they crossed the railway next morning and made their way to the river, where to everyone's relief Constable Huxtable found them.

Wayward juveniles occupied a good deal of the policeman's time. Regularly boys got into trouble for throwing stones. The boys who stoned the roof of the Aboriginal camp were birched; those who broke the windows of Mrs Herbert's old school building were reported to their parents, no doubt with similar conse-quences. When a boy was found to have stolen a flute from the government school his mother asked Mr Peel, the headmaster, to inflict punishment, and Mr Peel no doubt obliged. Guy Fawkes Night brought its temptations, and in November 1897 two boys of six and seven were in serious trouble for stealing £2 10s from the tent of a man camped near the school. Their big spending on fireworks at Koeppe's store had brought them under suspicion, and retribution followed.

The presence of a tent pitched somewhere near the corner of Bay View Terrace and Princess Road reminds us that even late in 1897, four or five years after the first fever of the gold rush, travellers were still arriving at Fremantle with little but their hopes and heading inland to find their fortunes. Huxtable was

Postcard showing two
children at Butler's
Swamp.

tolerant about allowing teamsters and individual travellers to camp on government reserves, but if they abused matters by staying more than two or three
weeks he would move them on. The camps of squatters who stayed longer were
apt to become an eyesore. As the warm weather approached he took action
against families such as the occupants of a hut on the foreshore whose litter
included not only a quantity of bottles and tins, but worse. They had no latrine,
and 'the family (7 people in all) has committed a nuisance all along the beach'.
The following year the health authorities heard that, because of the number of
tents pitched near the river at the Glebe estate, the bush was 'becoming foul'.

More than once Huxtable made a point of noting that there were a lot of
strangers in the district, and he recorded anything unusual about them. On
8 November 1897 he reports meeting 'four men known as Gatwood's push
walking from Perth to Claremont, these men is suspicious characters and known
to be idle loafers'. He advised them to keep moving. More often his encounters
were simply exotic. One day there might be four sailors, including a black
American, who had probably jumped ship; another day four Italians who could
not speak English and seemed to be wandering. Most remarkable of all, on a
March day he sighted two men walking from Claremont to Crawley *without
hats*. It is easy to forget how fashions have changed during the last hundred years.
Mistrust of the alien remained constant, however. Several times householders
complained about the presence of Indian hawkers, though they could seldom be

shown to have disobeyed any regulations. But there were also examples of cultural sensitivity. When 'Kella Sing, an Hindoo' died, the authorities gave permission for his body to be cremated in its coffin by Perth's leading funeral director, Donald Chipper, in a paddock near the Osborne Hotel. (There would be no crematorium in Perth for decades.) Huxtable was present at the ritual, and reported a large number present including many who were not Indians.

Some of these passing travellers required Huxtable to act as an agent of social welfare. Finding an old man, James McHugh, very ill in his tent, Huxtable organized his admission to hospital. There was a more tragic scene late one night in March 1897 when he found the priest from Fremantle, Father O'Rhyan, searching for a tent where a recent arrival from Sydney named Doherty lay dying. The priest arrived in time for the last rites, but the newly arrived widow and family were left destitute, with no furniture or effects. It is good to know that a fortnight later a concert and ball took place at the Osborne Hotel to raise funds for Mrs Doherty. In an age largely ignorant of psychiatry, Huxtable also had to look after the emotionally disturbed. He recorded only one suicide—a woman suffering from depression who took poison—but there were two or three other cases of troubled spirits who wandered off into the bush, including one man at Butler's Swamp who 'ran into the bush at 9.30 p.m. wearing only stockings, he has been going off his mind for some time now, saying the natives were going to kill him'.

By this time the remaining Aborigines in the Claremont neighbourhood were beyond threatening anybody, though they had permanent quarters at Butler's Swamp and two or three temporary camps. In March 1897 John Elliott Richardson was demanding the removal of a camp which he thought too close to his elegant home. After playing with Nyungar kids at another camp near Hammond Road a small boy, Douglas Caporn, came home with lice in his hair, and he could vividly remember more than eighty years later how his mother scrubbed him down and burnt all his clothes.[16] Constable Huxtable used to visit the Butler's Swamp camp regularly. Some of these visits were formal: in June 1897 he had to take a census of all the inhabitants, and he supervised the distribution of rations by the foreman of Hamilton's dairy. As it was the diamond jubilee of Queen Victoria, twenty-seven Aborigines each received provisions costing ten shillings, about a day's wages for a skilled working man.

If on some of his visits Huxtable was the firm hand of the law, for instance shooting their dogs if too many were out of control, on other occasions he was humane and fair. In June 1898, when an epidemic of measles swept the Butler's Swamp camp and the Aborigines could not go out to work and lacked food and blankets, Huxtable sought permission to distribute rations from the Claremont police station. At another time, finding a man called Johnny very ill with nobody to look after him, the constable gave him food and arranged for the police cart to transport him to Subiaco hospital. When an old lag stole money from an Aboriginal woman, Huxtable made sure he was charged for the offence.

From time to time complaints reached him when parties of Aborigines walking down the main road to Fremantle were in liquor and noisy, and once Joseph Langsford wanted something done about a loud corroboree because it was too close to his house—he lived near Katabberup, the site of the Halfway Tree, and this could well have been a traditional site for get-togethers. Huxtable usually managed to deal with such problems diplomatically and without force, but it is illuminating to reflect that a hundred years ago the owner of a select Claremont residence was more likely to be disturbed by Aboriginal merrymaking than by a neighbour's ghetto-blaster.

Huxtable's journal throws some interesting sidelights on Claremont's elite. They kept an eye on him. He showed no surprise when Horace Stirling, exercising his right as justice of the peace and Roads Board chairman, and with his satellite 'Tombo' Cooper in tow, paid the police station an unscheduled visit one afternoon and was pleased to comment that everything was highly creditable. Huxtable for his part visited all the 'silvertails' regularly, and on the few occasions when they voiced complaints dealt with them promptly. When Mary Burnside found a man and his son fishing without permission from her family's private jetty, she summoned Huxtable and he came at once. Edward Keane, ex-Mayor of Perth and high-rolling speculator, called for the constable after an encounter with a drayman who used impertinence when Keane upbraided him for driving on the wrong side of the Perth–Fremantle Road.

Huxtable was obliged to be in attendance when any of the local notables gave a major entertainment, and this meant late nights—as late as 3.10 a.m. when the McNeills of Peppermint Grove held a ball. At Alpin Thomson's ball in the early spring of 1897 'a large number of guests' overcoats, umbrellas, etc. were on the verandah. The Constable remained on duty until the dance was over, everything orderly, returned to station 1.30 a.m.' He was less tolerant of the amusements of the masses, and on one occasion peered in at the kitchen window of the Bay View Terrace newsagent, Peter Williams, to find him with the storekeeper Koeppe and 'some fellow wearing glasses' gambling for money; but he does not seem to have prosecuted them.

The upper-class residents kept up the tone of the suburb. Shortly after Claremont won the status of a municipality the good ladies of the district, including Mesdames Thomson, Richardson and Sandover, whose homes were on the cliffs overlooking Freshwater Bay, arranged a ball at the new Christ Church parish hall. In arranging such an event to raise money for the Hospital for the

Blind, they were following the time-honoured tradition that charitable works were among the duties of well-born women. Among the Perth notables who attended were Lady Onslow, wife of the Chief Justice, and her daughters. The compiler of the *West Australian*'s social notes was quite entranced by the planning that went into the occasion:

> The supper was arranged on the stage and the tables were a mass of lightly tinted carnations. Even the room itself was decorated with these sweet scented blossoms intermixed with the greenery... The dance was a Cinderella, and the programmes were ornamented with a clock, on whose face the hands pointed to 12 o'clock, and a small shoe, presumably the one Cinderella of the fairy tale left behind in her hurried flight.

There was no danger of the visitors from Perth being transformed into ragged maids, since 'most of them left by the 11.30 train'.[17]

A topic for discussion at the ball would no doubt have been the third meet of the Claremont Hunt Club, which had taken place just a few weeks earlier. As

Constable Huxtable's Village

After the hunt, members of the Fremantle Hunt Club enjoy afternoon tea at 'Norfolk', home of Mr and Mrs Horace Stirling, on the north side of Stirling Highway, Claremont, *c.* 1900.

in England, some members of the upper class found time to pursue hunting as a leisure activity and had sufficient funds to possess well-bred mounts and all the trappings necessary for riding to hounds. The Claremont Hunt Club followed a course extending from the gates of Perth Park (now Kings Park) 'over splendid galloping country…to an unknown point in the vicinity of Osborne'.[18] Among the followers of the hunt was the engineer C. Y. O'Connor, who on one occasion while galloping through the bush north of the railway line was thrown when his horse stumbled over a concealed tree stump. After their brisk exercise the members of the hunt often completed the day with afternoon tea in the gardens of Horace Stirling's home on the Perth–Fremantle Road. But as the 1890s drew to a close the Hunt Club was already becoming an anachronism: soon it would not be possible to gallop through open bushland at Claremont. And the colonial gentry who had controlled the affairs of the community would be receding into the background.

Chapter V

Creating a Council
1897–1905

AN OFFICIAL PUBLICATION, the *Western Australian Year Book* for 1896–97, described Claremont as a 'prettily situated … fashionable suburb', in contrast to Leederville, which was simply a 'rapidly growing municipality', Subiaco, which was 'thriving', and Bayswater, merely 'a growing hamlet'.[1] The Acting Premier, Edward Wittenoom, observed that Claremont was a 'fashionable place', whereas Subiaco was a 'working man's suburb'.[2] The Governor himself, Lieutenant Colonel Sir Gerard Smith, set his seal of approval on the suburb when he opened the Claremont Wild Flower Show in 1898. He thought Claremont 'an exceedingly picturesque and pleasant locality'.[3] A more perceptive observer noted that Claremont, while fashionable, included a wide range of residents:

> … here is the prosperous old West Australian gardener settled and tilling his own ground; here is also the government official of all grades filling the villas and mansions springing up around Freshwater Bay; here is the legislator, even the cabinet man, helping to give a conservative air to the place.[4]

He identified Claremont's most significant formative elements. The remnants of the pensioner guards had become 'the prosperous old West Australian' gardeners, though some prospered less than others. Their manner of earning their incomes still linked the smallholders of Butler's Swamp with their pensioner guard parents and grandparents, and artisan families such as the Caporns and the Effords were respectable rather than comfortably off. The upper class, in emulating their gentry forebears, lent 'a conservative air' to their suburb. But it was the new element he identified, the civil servants 'of all grades' moving into a range of housing, who represented a new force in the emergent suburb. Many of the newcomers chose to live there, at least in part, because of its prevailing social image. The upwardly mobile among them had no wish to rock the boat of established social custom. But they represented a force for change nevertheless.

As the Claremont Roads Board's responsibilities widened during the 1890s, the clique of old residents who had managed it found their grip loosening as the new men pushed forward. At the end of 1894 Burnside resigned to concentrate on his new responsibilities as Crown Solicitor and was succeeded by the 28-year-old Patrick Fitzpatrick, who, having arrived as a teenage migrant from Ireland, had worked his way up to become secretary to a timber firm—a background that distinguished him markedly from the likes of Burnside, Temple Poole and Alpin Thomson. At the same time Thomson resigned as chairman, to be followed after a short interval by the energetic Horace Stirling, who was to straddle the opposing forces of conservatism and progressivism in the emerging suburb with increasing uneasiness. On the one hand his entrepreneurial skills led him to invest heavily in the future of the suburb as owner or part-owner of subdivisions; on the other hand he enjoyed the pleasures of Claremont as a seemly suburban retreat and the considerable prestige that accrued to him as a community leader.

Late in 1896 four seats on the Roads Board were open to contest. Horace Stirling and Alpin Thomson renominated for two of them, but Temple Poole wanted to retire. One of the most acceptable among the newcomers, Joseph Langsford, was early in the field. An accountant and Wesleyan layman who had just built a home on the new subdivision next to the Congregational Hall, Langsford shared with other members an interest in the promotion of Claremont real estate, and at thirty he brought a youthful vigour to civic affairs. This cosy arrangement came under challenge from James Grave of the Osborne Hotel, who found an ally in a solicitor recently arrived from the east, William Smith. Another newcomer, James King, also threw his hat into the ring.

In those years the practice was that, when nominations closed, the returning officer would call for a show of hands from the electors present, after which a poll would be taken only if one of the unsuccessful candidates demanded it. With Grave's usual penchant for publicity, he planned that he and Smith should arrive with about twenty supporters just as the show of hands was requested. By an unlucky mischance their train from Perth was delayed, and they arrived after the show of hands from the few voters present had decided on Stirling, Thomson, Langsford and King. The returning officer refused to reopen proceedings.[5] Nobody commented on the coincidence that Alpin Thomson was Under-Secretary for Railways at the time, but maybe the driver and the fireman of the train were able to shout drinks all round for their mates that evening.

Smith wrote a furious letter to the press, asking Claremont's ratepayers: 'Are they going to abide by the hole-in-corner arrangements which have prevailed at Claremont for some years past, and allow the old hands to continue in the roost against new and independent blood, and this simply by a fluke?'[6] Grave also grumbled, but next year he succeeded in gaining election to the Roads Board. Its social composition had changed perceptibly over four years. Whereas in 1893 its members had included the Crown Solicitor, the Colonial Architect, the Under-Secretary for Railways, a member of the Legislative Council and a former mayor of Perth, by 1897 only Alpin Thomson and Horace Stirling remained of the 'ancient colonists'. The rest were Perth entrepreneurs: a land developer, the secretary of a timber firm, a mortgage broker and two merchants. Economic power was replacing social prestige.

By this time the boundaries of the Claremont Roads Board were shrinking, Peppermint Grove (including what later became the Town of Mosman Park) and Cottesloe having been carved out in October 1895. Another change in the local government arena took place when it became necessary to set up a local board of health. As an unwelcome consequence of the gold rushes, Western Australia experienced several epidemics, and typhoid was a recurring problem in an age of poor water supply and sanitation. Because these diseases showed themselves most conspicuously in the towns, rural ratepayers objected to subsidizing the new boards of health set up to monitor these problems, so it often happened that a board of health did not take responsibility for the entire local government area in which it was situated. This happened in Claremont. The boundaries created for the Claremont Board of Health covered only the settled areas on either side of the railway from Peppermint Grove on the western side to the lines of Loch Street and Bay Road on the east, with a deviation to take in the Glebe estate. These were the areas with established population, and they were practically identical with the present Town of Claremont. In March 1897 the board's members were appointed. There were the expected names—Horace Stirling, Alpin Thomson, Joseph Langsford and Patrick Fitzpatrick—together with those of George Edwards, a York farmer and storekeeper with Fremantle investments, James King and James Thomson, both subsequently destined to become mayors of Claremont.

The legend has grown up that the Town of Claremont separated itself from the rest of the Claremont Roads Board (now the City of Nedlands) because the snooty ratepayers of the built-up district centred on Bay View Terrace could not endure carrying the burden for the underdeveloped remainder, thus short-sightedly depriving Claremont of whatever glamour resulted from the later growth of Dalkeith and Nedlands.[7] Like most legends this is not quite accurate. The mundane truth is that at a period of rapid suburban growth the hard-pressed bureaucrats of Sir John Forrest's day carved out municipal boundaries and approved street planning with scant regard to the needs of future generations. The Claremont Board of Health levied a rate only on the populated parts of the Roads Board, and it proved difficult to administer the Health Act through a roads board that had to make regulations partly for the area covered by the Board of Health and partly not. Hence pressure arose for the partition of the Claremont Roads Board.

Probably Horace Stirling foresaw this; he was certainly a busy citizen in those autumn months of 1897. In mid-May he was to be found attending a registration court to protest successfully against the omission of the names of more than a hundred Claremont ratepayers, his own included, from the electoral roll for parliament. Once on the parliamentary roll, electors could also vote for local government. A few days later, on 19 May, the Roads Board endorsed a proposal to grant municipal status to the portion of Claremont covered by the Board of Health.

Why was Stirling so eager for Claremont to become a town? His explanation was ideological. A roads board, he claimed, was simply a servant of the Government whereas the members of a town council were servants of the people. But money was also involved. A roads board could strike a rate of only threepence in the pound, so that Claremont's revenue could be no more than £400 a year. A town council could strike a sixpenny rate, which the Government would subsidize on an equal basis, so that there would be £1,600 'to distribute for the advancement of the suburb'. Several of the large landowners in the Claremont Roads Board district were unhappy at the prospect of paying higher rates. By confining the proposed town boundaries to the area served by the Board of Health, Claremont would exclude property owners such as the Gallop family and the influential Sir George Shenton at Crawley House, as well as unrateable Crown Land such as the proposed cemetery at Karrakatta.

Taking with him his younger colleague Joseph Langsford, Stirling secured an appointment with the Acting Premier, Edward Wittenoom, requesting his advice and candidly admitting difficulty with the larger landowners. Wittenoom replied that if an influential and numerously signed petition was drawn up he would grant municipal status to Claremont. This was enough for Stirling, and on 8 July, as Chairman of the Roads Board, he convened a meeting at the Congregational Hall to frame such a request. It was a happy coincidence that the Stirling family still had influence with the *Daily News*, because on the very evening of the meeting the newspaper ran a leading article headed 'Progressive Claremont',[8] boosting the district in glowing terms. No roads board had striven more to carry out its duties, according to the article; no fashionable suburb possessed such beauty of scenery or easy access to the city. The following evening the *Daily News*, not without a compliment to Stirling for his clear and succinct presentation of the issues, duly reported: 'All doubts as to whether Claremont property owners and ratepayers desired to have their suburb awarded the dignity of a municipality... was set at rest last night by the almost unanimous verdict of a large representative meeting'.[9] Only four voted against the motion, and even they agreed to support a petition calling for the creation of a council with a mayor and nine councillors from three wards. 'In a suburb like Claremont', predicted the *Daily News*, 'there should be no difficulty in securing the honorary services of ten good men.' (Women could not vote until 1899.)

More than two hundred signatures were collected and a petition went forward. Then progress faltered. Later in the year Stirling had a change of heart. Perhaps he doubted whether the ratepayers would elect him mayor of Claremont; we do not know. He told the Government that Claremont wanted no further action for the time being. When the news leaked out in December, Joseph Langsford and other ratepayers wrote to the newspapers contradicting this statement, and for the rest of the summer Claremont split into two camps over the issue.[10] Stirling now argued that the boundaries of the proposed town of Claremont were too restricted. Besides, the Roads Board was giving good service, and the rates were far lower than in new municipalities such as Subiaco, Leederville and Victoria Park. These arguments appealed to some who regarded mayors and councillors as expensive luxuries and others who foresaw that there must be a gap of some months before the new council could collect rates. Stirling also asserted that a local contractor, a man named Carali, had offered to spend £1,000 on macadamizing roads and would await payment until the Claremont Roads Board collected a government subsidy for the purpose, but the deal would go through only if the Roads Board was in sole control. His motives puzzled many, but the bandwagon of municipal autonomy was rolling too fast for Stirling to stop.

During the autumn evenings of 1898 there must have been many lively arguments among the young professionals and businessmen of Claremont because on 22 April at a well-attended meeting at the Congregational Hall, under the chairmanship of the thriving hardware merchant Sydney Stubbs, a group banded itself together to create a Progress Association. Having made a good start by securing the support of the local members of parliament as well as three members of the Claremont Roads Board, the Progress Association then called for a further public meeting to press for a municipality. Stirling fought back, using the *Daily*

News to produce editorials in support of his stand and provoking a vigorous war of words with his opponents.[11] However his former allies Langsford and Stubbs mobilized support on the other side, and amply had the numbers at the second meeting, also at the Congregational Hall, on 13 May. At a rowdy but good-humoured meeting Stirling and Alpin Thomson were completely outgunned, as was Burnside when he urged a referendum on the question.

A little later Langsford led a deputation to the Premier, Sir John Forrest, who cordially supported the move to town status. Virtually his only query concerned the boundaries of the municipality: Would the new town of Claremont be too big?[12] It was one of Forrest's more controversial legacies to the future that he favoured the fragmentation of local government units—Peppermint Grove is an extreme example—and although Langsford and his colleagues promised to think about the matter no change was made. So the Town of Claremont was created in the shape and form which it would retain for the next hundred years.

Claremont was declared a municipality on 15 June 1898 and the first council elections took place on 13 August with sixteen candidates offering themselves for the nine vacancies. Horace Stirling did not contest the mayoralty, choosing to soldier on as chairman of the remnant Roads Board, but his brother consented to serve as auditor. Langsford, as secretary to the Progress Association, stood for mayor but was opposed by the president, James King. It was a lively campaign, and in old age Langsford remembered how 'for weeks before the election day candidates canvassed electors, addressed meetings, slandered opponents without worrying about the law of libel… The store and balcony of E. Massey at the corner of Bay View Terrace and Gugeri Street was plastered with electoral signs.'[13]

Despite frequent heavy showers, on election night hundreds of curious bystanders assembled outside the Congregational Hall, where counting took place. It took more than rough winter weather to deter the voters of a hundred years ago, but their vigil was in vain. Counting was incomplete by midnight, and in those God-fearing days no political activity could take place on Sunday. So it was only at 1.30 a.m. on Monday morning that King was declared victor over Langsford by 609 votes to 390.

King was typical of the 'new men' who were coming to the fore. A Scotsman from Ballarat, he had been only six years in Western Australia, where he made his money as a flour miller at Cottesloe and Beverley. He now had a grazing property at Mundijong as well as a fine Claremont residence. Old Claremont was represented on the Council only by that native son T. J. Briggs, who topped the poll. He was closely followed by James Grave and Patrick Fitzpatrick, who were now members of both the old Roads Board and the new Council. Among the newcomers, Edward Augustine Harney was a young lawyer whose 'silver tongue'

The first Town of Claremont Council, 1898. Public meetings were then held in the Congregational Hall, Stirling Highway. L–R J. H. Williams, A. G. Ross, J. de Castilla, A. Barrett, P. J. Fitzpatrick, Jas King (Mayor), E. A. Harney, G. W. Johnston, Jas Grave, T. J. Briggs and the auditors John Stirling and Mr Hill.

would soon win him a seat in the Senate of the first Commonwealth Parliament, but who rapidly grew bored with his Claremont responsibilities and resigned within a few months. The other new councillors—J. de Castilla, Albert Barnett, A. G. Ross, G. W. Johnston, and J. H. Williams—were less experienced, and it must have been surprising to many that they finished ahead of opponents such as Sydney Stubbs and the architect Edwin Summerhayes. The old guard that had run Claremont in the 1880s and the early 1890s seemed to have vanished from the municipal scene.

The new Council inherited its predecessors' concerns to make the most of Claremont's environmental advantages, but it was too late to preserve the Freshwater Bay foreshore. Whereas Peppermint Grove, undeveloped until 1893, had succeeded in banning subdivision on the river side of the Esplanade, Claremont was already compromised by the alienation of the original pensioner lots—now increasingly the site of expensive homes—and by later subdivisions authorized by the Roads Board to take advantage of river views. At least the public had unrestricted access to the river's foreshore, for Western Australia had learned from the example of Sydney and did not allow the alienation of land to the water's edge. Fortunately the grounds of Mrs Herbert's schoolhouse—'the 'Appy 'Ome' where those young bachelors resided—and another nearby block

Matheson's Terrace, 1898, later known as 'Bay View Mansions'. The building effectively blocked the view of the river from Claremont's main street, Bay View Terrace, thus making a mockery of the name.

(now Alex Prior Park but until the 1930s the site of a pensioner cottage) could be kept as reserves, but that was all. Even Bay View Terrace itself soon became a misnomer when a Scotsman on the make, the developer of Applecross and future baronet Alexander Matheson, put up a row of five maisonettes completely blocking any glimpse of the river from Claremont's main street. Nevertheless, the Council wanted to ensure that the built environment of Claremont lived up to its early promise.

Their initiative was the more remarkable because 1898–99 was a period of economic recession in Western Australia—a natural enough shakedown after the boom years of the early gold rush, but it had a dampening effect on Perth's market. The Council nevertheless pushed ahead vigorously with improvements. The section of the Perth–Fremantle Road that ran through the municipality was renamed Claremont Avenue and provided with a footpath. Tenders were let out for the making and metalling of a number of roads, including Bay, Princess, Goldsworthy and Stirling Roads, John and Bernard Streets and Pensioners Terrace. In an age when the hems of women's skirts swept the ground, and men prided themselves on the sleekness of their shoe polish, the dustiness of suburban streets was a constant cause of complaint.

Responsive to public needs, the Claremont Council also had a sense of its own aspirations for suitable municipal chambers, and on 24 March 1899 the mayor's wife, Elizabeth King, laid the foundation stone of a new building on the government reserve at the corner of Claremont Avenue and Bay View Terrace. The architect was Edwin Summerhayes, consoled for his failure to gain election to the Council. By the time the building was ready for occupation James King was no longer mayor. Driven into debt by the recession, he had been obliged to resign, and this time Joseph Langsford assumed the mayor's chain of office. He did not remain in the position for long, however, pressure of business obliging him to resign in 1901. He was followed for three years by Sydney Stubbs.

Local politics in Claremont was already reverting to the snug 'clubbishness' of the early 1890s, and there was even room for some of the survivors from that era. In 1900 Temple Poole resumed his seat on the Council, and in the following

Watercolour of Freshwater Bay, 1897, artist unknown. The painting shows Matheson's Terrace, Judge Burnside's home (top left) and Alpin Thomson's first home on the foreshore by the middle jetty.

- 87 -

TOP LEFT: Press Bros Grocers, on the north-west corner of Bay View Terrace and Stirling Highway, early 1900s.

TOP RIGHT: Intersection of Stirling Highway and Bay View Terrace looking towards Fremantle, *c.* 1910. Note Press Bros' new location.

LEFT: Mrs Nicholson's Confectionery & Fancy Goods Emporium, c. 1906. It was the third store from Bay View Terrace on the south side of Stirling Highway.

BOTTOM RIGHT: Intersection of Stirling Highway and Bay View Terrace looking toward Fremantle, c. 1899. The Council Chambers are on the left.

year, when Claremont became a parliamentary seat, he stood as a candidate; but he campaigned too much as an amateur gentleman and was defeated by the State Attorney General, W. F. Sayer. His presence on the local authority was a symbol of continuity with the ideas and aspirations of Claremont's municipal founders. Even Horace Stirling staged a comeback, bouncing back on to the Council at the end of 1901 at the head of a 'reform ticket' and unseating his old colleague Patrick Fitzpatrick.

If gentry attitudes still lingered among the members of the Claremont Town Council, the prevailing note was one of modern-mindedness. Admittedly they were still good loyal Anglo-Australians, and when Queen Victoria died in January 1901 the Council mourned her passing and unanimously resolved that 'The Mayor, Councillors, and People of Claremont moved by loyalty and love, desire to tender their humble duty and respectful reverence to His Majesty the King, Edward VII'.[14] They also decided to rename Pensioners Terrace Victoria Avenue in honour of the deceased sovereign. But when the Australian colonies federated into a Commonwealth in January 1901, Claremont insisted on marking the occasion with its own celebrations instead of mingling with the crowds in central Perth. As the local celebrations attracted five hundred adults as well as three hundred children from Claremont and North Fremantle schools, this was a sensible precaution against overcrowding. Claremont was also one of the first local authorities in Western Australia to take seriously the American innovation of Arbor Day, voting to provide fifty trees for planting on that day in 1900.[15]

Arbor Day ceremony, Claremont 1900. J. W. Langsford, a prominent citizen, is under the umbrella.

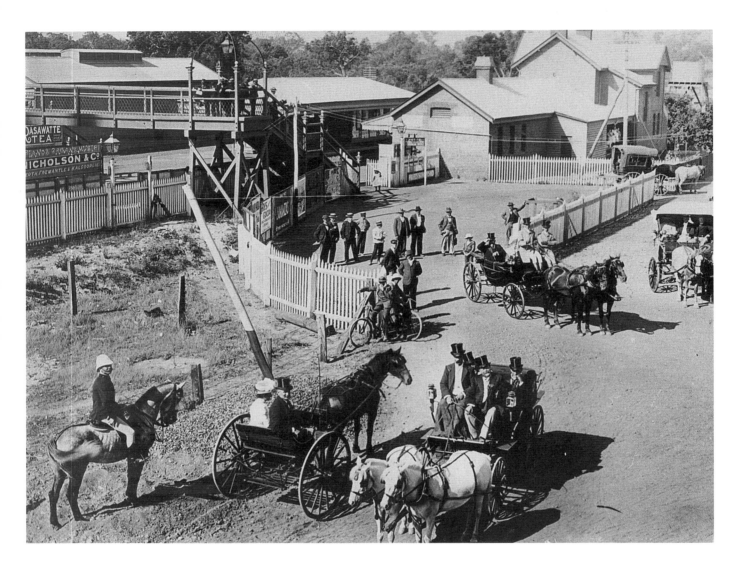

Sir John Forrest
leaving Claremont
Station in 1902 to
open the new road to
Cottesloe (North
Street). Constable
Huxtable and his
horse, Hector, are on
the left.

- 90 -

When the Council took over, Claremont still retained much of the atmosphere of a rural village, with no restrictions on the type or quality of building materials used. Artisans and tradesmen often used their skills to build their own houses, and in one street a number of social classes and lifestyles could co-exist. Among the first houses built in Goldsworthy Road in the 1890s was George and Eliza Caporn's home. The Caporns were an old Western Australian family from pre-convict times, the epitome of the respectable artisan class. They were boat-builders and ferrymen, carpenters, printers—all callings demanding sound practical skills. Some of the Caporns lived in their own houses in Victoria Avenue and Chester Road, but George's circumstances were more modest. According to family tradition his father, Henry Caporn, gave him a start:

The old grandfather—I'll never forget Dad telling me—he got all the tin, the wood and the bricks, and he said, 'There you are George, there's your bloody house. Build it!' That's all he said to Dad. So Dad got to work and built his home... He and old Joe Hossack built it—he was a carpenter, he lived next door...[16]

While they were building the house the Caporns and their three small children lived in a hessian shanty in the back yard. The house had a small living room and three bedrooms, and at the back a kitchen made of matchwood, a sleepout and a back verandah. An earth closet was in the back yard, and the only water came from a tap at the back verandah:

We never had a bathroom. We used to bath in a big tub; we used to take it into our room... My mother never had the pleasure of a washhouse. She used to do all her washing under a bit of a cover outside, used to boil the clothes in two kerosene tins over an open fire.[17]

The Caporns' family increased until they had eight children, but their home did not increase in size, although by the time the younger children came along some of the older ones had left home. George worked as a labourer and bush carpenter around Claremont until he eventually found employment with the Claremont Council. At no time would he or his family have identified with the 'silvertail' image of Claremont, and their modest 'do-it-yourself' weatherboard house did not accord with Claremont's residential image.

Not without causing some concern to the Council, a considerable number of the less affluent householders in Claremont were in fact choosing to build in jarrah weatherboards. Perth's first steam joinery shop capable of mass production had commenced operations in the early 1890s, and many working-class handymen found weatherboard the best medium for do-it-yourself home-building, but their architecture was often basic. Because jarrah was difficult to carve easily and quickly—and Western Australia lacked softwoods that might serve as an alternative—fine decorative timber products were not mass produced as in eastern Australia. Consequently, unlike Queensland and parts of Victoria, Western Australia never quite accorded weatherboards social acceptability as a building material.[18]

Nevertheless many small- and medium-sized Claremont villas already erected during the 1890s were made of jarrah weatherboard, perhaps because the railway made it easy to transport timber to the district. Some of them were in fact quite elegant. The Liddelow family's 'Kenwick' in Bay View Terrace, for example,

The Liddelow girls on their bicycles, 1898, outside 'Kenwick', Bay View Terrace, near the site of the present Old Theatre Lane.

featured a shingle roof, a considerable amount of wooden ornamentation and many of the stylistic features common in the Federation era. The rising sun motif, a widely used symbol of Australian nationalism, was incorporated into the gable end and echoed in the shape of a glass vent that allowed more light to penetrate the verandah near the entrance. This motif appeared also in narrow arched twin windows in the bay projecting from the house.[19] But some weatherboard houses had less to recommend them in a 'charming suburb' whose real estate agents were still proclaiming Claremont 'The daddy of them all for health, peace and pleasure', and a few specimens of cheap housing were positively incongruous. In Goldsworthy Road in June 1899 an iron house with a water tank was advertised for £45. (By comparison, a vacant quarter-acre block in Chester Road near the river was going for £105.)[20] Understandably the Council felt that the time had come to place its stamp on building standards.

On 28 March 1899 the Council proclaimed by-laws which ensured that brick and stone would henceforth be the dominant building materials in Claremont. It prescribed that in every one-storey house built of stone all exterior walls should be 14 inches thick, and all partition walls 12 inches; in brick houses the thicknesses should be 9 and 4.5 inches respectively. Basement walls were to be 20 inches thick for single-storey houses and 24 inches for those of two storeys.[21] The consequences of this policy were soon apparent. By 1903 the average value of a Claremont property was assessed at £217, in comparison with working-class municipalities such as Subiaco and Victoria Park, where 75 per cent of the houses were wooden and the average value £104. The number of dwellings in Claremont more than doubled between 1898 and 1907—from 391 to 822—so it was in vain that in the latter year a local newspaper complained that the restrictions were 'too draconian for the working man'.[22] Claremont's popularity was founded on its insistence on high building standards.

The Council kept abreast of new technologies, and was early into the provision of electricity. Perth as a whole was somewhat laggardly in this respect, having preferred gaslight for its streets, but with the introduction of a tramway system in 1899 electricity challenged gas for cost and convenience. In August 1900 a ratepayers' meeting endorsed the Council's decision to investigate the provision of local electricity, and in May 1901 a Mr A. Williamson, who claimed to be backed by a powerful financial syndicate, put forward a scheme for a Claremont Electrical Lighting Company with its headquarters in Gugeri Street. The Company secured Council's endorsement, but it was not until February 1905 that the plant was turned on by the acting mayoress, Mrs Whiting, and Claremont enjoyed clean power and, at least in Bay View Terrace, effective street lighting.[23]

MUNICIPALITY OF CLAREMONT.

LOCAL BOARD OF HEALTH.

SANITARY CONTRACT.

TENDERS are invited, and will be received by the above Board, for the performance of the necessary WORKS in the Collection and Removal of Night soil and Garbage, in accordance with the specifications for a term of three years.

Tenders close on Saturday, 31st August, at 12 noon. Copies of specifications obtainable from the undersigned, on payment of 2s. 6d.

P. A. HEPBURN,
Acting Secretary.

Council Chambers, Claremont,
August 9. 1907.

Guardian, 17 August 1907.

Good sanitation proved harder to achieve. The Council provided a rubbish collection system, but in January 1901 only half the households were using it. The Council's regulations also insisted that all new houses should be provided with a water closet or at least a well-constructed earth closet. Early in 1897 the Roads Board had hired a nightman with strict instructions to dispose of his cargo outside the boundaries of the municipality, only to find that he was dumping it on the Subiaco commonage, to the anger of the local progress association. A report of January 1901 stated that Claremont's privies were usually clean, but 40 per cent of them were badly built.[24]

In March 1898 acrimonious controversy broke out between the Roads Board and the education authorities when water from the Claremont school well, servicing two hundred children, was declared unfit for human consumption because nightsoil was buried only a short distance away. Although the well passed muster in May, by August its condition was 'worse than ever'.[25] This was not an isolated example. The majority of households relied for their water on rainwater tanks or wells, and some of the latter were very dubious indeed. As in much of the Perth coastal plain, Claremont's wells were liable to be affected by seepage, but despite the health hazards residents disliked criticism from official-dom. When in November 1898 the five wells servicing Alexander Matheson's terrace of maisonettes were pronounced unfit, he counter-attacked strongly. Why had his wells been singled out, he asked, and not those of such prominent citizens as the Burnsides, Sandovers and members of the Town Council? It was 'beyond dispute that the whole of well water in Claremont is an undesirable fluid for human consumption, though we are not prepared to say that it is any worse than the average in the Perth metropolitan district'.[26] The Council's response to such problems was to encourage householders to connect with James Grave's Osborne waterworks. This policy succeeded to the extent that, when the State Government purchased the facility in 1904, it was connected to 866 houses in Claremont, Peppermint Grove and Cottesloe. Only half of Claremont's households by then were serviced by the Osborne waterworks or a government bore, but the suburb was probably one of Perth's best in terms of provision of water supply and sanitation.

It was an era when infectious bacterial diseases were still a menace. Sometimes fever could be attributed to crowded and unhygienic conditions, as when two children were hospitalized from a Diver Street house with no fewer than six lodgers. But typhoid could attack even the affluent—ex-mayor King had one of his children stricken in the summer of 1899—and the health inspectors kept an eagle eye on Claremont's four local dairies as likely sources of the disease. The biggest, Rome's dairy (formerly Hamilton's) at Butler's Swamp, regularly received a good bill of health, but the smaller concerns, particularly one on the corner of Claremont Avenue and Vaucluse Street, were sometimes suspect.[27] Most sensational of all, in March 1901 a Stirling Road resident was taken to hospital with bubonic plague. The young man was thought to have caught the disease through working as a ratcatcher for the Perth City Council, though the health officer, Dr W. T. Hodge, was not impressed with the victim's living quarters, which, he reported, were in a very filthy condition. He was himself suddenly taken ill by the offensive smell. The house had only one room, subdivided by canvas partitions, but he could not order its demolition because it complied with existing regulations. He contented himself with quarantining the rest of the family and ordering such a thorough fumigation that the family later billed the Council for loss of and damage to its furniture. Far from abandoning their home, they remained in it until the 1980s, and the house itself was only torn down a few

Rome's Dairy, on the
corner of Davies and
Alfred Roads,
Claremont, *c.* 1905.

years later. In old age the victim's sister claimed that he had fallen ill because of over-indulgence in 'hot bush tomatoes' followed by ice-cream. It had taken twenty-four hours to get a horse-drawn ambulance to take him to the quarantine station at Woodman's Point, but once there he had passed an enjoyable six weeks idling and fishing. He may have been cracking hardy, or perhaps his sister's memory was faulty, as at that time a number of plague victims were dying at Woodman's Point, and it was generally feared as a terrible menace.[28]

By the turn of the century at least one forward-looking thinker was coming to realise that issues of sanitation might even affect Claremont's proudest environmental asset, the Swan River at Freshwater Bay. A memorandum exists from 1901—it is tempting to conjecture that the author was Walter St Clair Brockway, who had been taken on as part-time municipal engineer at the salary of £50 a year, thus commencing a long and distinguished career of service to Claremont—alerting the Council to the effects of unrestricted drainage on the quality of the river. For the majority of Claremont residents at this time it was the river that gave their suburb its special character. In old age Dudley Napier remembered with pleasure:

We made our own canoes (and had great fun making them) and went for miles in them. It was a lovely river – you could look down ten to fifteen feet,

crystal clear to the bottom. It was too far to go to the ocean, but we had this river and it was really a wonderful playground. We used to go crabbing, prawning and fishing… If I was asked whether I would like my childhood under the present conditions, I would say 'no'. I never look back to my childhood with any regret. I think it was wonderful…[29]

Clarence Braddock, a draftsman with the Lands Department, waited nine years after buying land in Claremont before he and his wife could afford to erect a Federation villa there, but his son remembered him as well pleased with his choice: 'I presume it was because he was always keen on fishing and crabbing… The end of Goldsworthy Road where we lived is only a quarter of a mile or so from the river'.[30]

At the beginning of 1898 the Claremont jetty was constructed near the foot of Bay View Terrace. That astute businessman T. J. Briggs was at once placing advertisements in the *West Australian* notifying the public that he had rowing and fishing boats for hire and could at a day's notice arrange the conveyance of picnic parties from the railway station to the jetty.[31] Ferry proprietors began to run excursions from Perth to Freshwater Bay, often taking in the Osborne and Point Walter as well. The growth of this river traffic led to the construction in 1899 of a second hotel, the Continental, not far from the jetty. This came about through the enterprise of Ansell Freecorne, a Polish migrant who within a dozen years of his arrival in Perth had advanced from a one-man tailoring business to prosperity and philanthropy through hard work and initiative. According to one story his shop was the first in Perth to display its wares behind a plate-glass window. He invested shrewdly in real estate, and was said to have 'large landed interests all over the city and suburbs and at Esperance'. He retained the Continental until 1912, when he sold it to a successful carrier, Tom Dunn.[32] Like

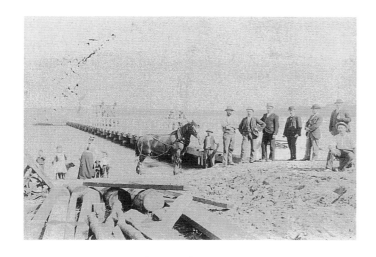

ABOVE LEFT: The opening of the Claremont Jetty, 1898.

ABOVE RIGHT: Claremont Jetty, 1903. The two men are collecting for the Home of Peace.

LEFT: *Yachting and Motor Boat Annual*, 1907–08.

BELOW LEFT: Hotel Continental, Victoria Avenue, Claremont, *c.* 1905

BELOW RIGHT: *Guardian*, 23 February 1907.

the Osborne, the Continental sought to build up a clientele among goldfields and pastoral families needing a change of scenery as well as catering for weekend holiday-makers. It was never as grand as the Osborne, but its style suited Claremont.

Freshwater Bay's growing popularity created a new demand for amenities. In simpler days the young men of the district swam in the river without troubling about costumes, but as fashionable residences spread along the foreshore and the tourist traffic became heavier, these free-and-easy ways were increasingly frowned on. More than once Constable Huxtable had to reprimand otherwise respectable youths for nude bathing, and after 1898 the Council minutes record several instances of members waxing indignant about this indecency. Good order was served by authorising the building of a regular swimming baths at the foot of Chester Road, and in November 1901 the Council accepted a tender of £583 for their construction. Mixed bathing was not yet accepted in polite society, and in its first summer the baths catered for male swimmers only. It was not long before the ladies of Claremont brought pressure to bear, and in July 1903 the Council found another £500 for extensions to provide a women's section. These baths were to serve Claremont for more than half a century, and even after ocean beaches eclipsed the river in popularity they were remembered by hundreds of youngsters in Claremont and surrounding districts as the venue where they learned to swim. Older and more affluent Claremont residents also made the most of the river. In March 1904 the Claremont Yacht Club held its first races, the riverside gentry being well to the fore: Mr Justice Burnside was patron, Alfred Sandover president and Sydney Stubbs commodore.

Young people at the river.

The river was not the only sporting amenity. As might have been expected in a suburb of Claremont's social character, priority lay with cricket. On 19

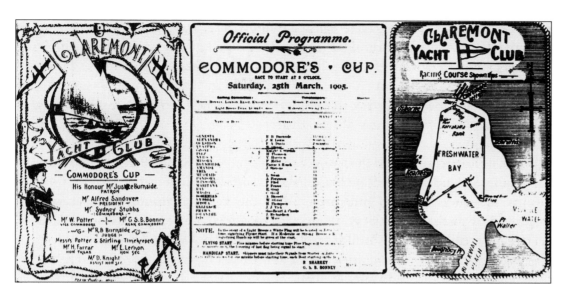

The first race program of the newly established Claremont Yacht Club, March 1905.

September 1898 three local notables—Freddy North, aristocratic brother-in-law and official Under-Secretary to the Premier, Sir John Forrest; Clayton Mason, Chief Collector of Customs; and Walter Gale, soon to be Clerk of the Commonwealth House of Representatives—convened a meeting at the Osborne Hotel to form a Claremont–Cottesloe Cricket Club. The club soon became one of the leading suburban sides, in 1902–03 losing the premiership to North Fremantle only—we have the word of mayor Sydney Stubbs for it—through bad umpiring.[33] Stubbs, during his term of office, was an active patron of sport. He supported the tennis club, formed in 1899, though when its courts opened in April 1902 he disapproved of their use on Sundays; but the club flourished, and by April 1903 was initiating pennant matches. Stubbs also approved the allocation of part of the municipal reserve on Bay View Terrace for the establishment of a bowling club in 1903, and, when some ratepayers objected to the alienation of this land, simply replied that the Council was 'prompted by the best interests, namely to make the district go ahead'.[34] With the same objective and at the same time, the Council reserved fifteen acres of land to the north of the railway for a football and cricket oval, and secured State Government assistance towards the cost of clearing and fencing the block. This oval would later become the home ground of the Claremont Football Club.

Until this time the land north of the railway had lain comparatively underdeveloped. On the high ground west of Claremont railway station, enough development took place to warrant the laying out of Shenton Road and a number of smaller streets named after the steamships plying the Western Australian coast: Saladin, Australind, Otway, Rob Roy and Servetus. In 1898 a halting place was provided on the railway line, at first named Osborne, but later changed to Swanbourne to avoid confusion with Osborne Park. It was not until 1903, however, when Legislative Councillors Henry Briggs and Robert Laurie bought 18.5 acres for £1,000 and commenced subdividing,[35] that the area began to take off. The writer Joseph Furphy, arriving from Victoria in 1904 to build a house in Servetus Street with his son's family, observed:

> A soft rain is falling on the roof; eastward, half a mile, the Perth–Fremantle trains are passing every fifteen minutes; westward, half a mile, the surf of the Indian Ocean is thundering on the beach; and the banksia and acacia scrub is thick in luxuriance all around, except where we cleared it away to plant melons and so forth. There are scores of palms within quarter of a mile, with innumerable varieties of shrubs unknown in the East, and all building for spring bloom. In many respects it is a beautiful country, but sandy—sandy…

'He was not indifferent to the appeal of the natural vegetation', writes Furphy's biographer, John Barnes, but 'the thick banksia scrub was grubbed out, the soil was dug and in only a few weeks radishes and lettuces were growing protected by a rabbit-proof fence.'[36]

Swanbourne's high position attracted a number of noteworthy residences, mostly along the line of Shenton Road. Probably the oldest, built in Saladin Street in 1895, was occupied by that unsuccessful candidate for the Roads Board, the lawyer William Smith. An unusual weatherboard structure built from pre-cut American redwood, the house with its elaborately turned verandah balustrades and friezes replicated a style favoured by eighteenth century landowners in the Southern States. Local legend asserted that it was built by an American sea captain who chose a site high on Swanbourne hill so that he could watch for ships rounding Rottnest to enter Fremantle, but there is no evidence to support this notion. After 1957 it was sympathetically restored by historians of architecture Ray and John Oldham.

Not far away, at the corner of Devon and Shenton Roads, an early mayor of Kalgoorlie and Legislative Councillor, R. D. McKenzie, built a house with stables and garage so imposing that the property was known as 'McKenzie's Folly', but it has survived for a century—since 1939 as a veterinary clinic. It was a satisfyingly stable neighbourhood. Amy Wright, who came as a girl of six with her family to their new house in Shenton Road in 1898, remained there until her death in 1985. During the intervening eighty-seven years she had risen to be a notable headmistress of Perth Girls School.

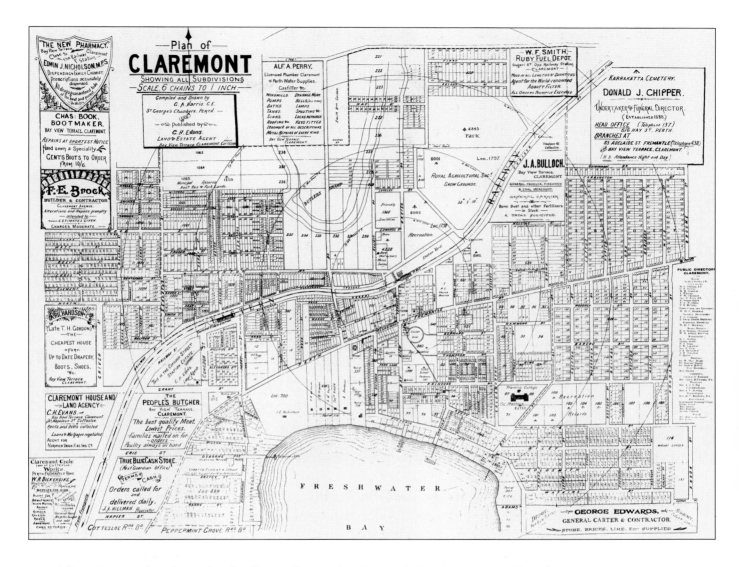

Plan of Claremont, 1903.

The Cairns family, who built 'Nyleeta' in Central Avenue in 1908, also remained there for over eighty years. Theirs was a tuckpointed brick home, whose architraves and fireplaces were decorated by Allan Cairns, a skilled amateur wood-carver. But elegance stopped at the front fence, its hedges screening the occupants of the house from the dust of Shenton Road. A daughter remembered that 'the locals used to hide rags in the bush at the top of the road to clean the dust off their shoes as they made their way to the railway station. Several times a week a water cart dampened the gravel sections of the roadway.'[37]

For the area further east on the 'wrong' side of the railway, somewhat further from the coastal sea breezes and access to the river, there was little residential demand; but as it lay halfway between Perth and Fremantle the northern part of

The first Grand Parade at the Royal Agricultural Society Showgrounds, 1905.

Claremont could be used for significant public purposes. In 1903 the State Government took two major decisions. An area of a hundred acres east of Claremont Oval was allocated to the Royal Agricultural Society, which had outgrown its old showgrounds in Guildford and needed an ampler site with good railway access for produce and visitors from the rural inland. This news was welcomed in Claremont, especially by the shopkeepers of Bay View Terrace, who could expect that the annual Royal Show would bring a healthy boost to their trade each year. More contentiously, the Government also fixed on the northern edge of Claremont as a fit site for a hospital for the insane. This was a major undertaking, since the asylum (which took five years to construct) was planned to accommodate over five hundred males, two hundred females and a nursing staff of nearly a hundred. The decision had logic, since the locality was healthy, accessible to the city, but far enough from built-up areas not to cause distress or offence to susceptible citizens.[38] But it was decidedly embarrassing that the institution would be 'Claremont', thus associating a respectable and upwardly mobile suburb with a collection of unfortunates who were 'not quite right in the head'. For decades afterwards, when hard-pressed parents anywhere in Perth yelled at their children, 'You kids, if you go on behaving like this, you'll have me in Claremont!', they meant that they would be driven to distraction, not that they expected to move up-market. Claremont ratepayers were unhappy at this usage, but it would be more than fifty years before authorities could be persuaded to change the name to the less fashionable 'Graylands'.

Claremont's sense of grievance was inflamed further by another government decision about the same time to relocate the home for old men—previously known as the Invalid Depot and situated in Mounts Bay Road—to a riverside site at Point Resolution. Again the location was chosen because it was both healthy and comparatively remote. Nobody seems to have foreseen that by the 1990s the Old Men's Home would find itself the centre of real estate of such opulence that

The Hospital for the Insane and its rural environs.

a money-hungry State Government would eventually oust the old men to a less desirable locality so that the land could be put to more profitable uses. Although the home was situated well within the Claremont Roads Board area, the Town Council was concerned because the main road to it ran from the Claremont station and shopping centre along Bay View Terrace and Victoria Avenue—which had all too recently discarded the name of Pensioners Row. Many of the inmates were ex-convicts, and Claremont citizens believed that they were 'an undesirable class, likely to escape, make themselves obnoxious with drink, and annoy residents'.[39] In June 1903 the Council protested, but in vain. It must be admitted that, with the coming of federal old age pensions a few years later, pension day saw the fulfilment of these gloomy forecasts. The old men were apt to draw their pensions at the post office before moving on to the Hotel Claremont or the wine saloon that gained a licence in Bay View Terrace in 1910. Their meandering path homewards is well remembered by those who, as small children, watched their progress.[40]

The Hospital for the Insane and the Old Men's Home were, after all, both on Claremont's periphery. In a central part of the suburb the Western Australian Government provided a building much more likely to nourish civic pride. In 1897 Cyril Jackson, a new broom recently arrived from England to sweep the Western Australian Education Department into the twentieth century, persuaded Sir John Forrest's Government that a teachers training college was required to cope with the vast influx of families following the gold rush. He told his officials to look for a site convenient to the railway between Perth and Fremantle, preferably close to either the Claremont or Cottesloe primary school, with space for recreation and the provision of boarding facilities. By August 1897 a piece of land was found between Bay, Princess, Goldsworthy and Agett Roads, zoned for residential purposes but not yet built upon. The Education Department secured the whole block, an area of approximately eleven acres. As usual, delays followed in funding and constructing the building, and Jackson was within months of returning to England when the Teachers Training College was opened on 30 January 1902.[41]

The college was an imposing two-storey limestone Tudor-style building designed by Hilton Beasley, the very competent Government Architect. It stood out as a fine piece of architecture, well capable of accommodating the fifteen young men and twenty-five women who, in return for free tuition, committed themselves to teach in schools throughout the length and breadth of Western Australia. Its appearance was enhanced a little later by the planting of avenues of fine sugar gums along its Bay Road and Goldsworthy Road borders, still one of Claremont's most admired pieces of landscaping.

Originally the plan had been that trainee teachers would gain experience by working with the children at the Claremont Primary School—hence the name 'Claremont Demonstration School'—as it was among the schools which not only provided a basic primary education but also prepared students for the primary and junior examinations conducted by the University of Adelaide. (The University of Western Australia did not exist then.) Between 1905 and 1912 the school premises were considerably enlarged to meet its new functions, and in 1907

Male students playing sport at Claremont Teachers College, *c.* 1910.

technical education night classes began in the senior school. Before long the need was felt for an alternative, and in 1905 a primary school was opened in the college's grounds. This was the East Claremont Practising School. In 1911 it was enlarged to include a one-teacher school intended to provide a model for the many rural schools of this type to which new teachers might expect to be sent. Under an able succession of masters-in-charge, the East Claremont 'rural school' came to find favour with many parents who liked the mixing of ages and the sense of belonging that it seemed to generate.[42]

Perhaps—at least by comparison with Claremont Primary School—East Claremont's teachers aimed more consistently at reinforcing middle-class standards of conduct. Often, it seems, working-class children had trouble in conforming. One such was Roy Caporn, who completed his first year of school at Claremont Primary and then moved to East Claremont when it opened in 1905. He remembered the crisis that provoked his leaving the school to return to Claremont in mid-1907:

> I was getting a 'yorky' nut out of a wild peach when it got in my eye. I screamed out 'Oh Jesus!' and a chap ran out of the schoolroom and went and told Gladman, the headmaster, that Caporn was swearing. He waited till school went in and he beckoned to me. I wouldn't move for a while: 'Caporn!' I went over and said 'What's the matter, Sir?' 'Come into the office.' I went into the office and thought to meself, 'Oh there's going to be a go here.' He had a cane in his hand, a cane about that thick. He said to me, 'Bend over that chair.' I wouldn't, so he made me, and he gave me two welts across the backside. 'Ooh!' I grabbed me behind and I ran out. That finished me with the schooling there. I said to Mum 'I won't go back there.' I showed her me behind, two big bruises right across... So I finished up going back to Claremont School.[43]

That year his elder brother also got the cane on several occasions, in his case for truancy as well as swearing. He too returned to Claremont School. Most parents and teachers would have approved of Mr Gladman's approach. School was not just a training ground for job skills and basic cultural background: education also embraced standards of behaviour.

The standing of a good State school headmaster in the community was attested at a ceremony in the Council Chambers in August 1907, when the mayor and about eighty citizens gathered for a presentation to H. J. Hughes on the occasion of his marriage. Hughes had been headmaster of Claremont Primary School since 1902. He was an inspiring teacher, who started a Latin class for the brightest boys and succeeded in firing them with enthusiasm for Julius Caesar's *Gallic Wars*. During that time Claremont students had done increasingly well in public examinations, but, said Mayor Saunders, Hughes was more than a teacher to the children: he was 'a comrade of them all, and one who has stamped the imprint of good moral character upon them'. Hughes in his reply acknowledged 'that the best work of a school teacher was to have an effect for good or evil upon the National Life of Australia'. They gave him and his fiancée a handsome side-board with a walnut frame and a massive top, two cabinets and three drawers, as well as 'three beautiful Doulton ware vases'. After the ceremony the Yacht Club entertained Hughes and 'drank his health in bumpers'.[44]

Middle-class parents often trusted fee-paying private schools to foster character and moral qualities in their children. Even before the opening of the Teachers College, Claremont was coming to be seen as the kind of healthy, central and attractive neighbourhood in which the better class of private schools might be established. The first to make its appearance was a relatively small affair started by a Miss Ross in 1896. She was followed by a Miss Allen in 1899, but the school reached viability only with the arrival of the redoubtable Miss Florence Parnell in 1904. Three years later, by leasing the Fergusons' riverside house, 'Dalnabrek', she provided the stability that would stimulate its evolution from Claremont Ladies College to the Claremont Girls High School of the 1920s and the St Hilda's of more recent years. Other ventures of this kind failed to survive. Mr A. C. Pritchard's Grammar School opened in 1901 and closed in the same year, while Miss Fenton's Ladies College in Bernard Street lasted from 1901 to 1903. In 1907 the Methodist Church purchased six acres of J. E. Richardson's 'Corry Lynn', on which in the following year another girls' school was opened: Methodist Ladies College.

These were not the first of Claremont's opulent homes to find a second career as a private school. An even grander landmark, the Osborne Hotel, underwent the same fate as early as 1901. Despite, or perhaps because of, his lavish invest-ment, James Grave had not been able to turn a consistent profit on his palace. In 1898 he had to discontinue the steamboat service to Osborne because the cost of repairing the launch *Alpha* was beyond him, and in August he sold the property to the Fremantle merchant William Dalgety Moore, retaining with his wife the management of the hotel. Either because of a recession or through increased competition, the customers still failed to come in sufficient numbers, and in August 1900, pressed by his overdraft with the National Bank, Moore put the hotel up for sale.

After six years the Osborne had lost its first bloom. The lath and cement ballroom was advancing into dilapidation, and the gardens were no longer so

View from the tower of Loreto Convent, formerly Osborne Hotel, looking down Bindaring Parade toward Keane's Point, *c.* 1904–05.

carefully maintained. Yet, with 'an existing building of large dimensions and a number of small cottages all set in beautiful and sizeable well-kept grounds' Osborne looked like opportunity to Mother de Salis Field, principal of the Loreto Convent school set up four years earlier in Adelaide Terrace. Requiring more suitable premises than a rented house in central Perth, the Loreto nuns had been contemplating a move to the land owned by the Catholic Church on the north side of Claremont Avenue, between Mary and Notre Dame (now Langsford) Streets. When Osborne came on to the market with suitable ready-made buildings, the Loreto sisters were quick to make a bid. After months of dignified haggling Moore agreed on the price of £12,000, which was the amount he needed to satisfy the bank. On 15 August 1901 the Loreto boarders moved into their new building with Bishop Matthew Gibney celebrating Mass.[45] James Grave, whose daughters went to Loreto, was not displeased with the outcome, but his spirit was broken. He soon succumbed to a lingering illness, and in 1906 he died.

Other schools cramped in unsuitable premises in central Perth noticed this example. Scotch College, founded in 1897 with a somewhat inadequate headmaster, needed space to grow by 1903. The college council asked the State Government for a grant of land in Claremont in May 1903, but this was refused. Matters came to a climax in June 1904 when, with no solution to the accommodation problem in sight, a new headmaster was appointed—the young and dynamic P. C. Anderson. Before his arrival in July, the philanthropic John Maxwell Ferguson offered to provide a deposit and raise a mortgage for the purchase of a large house in Shenton Road, Claremont, then on the market for £4,700. A twelve-roomed mansion standing on about eight acres, it had been built in 1900 by the chairman of the Perth stock exchange, Richard Barrett, who entertained lavishly with a retinue of servants including a butler and a coachman. By 1903 the money had gone, and Barrett, who had hoped to profit from sub-dividing the adjacent real estate, found himself obliged to sell up. It was bought as an investment, and for a time lay vacant. Small boys amused themselves by sliding up and down the polished floorboards of the ballroom, and the house was at risk of being vandalized. The new owner was willing to close with Ferguson's offer, and Scotch College received the news with 'a hearty vote of thanks'. In February 1905 the school, with seventy-eight boys, moved into its permanent home. Where Bishop Gibney had led the ceremonies with Mass at Loreto, the main speaker at Scotch was Sir John Forrest, booming prophecies that the school would be 'productive of much good to Western Australia and the Empire'.[46]

In such ways Claremont found itself integrating into the wider perspectives of Western Australia, if not as yet the larger British Empire, and thus becoming more than a pleasantly situated residential suburb. Claremont would be the background against which hundreds of young people—at Loreto, at Scotch, at the Claremont Ladies College, and later at Methodist Ladies College, St Louis and Christ Church—would be educated through some of the most formative years of their lives. It would play host to thousands of country dwellers—schoolchildren and their parents—who converged each year on the Royal Show. Claremont would also have to cope with marginalized groups such as the institutionalized insane, the veterans in the Old Men's Home, and the remaining few Aborigines.

But increasingly it was the professional middle class who were setting the tone of Claremont. If we follow the State electoral roll for 1904 we find that no fewer than 28 per cent of Claremont's male voters were members of the upper middle class. As well as wealthy merchants, manufacturers and financiers there was a large number of senior professionals—doctors, lawyers, architects, engineers—some retired pastoralists and many influential civil servants. Civil servants were also heavily represented among the 45 per cent of Claremont men who could be described as middle class. The local newspaper claimed that 'the civil service vote in Claremont, if cast in block, would largely influence the result of an election in the constituency'. There was a small group of semi-professionals such as journalists and draftsmen, but most of the white-collar workers were clerks in banks or insurance companies, managerial staff, salesmen and commercial travellers. There was also a large group of small businessmen ranging from master builders to drapers and storekeepers. Only 27 per cent of Claremont's voters were working class, and most of these worked in the building industry. Fewer than 10 per cent were unskilled or semi-skilled.[47]

The core of Claremont lay in such families—the men in three-piece suits travelling by train each day to Perth, the housewives in their long skirts bargaining cannily in the Bay View Terrace shops, the children exploring the delights of the river in summer, and the tradespeople, artisans and domestic servants earning a living there. These are the people whose experiences we should explore in the easy Edwardian years before World War I placed its imprint on Australian society.

Chapter VI

Consolidation
1905–1914

THE DECADE BEFORE the outbreak of World War I was a good one for Claremont. Western Australia continued to thrive, for although gold production was declining the State's politicians had found a new attraction for migrants in the opening up of the wheat country east of the Avon Valley. Although fewer new families came from the eastern States, their numbers were balanced by an influx of English migrants who, between 1910 and 1914, responded to the call to gain yeoman independence by farming the broad acreages of Australia. But the Perth metropolitan region continued to grow also, the population of the Town of Claremont increasing from about 2,500 to roughly 7,000 between 1905 and 1914. This growth made for lively times on the property market, as well as attracting numerous small businesses, not all of which survived in the long term.

A dozen real estate agents were now active in Claremont and a number of them had opened agencies in Bay View Terrace. These included John Bulloch, who in 1903 had been in business as a general produce, firewood and coal merchant with an office in the same street, but who had seen greater opportunities for profit in real estate and was now Claremont's busiest agent. Others operating from Bay View Terrace were James Arter, J. W. Holmes and Charles Evans, who traded under the name of Claremont House and Land Agency. A slightly later comer to Bay View Terrace was the firm of Ferris, Forbes & Ewens, ancestor of the present firm of Shellabear & Son. Around the corner in Gugeri Street, opposite the railway station, was Thomas Bow. Despite the presence of these local firms there was sufficient business in Claremont to warrant competition from larger city agents, including A. N. Geere (who lived in the suburb), W. Charles Hood, Wolridge and Roberts, Learmonth Duffy & Co., Hyem Hester and Toy, and W. Wilford Mitchell.[1]

Corresponding to the increasing number of homes under construction in Claremont was a vast increase in the number of builders and contractors living in the suburb. By 1908–09 there were seven builders, nine contractors, two plumbers and two painters and decorators, most of them located in Bay View Terrace, but a pocket of building-related businesses still remained in the Claremont Avenue section of the Perth–Fremantle Road near Millar's Karri and Jarrah Company, which had bought out a local timber yard in 1903. Other builders were scattered throughout the suburb, usually operating as backyard businesses, sometimes on a block adjacent to the builder's home. One group was concentrated in a comparatively low-lying area where the land was subdivided into small blocks: James Caporn (Chester Road), Matthew Goy (Pennell Road), J. D. Hossack (Goldsworthy Road) and Frank Allum (Princess Road). Others settled east of Bay View Terrace and north of Claremont Avenue: William Williams (Reserve Street), Thomas Bros (Vaucluse Street) and M. F. Sage (Walter Street).[2]

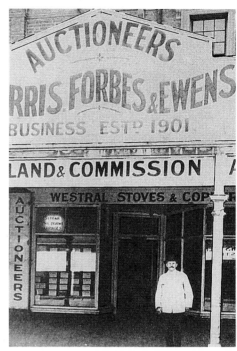

The office of Ferris, Forbes and Ewens, auctioneers and land agents, Bay View Terrace, 1912.

Architects were involved in the development of only the largest homes, most being designed by builders, who tended to copy architectural designs (after a time-lag during which they gained popularity) or took their inspiration from patent books and catalogues. Their inventiveness tended to be tied to the availability of building materials and mass-produced decorative items. Details of the work of only one Claremont builder have survived, perhaps largely because his designs were quite different from the more typical Federation villa. William Williams had come from Victoria in the mid-1890s and appears to have operated as a speculative builder. He is reputed to have bought a block of land and built on it while at the same time living on the site. He then sold the property and moved on to another block. This was not uncommon practice.

Two homes built by Williams still stand: 16 Agett Road (completed about 1905) and 9 Brae Road (1918). In addition he added a characteristic shingle-clad second storey to his own home at 24 Reserve Street (1907). The Agett and Brae Road houses are almost identical. Both are of two storeys, with a shingle-clad upper storey and either a whitewashed bagged brick or roughcast plaster-clad brick lower storey. Both have a small square porch with square wooden posts at the entrance; both have small bay windows with a wooden shingled window hood on the lower storey, the structure of which climbs upwards to form another

TOP LEFT: 'Norfolk', Stirling Highway opposite the Council Chambers, home of the Stirling family, 1904.

TOP RIGHT: 'Kilkerran', Shenton Road, home of E. C. Shenton and family, *c.* 1910–20.

CENTRE LEFT: 'Wainomi', 3 Victoria Avenue, home of the Sharkey family, early 1900s.

CENTRE RIGHT: The home of the Prior family, Victoria Avenue, on the riverside east of Chester Road, *c.* 1904.

BOTTOM LEFT: 'Karouil', 3 Riley Road, home of the Baker family, *c.* 1920s.

BOTTOM RIGHT: Croquet and tea at 'Hillside', 2 Agett Road, home of the Beart family, *c.* 1910.

bay on the second storey; and both have tall brick-strapped roughcast chimneys. There were two main influences on Williams's designs: the English Arts and Crafts style and the American Shingle, then popular especially among Sydney architects. With its extensive use of timber, his work is not typical of houses constructed in Claremont before World War I, the vast majority of which were brick villas.[3]

Location was still the main factor determining the price of a villa. This affected the initial value of the land and thus the size and quality of the home built on it. An analysis of house advertisements in 1908–09 indicates that those offered for sale were now almost exclusively pitched at the middle class. In the advertisements in which the price was quoted, 30 per cent were for sale at around £450 and another 30 per cent at £675.[4] Typical of the higher price range, perhaps aimed at the senior civil servant, was the following:

> Claremont, Victoria Parade [now Freshwater Parade] Pretty brick villa, six rooms, good garden, splendid workshop, land 49.6 x 165, £675, beautiful home.[5]

The lower middle class family seeking a home in the £450 bracket might consider the following:

> Claremont (on rise). Double fronted brick house, five rooms, kitchen, wash house, etc., land 50 x 150, £450.[6]

In general brick villas near the river fetched higher prices, as long as they were not too far from transport.

Although many new homes were under construction in Claremont in 1908, the more established nature of the suburb can be seen by the features identified in advertisements. Gardens with paths, lawns, fruit trees and vines were now common; a few even boasted ornamental trees and flower beds. Fences were so common as scarcely deserving mention. The water supply had improved with the building of a high-level reservoir in Congdon Street, where hills water, pumped from the reservoir on Mt Eliza, was stored. In summer this was augmented by supplies from two bores at Butler's Swamp. Many homes now had power and light from the electricity station, which had soon passed from private ownership to the municipality.

The appeal to status was very strong. Houses were frequently described as 'splendid', 'fine' or 'handsome'. The increasing number of smaller villas in Claremont was reflected in the appearance of the now rare adjective 'bijou',

- 113 -

meaning small and elegant, and the frequent use of 'pretty'. Other terms such as 'modern', 'convenient', 'handy' and 'ideal' gave the sense of a modern, efficient and progressive suburb, and were backed by descriptions such as 'substantially built' and 'perfectly finished', suggesting that shoddy workmanship had no place in Claremont—a consideration much in the minds of prospective buyers when so many houses were springing up rapidly. A small number of villas catered for less affluent families; these were described as a 'gift', a 'sacrifice' or just plain 'cheap'.[7]

Advertisements were more revealing than they had been earlier about the financial terms under which a house could be purchased. In 1908 the Perth Building Society offered loans on the security of houses—but only if they were brick—at 7 per cent over an eight-year term. Private lenders often charged higher rates. Some loans were arranged by the estate agent. A seven-roomed villa in Victoria Avenue, 'Riverside', was auctioned in 1908 for 33 per cent cash deposit with the balance to be repaid over five years at 6 per cent. What was it like to live in such a house? The catalogue for this property affords a rare glimpse of the image created within middle-class homes in the early years of the twentieth century:

Auction of Household Furniture and Effects
Owner leaving for the East
'Riverside'
Victoria Avenue, Claremont

Drawing room, dining room, breakfast and no. 1, 2 and 3 bedroom furniture and kitchen utensils, viz.

Pretty suite 7 pieces, bamboo occasional tables, walnut occasional tables, pretty bamboo chairs.

Handsome overmantle, rattan chairs, standard lamp (double burner), pair large vases, large cedar table (occas.).

Tapestry, Axminster square (10 x 10), door mats, hearthrug, pictures, ornaments.

Dining room suite (9 pieces) upholstered in morocco, nearly new.

Extension dining table (6ft), 8 day clock, child's combination chair, linoleum on floor (17 x 14), best quality go cart (springs) with hood, Gramophone (Edison) in good order, about 25 records, linoleum on passage (33 x 4) best quality, bamboo hall stand, pair hall curtains.

Handsome Huon pine bedroom suite (4 pieces), A & G and Vienna chairs, toilet sets, cedar chest of drawers.

TOP LEFT: The home of the Schruth family, Bishop Reserve.

TOP RIGHT: Mr and Mrs Schruth take tea in their elaborate sitting room.

CENTRE LEFT: 'Sandgate', 4 Goldsmith Road, home of the Moullin family, said to be one of the first tiled houses in Claremont, c. 1905.

CENTRE RIGHT: 74 Davies Road, rented by Thomas Fletcher.

BOTTOM LEFT: 29 Davies Road, owned by Mrs Mary Gallagher.

BOTTOM RIGHT: Interior, 6 Langsford Street.

Massive 4'6" half Tester bedstead, brass mounted, wire mattresses, kapok beds, Huon pine wardrobe.

Dinner service 60 pieces, gold edged with red flowers, Kerosene stove, mincing machine, primus stove, pretty tea service (34 pieces) gold edged with blue flowers, verandah blinds, 11 choice fowls, iron stable (for removal) and all the usual kitchen utensils.[8]

Amongst the trivia of middle-class domestic life is evidence of a comfortable world of considerable charm and elegance.

Memories, from a child's perspective, suggest that not all was formality and elegance. The Federation villa of Clarence Braddock, a civil servant and later a manufacturer, was just as spacious but adapted to a more casual living style:

The hall went straight down, and on the other side of the hall was my parents' bedroom. Going down the hall the next on the left was my bedroom, opposite there was my sister's bedroom, both big rooms. I used to sleep out a lot — people did in those days — on the front verandah. A lot of people slept out; that's why there's so many old houses with sleepouts. Everyone slept out, all year round: the fresh air was very good for you.

But there were refinements.

There was a verandah right across the front, the old bullnosed iron verandah roof. Then as you opened the front door there was a drawing or lounge room, the old family lounge with the photographs all around. You were only allowed in there on special occasions — you couldn't get in there and play or anything like that… It was very seldom used. The piano was in there. That was one of the early things they had me taught, the piano and the fiddle. But I'd no idea of music. I had to practise for so many minutes or hours a day and no-one could understand why the clock gained so much time. I'd wind it on! I used to hate the piano!

The sitting room had little practical function, but was a place of social display. Families eschewed its formal arrangement in favour of the restful and comfortable vestibule, forerunner of today's family room:

We mainly lived in the big vestibule. There was a big fireplace over in the corner; in cold weather we'd have a big log fire. Everyone would grab a chair, if they could, and sit around it. I used to get pipped to it and I'd go to sleep in front of the fire on the floor… We also had a very big table in the vestibule; we had our evening meal there…

The vestibule was the heart of the home. It was closely linked to the nether regions of the house where the cooking and washing took place, and in these sections the formal symbolism and carefully contrived appearance of the front room broke down when faced with the reality of everyday life:

> …from the vestibule, on the left was the kitchen. There was a big wood stove in the kitchen to start off with. There was no refrigeration… The ice chest was kept in the vestibule, or in a part of the kitchen that was handy…
>
> The kitchen led out to a big back verandah, a lot of it built in… On the left hand side there was the laundry, with the old troughs. At the other end of the verandah was a bathroom, and then another bedroom, a spare bedroom… In the bathroom originally—it improved as we got older—we had a tin bath, only tin, and a chip heater… There was no sewerage; there was an outside lavatory…

Outside, male activities tended to predominate.

> We had a garage built onto the side of the house when we got a motor car, a Ford, in 1915 or '16…
>
> There was a reasonable sized back yard with a big workshed down at the back. Dad was very handy with his hands… Occasionally we had chooks, and Dad built me a two-storey loft for my pigeons.
>
> We had lawns back and front and someone to weed them for clover. The old man occasionally used to plant things, but he wasn't wrapped up in the garden much—it was always a chore… But my mother was mad on plants. I think she was the major one who looked after the garden… She'd shuffle up everyone to try and get something done in the garden…[9]

Although material possessions might imply an elegant standard of living, at least one wife and mother in Claremont felt it necessary to struggle against the recalcitrance of her menfolk in order to maintain an image appropriate to the family's position in society. Another way in which the social image of private domestic space was signalled was by use of house names. Before World War I houses in Claremont were known by names rather than street numbers. These names provided a valuable indication of the personal values and preoccupations of the householders, as well as the image they wished to present.

Over two-thirds of the names chosen for Claremont homes before World War I had British associations. Names such as 'Norfolk' and 'Maxwellton', for instance, probably commemorated family links with England and Scotland. Many names appealed to status by their strong association with the country estates of the British aristocracy, such as 'Stanhope' and 'Rothesay'. Others had rural connotations, such as 'Cotswold', 'Grassmere', 'Glen Isla' and 'Ben Nevis'. Almost as many names suggested a love of nature, again in most cases linked with the British countryside, a countryside of untamed romantic woodlands, as in 'Hazeldene', 'Ashlea', 'Elderslie', 'Woodside' and 'Oaksea', rather than more ordered manmade pastures, although a few houses with names such as 'Cloverley' and 'Roseview' made this symbolic connection. On the other hand names such as 'The Manor', 'The Gables' and 'Gateshaw' revealed a firm link with both status and rural England. Other names revealing a love of nature were linked with natural features, again with British allusions. 'The Knoll', 'Riverside', 'Riverview', 'Hillside' and 'Hillview' reflected topography, and 'The Lookout' and 'Portsmouth' conjured up an English seaside. 'The Haven', on the other hand, was a haven from both the storm-tossed seas and the public world.

In contrast some house names revealed that, for a minority of residents of Claremont, Australia was indeed home. 'The Wattles' and perhaps 'The Pines' suggest an awareness of local botany. One-tenth of house names were based on Aboriginal words, such as 'Cooringa' and 'Goongaree', thus linking their European inhabitants firmly with their adopted land. Allan and Mary Cairns named their home in Central Avenue, Swanbourne, 'Nyleeta' meaning 'place of wild honey', because beekeeping was among their hobbies. But such names as 'Wahgunyah', 'Menindie', 'Kyneton', 'Wendouree' and 'Eureka' are more likely to reflect a family's origins in eastern Australia, especially the Victorian goldfields. Maori names such as 'Te Kohanga' and 'Pipiriki' suggested either New Zealand origins or memories of honeymoons or holidays. If the latter, they were also perhaps an indicator of status, for who but the affluent could afford the luxury of overseas holidays?

A small proportion of house names were more high-minded, revealing educated families who made use of classical allusion ('Elysium'), literature ('Milton House' or 'Ivanhoe') or even the operettas of Gilbert and Sullivan, written with the British middle class in mind ('Iolanthe'). Occasionally house names suggest a religious affiliation, as with 'Loyola', 'St Elphin' and 'Havilah'. The last was a Hebrew place name associated with gold and lapis lazuli, treasures appropriate to a home whose name was linked to the Garden of Eden. Another small group of house names revealed the strength of the ideal of marriage in middle-class suburbia. Names such as 'Jessmond' and 'Bryans' commemorated the linking of husband and wife in marriage, the union of male and female Christian names affirming the home as symbol of the marital bond. On the other hand a name such as 'Bethhaven', while no doubt flattering to the young wife, sited her firmly in the home, providing a haven of peace and domesticity to which the husband could retreat each evening from the stress of his urban world of business.[10]

Above all, the names of Claremont homes reveal the strength of British connections in the suburb, and especially a nostalgia for the British countryside. If fewer house names commemorated the union of marriage, the domestic ideal still permeated most. This is consistent with Graeme Davison's findings in the late nineteenth century suburbs of Melbourne, for he argued that the choosing of a house name was a popular ritual, and that most reflected 'distant aspirations towards the forests and gardens of the ideal gentleman's estate', while others spoke of the peace and repose of the domestic sphere.[11]

One group had little luck in their search for peace and repose. About twenty Nyungars were permanently camped at the south end of Butler's Swamp, probably on the Atkinsons' property. At such times as the Royal Show they had a large number of visitors from the country. Their tenure was never secure, and in 1912 their camp was shifted 'because of the fly nuisance'. Next year Tommy Pinbar, reviving Tommy Dower's initiative of the 1880s, asked for a reserve of ten acres on Claremont Council land. He approached Sir John Forrest for support, telling him that 'they have no regular place to camp, and seem to be in people's way'. Forrest sympathized, and wrote to the Under-Secretary of the Premier's office—who happened to be his brother-in-law—urging that the Nyungars should have a camping place 'in a locality that is liked'. His word was enough to stir inquiries. Council considering the proposed site unsuitable, the request went to the newly founded University of Western Australia, the Lands Department asking for a corner of its endowment lands, 'thereby benefiting some of the original owners of the soil, who recognize this part of the State as the centre of their tribal district, but have at the present moment no place that they can call their own to live in'.[12]

Unfortunately nothing was done, and for nearly forty years longer the Nyungars continued at Butler's Swamp under precarious tenure and always under the oversight of the police. They were not yet completely marginalized from the rest of the Claremont community. In old age Fred Doepel remembered how Aboriginal women regularly visited his parents in Bay View Terrace to wash the laundry on Mondays. Sometimes they brought with them family members who sat as subjects for the artistically gifted Alex Doepel. Young Fred recalled with greatest relish how the washerwomen were sometimes rewarded with three sheeps' heads from the neighbouring butcher. Removing the brains and tongue, they would boil up the heads in a half kerosene tin, adding barley, onions and potatoes to create an excellent stew.

The Nyungar community at Butler's Swamp was the casualty of an accelerating suburban development which at the same time was bringing an increase in amenity. The expansion of Claremont between 1904 and 1914 had its inevitable effect on the character of the main shopping area. By 1905 Horace Stirling's fine house, 'Norfolk', was flanked on both sides by commercial buildings and potentially noisy tradesmen, and he sold up for demolition and subdivision. Bay View Terrace in 1905 still had its semi-industrial open spaces. As well as Bulloch's firewood and coal business on the western side of the Terrace a few blocks up from Claremont Avenue, next door the ever-enterprising T. J. Briggs was running an aerated water factory, and nearer the station Braack and Sons were operating another wood-yard. By 1915 all three had given way to the demand for retail space, and there were now over forty shops in Bay View Terrace, sixteen on the western side and twenty-six on the eastern. These included

RIGHT: *Guardian*,
31 December 1904.

BELOW: *Guardian*,
24 September 1904.

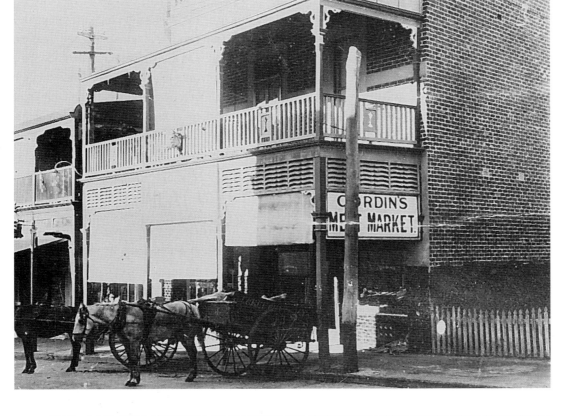

Cordin's Meat Market,
Bay View Terrace,
c. 1914. Note the gold
bull's head above the
shop.

Bay View Terrace
looking towards the
station, *c.* 1915.

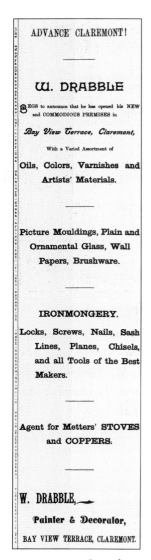
Guardian,
19 September 1903.

four tearooms or dining rooms, three grocers, three greengrocers/fruitmongers, two butchers and two tailors. The Wing Hai laundry still survived, despite the efforts of councillors to chivvy them with regulations and encourage non-Chinese competitors. By World War I it was probably the oldest surviving business on the Terrace, though pressed pretty closely by the Claremont newsagency, which under a number of different owners has survived until the present day on the same site. The Hotel Claremont was also thriving, though its founder, Edward Massey, soon severed his association with it in favour of the less demanding job of managing the Claremont swimming baths. He was followed as licensee first by C. H. Jackson and then by a family named Fink.

Dominating the southern end of Bay View Terrace was Walter Drabble, who claimed that his hardware business was established in 1885. In fact he was only ten years old at that time, youngest of four sons of a painter and glazier who, having been transported for larceny, married and rehabilitated himself. All the boys followed the father's trade. Walter, after serving as a junior at Sandover's and then working for his father, married in 1900 and branched out in a hardware and ironmongery business of his own. His first premises consisted of a very spartan iron building on the west side of Bay View Terrace. He ventured into large-scale importing, and caught the tide of fortune as Claremont grew.

He was in a larger store across the road by June 1914, when he opened the Princess Hall, for a generation a noted venue for public functions. Nearby his wife ran a tearoom. The children of Claremont remembered her as bad-tempered, but since she had a deformed foot ('Bumble Foot' they called her behind her back) this was excusable: it is easy to forget the callousness of the young towards personal deformity. Drabble was moving up in the world. He was elected to the Council in 1910, and became a justice of the peace in 1916. His favourite recreation was hunting, but not as the grandees of the old Hunt Club had known it. 'In the indulgence of this penchant' according to Dr Battye's *Cyclopedia* 'he makes prolonged excursions into the heart of the bush in company with other kindred spirits, and being an excellent shot usually bags his full share of game.'[13] He was not one of those who wanted a house with river views. Instead he and his wife built their residence at the Nedlands end of the Perth–Fremantle Road, and it now forms part of the complex of Nedlands City Council buildings.

More recent arrivals who would become household names in Claremont were starting to come to the fore. Mrs Rickard's boot store was established before 1910. George Cordin's notably decorated butcher's cart was plying its round in Claremont shortly afterwards. Ernest Pulham the signwriter, with his distinctive signature 'Pulham did it', was operating from about the same time. Behind his consistently cheerful façade there was a sad story, since in early middle age he had married a young wife who died in childbirth. Between the forty other businesses that lined Bay View Terrace, competition was keen. Grocers, bakers, butchers and icemen all delivered their wares to their customers' houses, and in return received local loyalty. 'Claremont shops were as good as Subiaco', recalled Sarah Olive Shaw. 'It wasn't the done thing to shop elsewhere.'[14]

Despite the ties of loyalty between shopkeepers and their customers, the gap between rich and poor was still wide and there was little direct contact between the two groups. Although, for example, the son of a labourer who grew up in Claremont between 1896 and 1911 thought 'it was a nice suburb, better than Subi, better than any of the other suburbs', when asked whether he had any contact with the people who lived in the large houses of Claremont, he replied: 'Nothing whatever'. But when the question was focused specifically on a family for whom his mother had worked as a servant, he commented, 'I only went down to see him about a job'. He recalled, with some wonder at both his mother's intrepidity and the surroundings in which the interview took place, that when he turned fourteen in 1910 and was old enough to work:

> I'll never forget it, she took me down to see old Stubbs, down in his house —big place, 'Ivanhoe', with a lovely big ballroom—down on the river. She took me down there.[15]

The result of this visit was a job on Sydney Stubbs's farm at Wagin: 'I got stuck there. Most of me work was goin' out after the sheep'. For a working-class lad, this was the only intimate contact he could recall with the upper class of Claremont.

It was a sign of the times that both Stubbs and the lad believed that opportunity could be found by going on the land. These were the years when enthusiastic politicians such as James Mitchell were trumpeting the promise of the wheatbelt to all who would listen, and some affluent citizens of Claremont were among those who listened. Stubbs, for instance, sold his hardware business to Sandover in 1907, and put all his efforts into setting up as grazier and storekeeper at Wagin. John Elliott Richardson retired from parliament in 1904 and went back into grazing, this time in the mild southern environment of Broomehill. In 1909 the Richardsons sold 'Corry Lynn' to that successful native Western Australian T. J. Briggs and his wife, Emma. Other prominent residents such as Walter Brockway and William George took up substantial properties in the South-West but continued to reside in Claremont. It does not appear that this diversification of their interests lessened their interest in the well-being of their city suburb.

Greeting card by Teddy Pulham, the local signwriter. None of his signs, which bore the motto 'Pulham did it', survives.

The Trigg family in
their home, 'The
Grange', on Claremont
Hill, Stirling Highway.
The home burnt
down in 1922 when it
was owned by the
Rose family.

Claremont was still home to many of Western Australia's decision-makers. David and Mary Forrest remained at 'Minderoo' until his death in January 1917. He was remembered as a hospitable old squatter addicted to cigars, especially when his brother Sir John came to yarn with him on the verandah. Dorothy McClemans recalled that as a small girl of four, visiting with her father, the rector of Christ Church, she could take shelter from the afternoon sun by sitting in the shadow thrown by the statesman's paunch.[16] Further down Bay View Terrace were Edgar Owen, Commissioner of Taxation, and Harry Swan, member of parliament for North Perth and, rather remarkably for Claremont, a Labor man.

Other successful pastoralists to settle in the area included George Rose, pioneer of the West Kimberley, who purchased 'The Grange' from the Cargeeg family. Built by Henry Trigg for his family it was a large wood and stone house on a two-hectare block with gracious formal gardens with stone lions, a rotunda and fountains with angels. The property required a full-time gardener, who lived under the tankstand. There were too many stone busts for George Rose's taste, so he broke some into rubble to make a path to his fowlyard, but retained the croquet lawn and fruit trees. After 'The Grange' went up in a spectacular fire in 1922, he lived in nearby Albert Street, dying in 1959 at the age of ninety-eight.

M. J. Durack's house, on Stirling Highway nearly opposite Congdon Street, was named 'Lissadell' after his East Kimberley property. His cousin, M. P. Durack of Argyle and Ivanhoe, brought his young and growing family to 'Bimera' in Goldsmith Street between 1915 and 1919, a childhood landscape for the toddlers Mary and Elizabeth Durack, who, as writer and artist respectively, were to become in later life influential interpreters of the Western Australian environment.

The residences of such notables were scattered across the district among others less affluent. They did not form a precinct of the kind that Alpin Thomson had envisaged when he subdivided spaciously between Claremont Avenue and the river: that phalanx of gentry houses was becoming depleted by 1910. On retirement Alpin Thomson himself had returned to England, and his residence later became the nucleus of first Lucknow and then Bethesda Hospital. Ferguson's 'Dalnabrek', future site of Christ Church Grammar School, now housed Miss Parnell's Claremont Ladies College. T. J. Briggs sold the 'Corry Lynn' estate for subdivision into a precinct planned around three short narrow streets, Corry Lynn and Brae Roads and Cliff Way, in time producing a Mediterranean effect not unlike the ambience of parts of the eastern suburbs of Sydney. Alfred Sandover disposed of 'Knutsford' somewhat later, and by 1915 he and his family had moved to Mount Street, within walking distance of his city business. Only Judge Burnside remained, still full of peppery panache, sailing his yacht *Genesta* at weekends and making a reputation as a conservative but humane judge. A skilful amateur metalworker and carpenter, he showed a probing curiosity about the techniques of the trades whose practitioners appeared before him in the Arbitration Court. He was reported to travel second class on the train to Perth so that he could get into conversation with working-class passengers and understand their point of view, and he was to display surprising leniency to political radicals even during the fraught years of World War I.[17]

Victoria Avenue and the adjacent streets with river glimpses nevertheless continued to be seen as the pick of Claremont, especially for those who could afford motor cars. John and Annie Conochie, for instance, moved to 43 Victoria Avenue in 1913 after John's purchase of a car meant that it was no longer import- ant to live near the railway to travel to his work as manager of the Foy & Gibson

Portion of a real estate poster advertising for sale Corry Lynn Estate and showing owners of land between the river and Stirling Highway.

department store. This house had a square lookout on the roof with an iron canopy and a protective balustrade around the open sides, so that views of the river could be enjoyed.[18] At the far end of Victoria Avenue resided Frank Wilson, Liberal premier for twelve months in 1910–11 and again in 1916–17. He was the first city businessman premier, a sardonic, self-confident product of the north of England with a finger in many pies. The Labor Party saw him as a tough antagonist, but at home with the younger of his nine children he was very much the simple family man enjoying the pleasures of the riverside. His colleague William George, once Commissioner of Railways and later Minister for Public Works, had a house with a large block on the corner of Princess and Bay Roads. White-haired and white-moustached, he was an irascible bantam-cock of a man, sworn foe of the small boys who dared to raid his fruit trees but a staunch patron of the Anglican Church. He would endow Christ Church with stained glass windows at its west end in commemoration of a son killed in World War I.[19]

The Claremont Town Council tended to be dominated by men between thirty-five and fifty-five who had done well in business, or less commonly the public service, and wanted to exercise their skills in approved civic-minded ways. Women took no part. In 1913 the Women's Service Guild wrote requesting Council's backing for the right of women to stand for municipal elections, but a resolution of support was lost on the mayor's casting vote.[20] It was 1920 before the right was granted, and another fifty years before a female councillor was elected.

In the early years municipal service was sometimes seen as a stepping-stone to politics. Joseph Langsford, after finishing his term as mayor, secured election to the Legislative Council in 1904, and Sydney Stubbs followed in 1908. Both men resigned in 1911 to contest seats in the Lower House, but where Stubbs succeeded in gaining one of the new wheatbelt seats, Wagin, and holding it for thirty-six years, Langsford was not as lucky in Claremont. He was beaten by a fellow Liberal from the Cottesloe end of the constituency, Evan Wisdom. Wisdom's career had an unusual trajectory. He began as a goldfields publican, would rise during the war to the rank of major-general, and ended his career as administrator of the mandated territory of New Guinea for eleven years. Curiously, although Claremont was a safe seat for anti-Labor candidates, none of its members achieved cabinet rank, and in the years between 1901 and 1924 most served for short periods.

Although few who served on the Claremont Council cherished political aspirations, most would have seen themselves as citizens of some prominence. For T. J. Briggs it was a natural consequence of his imposing civic presence in Claremont that he should take his turn as mayor, which he did between 1907 and 1909. Horace Mofflin had built up a successful firm that traded in wool, hides and skins. He had already seen service on the Fremantle Town Council before coming to live in Claremont, where he was elected mayor in 1909–11. He was followed by Walter Brockway, who, having served as Council engineer until 1907, had set up in private practice in Perth but succumbed to the temptation to stand—successfully—for Council two years later. Other prominent councillors included Harold Tuckfield, a dentist who boasted five gold medals for oratory, and George Philip Stevens, who as a young man was in charge of the Nullarbor Plain telegraph line, which linked Perth with the outside world. As electrical engineer with the new Commonwealth Post Office, he became involved in a spectacular and lengthy row over telephone technology, which resulted in his retirement on pension. He threw himself into nearly thirty years of service as the forceful general secretary of the Civil Service Association, with plenty of surplus energy for pennant bowls and the Claremont Council, and it was mainly through his exertions that Claremont's electric light system was taken over by the municipality. He was also keenly supportive when Claremont got its own telephone exchange in 1912. He would serve as mayor during the years of World War I.

Claremont's civic leaders were for the most part active in support of one or another of the Protestant churches. These were now quite numerous, as the Baptist and Methodist churches had both established themselves on the Perth–Fremantle Road in the early years of the century, and a Presbyterian congregation was established in 1903, but it was not until 1911 that John Maxwell Ferguson laid the foundation stone of the handsome St Aidan's at the corner of Princess and Chester Roads—another example of his philanthropy. The Masonic presence was strong in Claremont: Sydney Stubbs, Walter Brockway and G. P. Stevens being among those who belonged to the craft. Stubbs was also an active worker in the Congregational Church, where his wife was noted for her fine singing. Joseph Langsford was superintendent of the Sunday School and a trustee of the Methodist Church. So was Horace Mofflin, who married a minister's daughter. These men and their wives would have spurned any thought that their church activities promoted their public careers, but all would have agreed that respectability could be attested by churchgoing. Something of the flavour of this ethos is given in David Conochie's account of his parents:

> John and Annie were strict Presbyterians, as were their parents before them, and they brought up their children in the same way. Sunday, being the Lord's day, was strictly a day of rest from all work such as cooking, gardening or home maintenance. Parents and children wore their best clothes all day and went to St Aidan's Presbyterian Church, at the corner of Princess and Chester Roads, for both morning and evening services. After the

morning service, it was John and Annie's custom to invite a few others of the congregation home to lunch.[21]

Fred Doepel recalled of the Sundays of his youth: 'The whole family used to march into church behind father, who sang in the choir'.[22]

Significantly the Catholics were slow to establish a presence in Claremont, where they were under-represented. The nine acres between Notre Dame, Gugeri and Mary Streets and Claremont Avenue were kept undeveloped until 1911, when, believing the property to be more of a liability than an asset, the Loreto order placed the land on the market in thirty-six blocks ranging in price from £90 to £130. (A triangular block on Gugeri Street was priced at £250 but later retained as a possible site for a church.) Fifteen of the blocks went by April 1912, but it was not until 1924 that the last was sold. By that time, ironically, Notre Dame Street had been renamed Langsford Street in honour of that good Wesleyan Methodist Joseph Langsford. It was not until 1936 that a permanent Catholic Church, St Thomas More, was built.

Outside the churches Claremont offered plenty of opportunities for culture and recreation. No attempt seems to have been made to resurrect a Literary Society which met between 1899 and 1902, but the municipality had run a public library since 1904 and it was a popular and well-regarded resource. For the younger set a skating rink was established in 1913, but in the following year it was replaced by a Drill Hall—a reminder that Australia had introduced compulsory military training in response to a deteriorating international situation. And 1914 saw the coming of the cinema. First came a short-lived venture, Globe Pictures, and then from 1915 the open-air Claremont Picture Gardens on the site of Bulloch's wood-yard. In the cooler months of the year the pictures were shown at the Princess Hall, which was to remain a venue for films for the next forty years.

For most of the people of Claremont, whether prosperous citizens in their riverside residences or working-class families in the weatherboard cottages of the narrower back streets, it might have seemed that stability had come to Claremont. The pioneering rough edges were smoothed away. There were no longer itinerants camping in tents nor Afghans urging their camels along the main highway.

SWIMMING !   SWIMMING !

CLAREMONT AMATEUR SWIMMING CLUB will hold a

Grand Electric Light Carnival

On 24th FEBRUARY, 1904, At the CLAREMONT BATHS, commencing at 8 p.m., under the control of the W.A.A.S.A.

PROGRAMME.

1. MAIDEN HANDICAP, 50 yards. First prize, trophy, valued £1 1s.; second, 10s. 6d.
2. BOYS' RACE (14 years and under), 50 yards. First prize, trophy, valued 15s.; second, 7s. 6d
3. 50 YARDS OPEN HANDICAP. First prize, trophy, valued £1 10s.; second, 10s 6d.
4. NEAT DIVE CHAMPIONSHIP OF W.A. First, gold medal, valued £1 10s.
5. CLAREMONT SCHOOLS CHAMPIONSHIP, 100 yards. First, trophy, valued £2 2s.
6. 880 YARDS CHAMPIONSHIP OF W.A. First, gold medal valued £3; second, silver medal, valued £1.
7. 200 YARDS TEAM RACE. First, silver cup and four bronze medals, valued £1.;
8. OBSTACLE RACE, 50 yard. First prize, trophy, valued 15s.
9. 100 YARDS LADIES' NOMINATION RACE. First prize, trophy, valued £3 3s.; second, trophy, valued 15s.
10. 50 YARDS SCRATCH RACE. First, silver cup, valued £2 2s.

Entries close with the secretaries of the Perth, Fremantle, and Claremont clubs, also with the proprietors of the Perth, Fremantle, and Claremont Baths on Wednesday evening, 17th February, 1904. The committee retain the right to refuse any entry. Association costume must be worn.

Popular Prices—Adults, One Shilling; Children, Half-price. H. PENDLEBURY, Hon. Sec.

Guardian, 13 February 1904.

Gardens grew every year more established behind picket fences. Gas, electricity and piped water brought ease and comfort to more homes as more families could afford them. Even the cinema was losing its novelty, as were the high-backed automobiles that stirred up a dust on the major roads.

Though the goldfields were in decline and the wheatbelt suffered three dry seasons, Western Australia saw itself as a State on the move, welcoming hundreds of British migrants to a promising future. These newcomers were witnesses to Western Australia's role as part of a benign British Empire, over which the bearded George V reigned in succession to the bearded Edward VII, symbols of stability and continuity. There seemed nothing worse to fear than calamities such as the loss of the *Titanic* in 1912, or the even more mysterious disappearance at much the same time of Western Australia's own *Koombana* off the Pilbara coast—tragedies to read about but not likely to affect many lives in Claremont.

And then in 1914 an archduke was shot in remote Sarajevo, and nothing was ever quite the same again.

Chapter VII

War, Peace and the Search for Stability

CLAREMONT DURING WORLD WAR I was a stronghold of loyalty to King and Empire. Given its middle-class ethos this was not surprising, though there were other factors as well.

By this time most Claremont families had formed an attachment to their suburb, its seven thousand residents constituting an extremely stable population whose core was 'born and bred Claremontites'.[1] One statistic is illuminating: of the children attending East Claremont Practising School between 1905 and 1920, 60 per cent were born in the Perth metropolitan area, half in Claremont itself. These people grew up in a Western Australia that prided itself on being more steadfastly attached to the British connection than was any other part of the Commonwealth. They were reinforced by a recent intake of migrants from Britain: of the 18 per cent of East Claremont children born outside Australia in the years before 1914, by far the majority were 'Poms'. Since Claremont's population was young—even after the war, at the 1921 census, 45 per cent of its residents were under twenty years of age—many families had sons who thought it their duty to join up. At least 18 per cent of those eligible—219 young men from the district—served overseas, considerably more than the national average. The civilians who remained at home saw it as their unquestioned duty to support the cause for which their sons and brothers were risking their lives and futures.

The war's presence intruded early on Claremont. In October 1914, two months after its outbreak, the 10th Light Horse came into being and two of its

War comes to Claremont: troops marching near the Showgrounds.

Postcard showing World War I troops on parade at the Showgrounds.

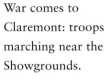

squadrons were stationed at the Royal Agricultural Society's Showgrounds. Here recruits were enlisted, tested on their riding skills and started on dismounted training. On 25 October these units went on church parade at Christ Church, with all the trappings of hats plumed with emu feathers, polished leather leggings and spurs. Three days later they marched twenty-five kilometres to join the rest

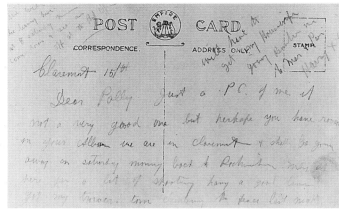

It was common for servicemen to have their photograph taken professionally after enlisting. In this case Harry Ferris of the 10th Light Horse had a postcard made which he sent to Polly Carter.

It read:

Dear Polly, Just a P/C of me if not a very good one but perhaps you have room in your Album. We are in Claremont and shall be going away on Saturday morning back to Rockingham. Only up here for a bit of shooting having a great time got my trousers torn climbing the fence last night. We will be leaving here at 8 Saturday morning. Come down and see us off at the Post Office. We'll have to get my housewife going. Remember me to Mar and Par.

Harry xxx

of the regiment at Guildford. 'They might easily have gone by rail', remarks the regiment's historian, 'but they preferred to march, just for the purpose, the men said, "of trying themselves out".'[2] The whole regiment, mounted and fully equipped, was back at Claremont before Christmas, and after further training marched on 8 February 1915 to the Fremantle wharf to embark for Egypt. Nearly four years of service against the Turks awaited them, culminating with the surrender of Damascus in October 1918.

Other units underwent training at the Showgrounds, and many years later Les Dolton of the 16th Battalion was moved to set down his memories of the old wooden pavilion where they camped:

When the bugler sounded reveille, troops billeted in the fowl-house would run out, crowing and cackling. The men in the dog pavilion would yap, bark, and lift a leg against any convenient post.

After physical training and a jog around the ring we performed our ablutions under a tap or, if you were very lucky, from a tin dish. Breakfast was taken in the open with great mugs of tea from coppers set in long rows.

We dug trenches in the bush about where the Graylands School is today and learnt the art of camouflage among the swamp and paper barks. At night half the troops would try to capture the trenches from the remainder. This exercise ceased when the casualty rate became too high.

Most of the 'casualties' recovered miraculously and returned to camp under their own steam when the Claremont hotel closed for the night...

'The local people were very friendly and hospitable', he added, 'and invited us to their homes.'[3]

Even more strongly connected with Claremont was the 44th Battalion, formed in February 1916, as its recruits were enlisted from the western suburbs between Subiaco and North Fremantle. The colonel commanding, 'Old Bill' Mansbridge, was a Cottesloe resident, and the Claremont architect Edwin Summerhayes was major and second-in-command. For want of khaki this unit was at first kitted out with blue dungaree uniforms 'with trouser buttons on the coats, no pockets in the trousers, and plenty of play around the ankles'.[4] The men could not be persuaded that they looked like soldiers, and morale duly improved when they were fitted out with proper uniforms. After drill and training at Claremont, ten drafts of the 44th were sent overseas between June 1916 and October 1917. They served in the trenches of the Western Front throughout 1917 and 1918, seeing action at Armentières, Messines and Paschendaele and playing an important role in the push against the Hindenburg Line in the last months of the war. Claremont took pride in reports of such local men as Lieutenant Eric McKenzie, in charge of signals, and Sergeant 'Yak' Ingvarsen, whose impetuous heroism won him a Distinguished Conduct Medal and bar, though it was commonly said he deserved the Victoria Cross.[5] Many were killed in action and many more wounded, and the families of the men at the front came to dread the unexpected arrival of the telegraph boy or the clergyman. More than one in eight of the Claremont men in the Australian Infantry Force died, some families losing two or three members. The Weedons gave three sons; two Chipper brothers were killed in action at Lone Pine on the same day; and it is said that every house in Agett Road suffered a casualty.

Support for the war effort was widespread. Within a week of the declaration of hostilities the Claremont Council undertook that the jobs of employees who volunteered for service would be held open against their return. Patriotic funds and a fund for the Belgian victims of invasion were well subscribed; the Red Cross became a focus for continuing activity throughout the war; owners of riverfront houses threw open their grounds for fundraising afternoon teas. When the 44th Battalion was formed, the citizens of Claremont presented it with a flag which was placed in the custody of the Bishop of Oxford until the end of the war. With a gold fringe, it was emblazoned with a motif of gumleaves and gumnuts, with the battalion colours and a Latin motto borrowed from the Christian church: '*In hoc signo vinces*' (By this sign shall ye conquer).[6] More pragmatically, the people of Claremont also formed a battalion committee to provide warm clothes and other comforts for the men of the 44th in the trenches. Established organizations such as the Victoria League at first opposed this new initiative for fear that it would spread the war effort too thin, but G. P. Stevens, as mayor of Claremont, fought pugnaciously for the idea and eventually the critics were won over.[7]

More than one in eight young men from Claremont who enlisted in the Australian Infantry Force during World War I died, but the death of more than one son from the same family was an especially bitter sacrifice. The two Chipper brothers, Ross and Lindsay, were killed on the same day at Lone Pine.

On the home front, the people of Claremont did their bit. Mrs Sydney Stubbs held a fete at her Victoria Avenue home, 'Ivanhoe', in December 1917 to raise money for the Red Cross.

Stevens was probably right in insisting that people would identify more strongly with their local battalion and work harder to support it, but sometimes this patriotic imperative had its unpleasant side. Desmond Abraham recalled that a German family who had lived in the district some years was ostracized: 'Every-one wanted them locked up as enemies of the people'.[8] The Koeppe family, already hard hit when their shop was destroyed by fire in 1911, were further dismayed by suggestions that the street named after them should be called something less Germanic-sounding. Even the respected Mengler family, who in later years would provide Claremont with a highly regarded mayor, had their moments of difficulty because their grandfather had emigrated to South Australia from Hamburg in the 1840s. It was not surprising that Claremont registered one of the strongest 'Yes' votes in the conscription referenda of 1916 and 1917.

As the war dragged on, the feeling strengthened among many civilians that the sacrifice endured by the troops at the front called for an answering self-denial, and this was expressed in a number of ways. All forms of sport were banned on Sundays in Claremont's places of public recreation, and mixed bathing at the Claremont baths also stirred up a lot of public attention. In January 1912 Council, aware that men and women often swam in each other's company at the beaches, had resolved to permit mixed bathing at the baths three evenings a week.

Not all residents had approved, and in 1913 an unsuccessful attempt had been made to rescind this permission. By 1918, perhaps reflecting a view that young men fit enough to swim should be away at the war, the opposition to mixed bathing was strengthening, and in the end a petition was got up protesting that this pastime was not in the best interests of residents and their children. It secured 350 signatures, including that of Canon McClemans, home from his experience as an army chaplain and much affected by it. A counter-petition could muster fewer than a hundred signatures, and Council accordingly agreed to do away with mixed bathing—though it was restored a few years later.[9]

The liquor trade came under the heaviest fire. Patriotic citizens found inspiration in the example of King George V, who pledged that during the war he and his family would abstain from alcohol (though it was whispered that he was angry when neither of his prime ministers followed the good example). More practically, it was believed that drink sapped the prowess of Australian soldiers and seduced some into venereal disease. If enlisted men stayed sober, civilians should follow the example. Prominent citizens such as J. W. Langsford and George Stevens were heavily involved in the Citizens National Movement, whose members urged the State Government to take an active part in liquor reform. In 1916 twenty-three ratepayers petitioned for a meeting in the Princess Hall to advocate the closing of all bars and liquor outlets at 6 p.m. The following year Council decided to ask the Government to suspend all traffic in liquor until post-war demobilization, as well as legislating a ban on the practice of 'shouting', which led to one round of drinks following another.[10] Before Parliament moved in the matter, the war ended.

Others prepared for peace more practically. The oddly named Ugly Men's Association, a very active voluntary organization in a number of districts in those years, took the lead in building an Anzac Cottage at 16 Saunders Street, Swanbourne, for a war widow and her family. Voluntary labour built the house in 1918, the materials being provided without cost by local tradesmen. It was a heartening gesture at a time when community morale was feeling the pressure of four years of war.[11]

When peace came in November 1918 it was zealously celebrated. The boarders at Methodist Ladies College sat up half the night singing such tunes as 'Keep the Home Fires Burning' and 'Tramp, Tramp, Tramp the Boys are Marching', and were not rebuked for it. The Scotch College boys roved the streets of Claremont and Swanbourne banging tin cans in celebration. The girls at Claremont Girls High School were astonished, when they went to a thanksgiving service at Christ Church, to find their formidable head teacher, Florence Parnell, dissolve in silent tears in relief that the war was over.[12]

Peace brought no easing of the demands on the Claremont Council. It was not just that the returning servicemen had to be given suitable entertainment on their welcome home, and that letters of condolence went to all the bereaved in the district. The provision of employment for the returned men proved more of a problem than had been expected, and £220 was set aside for such public works as the tar paving of roads and footpaths, thus providing temporary jobs for some. The Council faced another concern when, in the wake of the war, a lethal strain of pneumonic influenza swept Australia.

Even the victory celebrations were hard to organize. The Council at first nominated the second Saturday in February 1919 as a day for celebrations by the local children, but the Commonwealth Government announced that it would be taking an initiative in the matter, and so the local plans were set aside. Then the Commonwealth cancelled its arrangements, and it was Council's responsibility once again.[13] Weary of all this extra work, the Council responded hopefully to the news that in recognition of the Empire's loyalty Edward, Prince of Wales, would be sent to tour Australia and New Zealand in 1920. Council hoped that while travelling between Fremantle and Perth the Prince might stop at Claremont, and plans were made to entertain the children. When the Prince arrived in June 1920 this could not be fitted in, but the citizens of Claremont were among those who responded eagerly to his charisma. Several young Claremont ladies were invited to the Government House ball given in his honour, and Rose Bindley's disappointment was lifelong when a few days before the ball she developed measles and had to miss it.

William George had his finest hour as minister in charge of the royal tour. Undeterred by constant heavy rain, he made sure that the train conveying the royal visitor stopped at every siding and village in his South-West electorate, basking damply in the loyal tributes to the Prince. It was a pity that, when at length the train was derailed by a washaway south of Bridgetown, Mr George was trapped in a lavatory from which he could not be easily extricated despite his cries for help. The episode remained one of the Prince's most vivid memories of the trip.[14]

It would be graceless to sneer from the hindsight of the late 1990s at this outpouring of loyalty. Claremont had sent its young men to be killed or maimed for King and Country, and needed a focus for emotion. A war memorial was designed by the suburb's leading architect, Edwin Summerhayes, himself returned from the 44th Battalion. He chose an unusual form, with flying buttresses ornately carved in Donnybrook stone. Professor Walter Murdoch was invited to provide an inscription, and offered a choice of four. 'Do get them to avoid cheap jingles and all that is hackneyed and trite', he wrote.[15] As inscribed by the Returned Services League memorial works at Karrakatta, the memorial bore the words: 'Our life is but a little holding, lent to do a mighty labour, we are one with heaven and the stars when it is spent, to serve God's aim; else die we with the sun'. At the laying of the foundation stone on 24 September 1922 there was a large turnout of citizens despite poor weather. The ceremony was performed by General Sir Talbot Hobbs, with Archbishop Riley in attendance as well as the band of the 13th Brigade (formerly the 11th Battalion) and numerous schoolchildren. Halfway through the ceremony a violent squall of rain had the spectators, the band and the cassocked Archbishop hastening up Bay View Terrace to seek shelter at the Princess Hall. There, undeterred by the elements, the band led those present in spirited singing of the 'Recessional' and 'O God Our Help in Ages Past', while the schoolchildren rendered 'Land of Hope and Glory'.[16] The memorial was unveiled by the State Governor, Sir Francis Newdigate-Newdegate, in March 1923.

It is no coincidence that World War I is the point at which Claremont stopped growing. Indeed between 1915 and 1921 its population fell from 7,000 to just over 5,500. It is not possible to account satisfactorily for this drop, although similar trends have been noted in the nearby suburbs of Peppermint Grove and Subiaco. As in those districts, many young men were killed or incapacitated, and so fewer survived for marriage. A very telling statistic is that in 1921 Claremont women between twenty-five and twenty-nine years of age outnumbered men by almost two to one. This drastically reduced their chances of marriage and parenthood, and certainly accounts in part for the decline in population. Demand for new houses in Claremont accordingly slowed. Only a hundred were built between 1915 and 1921, less than half the pre-war rate of construction.

To judge by the real estate market at the end of the war, this check to Claremont's potential for growth was not yet realized, promotion of the housing industry continuing as vigorously as ever. At least twenty-one agents were advertising land and housing in the district, although only two operated from Claremont itself: Bulloch Brothers, who still retained a considerable share of the market, and Ferris, Forbes & Ewens, who were by far the most active. Building tradesmen continued to make a livelihood, and there were now fourteen builders, four painters, two plumbers and a carpenter, several of them by now long established. The centre of activity had shifted back to Claremont Avenue near the intersection of Bay View Terrace, which was becoming a more up-market commercial centre, while small pockets of these trades existed outside the commercial centre, notably in Gugeri Street near the railway station. Two of the most respected were the veteran Joseph Hossack in Goldsworthy Road and Samuel Rowe in Langsford Street, who would live to be 107. Probably many of these men worked on building sites on the outskirts of Claremont, such as Nedlands and the new estate at Mount Claremont.

Within Claremont itself most houses were still described as 'villas', though the term 'bungalow' was beginning to creep into the language of real estate agents. They continued using adjectives related to status, to project to the buying public a positive image of the suburb. Houses were 'beautiful', 'ideal', 'charming', 'gentleman's', 'handsome', 'splendid' and 'excellent'. Significantly, there was an even greater emphasis on Claremont as a garden suburb, while there were no hints of its earlier image as a rural retreat. A good atmosphere was guaranteed by the shared attitudes and behaviour of a large number of middle-class residents and the presence of European-style gardens. The Anglo-Australian community was well on its way to taming the original rural landscape and replacing it with European shrubs and trees to form a softer, more familiar environment. Lawns and gardens were no longer a rarity, and most houses boasted fruit trees and vines. Hedges were replacing fences, these featuring in almost one-third of advertisements after the war. Even aspects of home design reflected the creation of a safe, ordered environment, for now 'sleeping out accommodation' was as common a feature of homes as verandahs. The less ordered atmosphere of the suburb's earlier years was also changed by technology, for, although some advertisements still mentioned stables and sheds, a small number of properties now boasted neat motor garages.

Despite these changes the price of land and housing in Claremont did not alter much between 1909 and 1918. The availability of credit eased, however.[17] While interest rates had stabilized at between 6 and 7 per cent, the deposit required by vendors had fallen considerably—to between 17 per cent and 25 per cent of purchase price. Often the balance was quoted at a weekly rate, usually between 15 and 20 per cent.

The housing market in 1918–19 ranged from homes like the three-roomed jarrah weatherboard house on the outskirts of the suburb for sale at £160, through various gradations of middle-class residence ranging from £400 to £899, to an eight-roomed 'gentleman's residence' going for £1,550. At the turn of the century a gentleman's residence had often formed part of a small estate, with a substantial residence—built of stone and overlooking the river—set off by several acres of land laid out in lawns and gardens with gravel walks and a kitchen garden with an orchard. Twenty years later the gentleman's residence was more likely to have been built of brick and much of the land surrounding it had been sold off. At the other end of the market, workers' homes had improved somewhat. From the iron house of 1899 in Goldsworthy Road it was now likely to have become a two- or three-roomed jarrah weatherboard cottage, sometimes on a small block in one of the later subdivisions on the outskirts of the district.

The characteristic Claremont home, the perfect middle-class residence, remained the five- to seven-roomed villa with kitchen, pantry and bathroom, located between the river and the railway station. At the turn of the century it was likely to have been set on a fairly bare patch of land with a few outhouses and struggling shrubs and surrounded by a picket fence. But by the coming of peace in 1918 the middle-class householder could sit on the wide verandah of his 'charming' villa and view with satisfaction a flourishing garden with green lawns covering the once bare soil, annuals flowering gaily in their ornamental beds, fruit or sometimes ornamental trees offering shade in the hot summer, a neat gravel or granolithic path leading to the front gate and a cypress or plumbago hedge providing privacy and filtering the dust from the wide gravel footpath and the sandy verge.

Despite the often manicured appearance of the front garden, the back yard more closely kept the appearance of earlier years, with a clutter of outhouses—a toilet, a washhouse, a woodshed—a fowl run, a water tank on an unsightly wooden stand, sometimes a windmill and maybe a shade house or potting shed as well as the ubiquitous fruit trees and grapevines. The reality of the rural environment of the village of Claremont in the nineteenth century was generally being replaced by symbols of an idealized rural past.[18]

Remnants of that past survived into the 1920s. Consider the terms in which Elsa Rooney, youngest daughter of the principal of the Teachers Training College between 1903 and 1927, described the surroundings in which she grew up:

In those days that beautiful building stood stately and peaceful in its eleven acres of lovely grounds.

It was completely enclosed with a four feet high white picket fence, each picket shaped and carved at the top. Across the corner of Princess and Goldsworthy Roads were the big double gates of heavy timber, with small gates on either side. Outside the fence, the whole distance around those acres, were tall young gum tree saplings...alternating with them were Norfolk Island Pines. The gum trees bushed naturally at the top, while the pines spread nearer the ground, enclosing the whole College. Quite a lot of natural bush was left in the grounds and I loved the Kangaroo Paws, Spider Orchids, pink and yellow heaths—all of the native wildflowers.

The driveway from the front gate, edged with the same double row of gums and pines, swung around and opened into a double drive at the entrance to the College, with a large oval flower garden in the middle. Broughams and other horse drawn vehicles could turn there to return to the College gates...[19]

If this description suggests a colonial echo of the English country house, we must also remember the spider orchids and the kangaroo paws. More than one child who grew up in the Claremont of 1920 recollected with pleasure in old age the wealth of bush flowers, and especially the spider orchids, which could still be found profusely in the neighbourhood by those who knew where to look at the right time of the year. As for the sugar gums surrounding the Teachers College, they were already tall trees in the 1920s, shedding dappled light and providing welcome shade in midsummer. Along the Bay Road frontage they were never pruned, but on the Goldsworthy Road side they were 'pruned back annually, becoming nuggetty with thick trunks'.[20] The sugar gums on the Princess Road side were eventually removed and replaced by the more commonplace Queensland box, but during the 1920s the entire College precinct added to the pleasant rural —Australian rural—ambience of parts of Claremont.

Some were still convinced by Claremont's claims to a gentry image. 'All the important people lived in Claremont or…Mount Lawley', said Desmond Abraham in old age, and he especially singled out the Anglicans of Christ Church as stand-offish—'the nobility went there'—and disinclined to fraternize with the other churches.[21] In 1923 a Fremantle weekly was moved to satire when members of the Claremont Council made a bid for free rail passes:

> Classy Claremont nestles on a bank of the Swan. It prides itself on the quality and social status of its inhabitants. It embraces the district within which all the hobnobs live—all the pooh-bahs, dontcherknow.

The *Western Chronicle* hit back, disdaining 'the bad taste displayed in attempting to set up social questions as between two sets of readers', and revealing that:

> 'Classy' Claremont's proud aristocratic council consists of three store-keepers, one plumber, one dyer and cleaner, one dentist, one secretary, one journalist, one architect and one optician.[22]

It is striking that the membership of the Council was still all male, and would remain so for nearly another half-century. Yet from its earliest years Claremont's middle-class women included a number who took initiatives in public life. Janetta Griffiths-Foulkes, whose husband was the member for Claremont from 1902 to 1911, was a campaigner for women's political rights as well as a prominent early member of the Karrakatta Club. In the next decade a number of Claremont women, among whom for a time Bessie Rischbeith was numbered, took a prominent part in the National Council of Women. Their links with the rural community of Western Australia led to their particular involvement in a committee of the NCW formed to provide clothing for distressed farmers and settlers hit by the 1914 drought. Many of the Claremont members of this committee were also active in the WA Braille Writers' Association, a tradition dating back to the 1890s. Claremont also provided an early home for a branch of the Girl Guides, only one year after the inauguration of the movement in 1915 under vice-regal patronage. Among the most strongly supported movements was the campaign to ban or restrict alcohol, which gained strength during the war to the extent that in 1917 there were sufficient local organizations to warrant a combined meeting of temperance workers in Claremont.[23]

Evidence of the force of what was largely a women's movement may be found in the State elections of 1921. When the sitting member for Claremont, Tom Duff, a Merredin publican who tended to regard his parliamentary duties as a hobby, decided to retire, six candidates contested the vacancy, among them a partner in a Bay View Terrace drapery business, Ada Bromham. Women had been given the right to stand for parliament only in the previous year, but Ada Bromham was already known as a forthright and active personality. She was a foundation member of the Australian Federation of Women Voters and a great supporter of the temperance movement, eventually becoming State secretary of the Women's Christian Temperance Union. Some Claremont males disapproved of Bromham's ideas. Esmee Templeton's father warned her not to be like Ada Bromham, as she was 'too bossy' and 'always talking about different political things'. But the children remembered her kindly because she used to give them scraps for doll's clothes.[24] Perhaps it helped also that Claremont was a constituency with a majority of women voters. At any rate she stood as an independent and came a good second, losing to the mayor of Claremont, John Stewart, only after the distribution of preferences. With a little more luck she might have joined Edith Cowan as Australia's first woman parliamentarian. She tried again in 1930, but by this time the seat was firmly in the hands of the popular and energetic Charles North, who would retain it for over thirty years.

The younger generation was also apt to challenge pre-war values. In 1923 the Methodist Minister, Eric Nye, was shocked to find his hall being used for a twenty-first birthday dance by forty or fifty young people. It was all very innocent, but he denounced them for 'pampering to the Devil' and, as one of those present recalled, 'In those few minutes he did more damage for the Methodist cause in Claremont than anyone had done before him'.[25] To dance, to go to the

Ada Bromham, leading member of the Women's Service Guild and the Women's Christian Temperance Union. A strong advocate of social welfare policies, she stood unsuccessfully for the seat of Claremont in the State elections of 1921 and 1930.

- 141 -

The Fire Station,
Claremont, designed
by architect J. L.
Ochiltree and built by
A. Rennie in 1914.

beach in mixed parties, to smoke cigarettes in public, were no longer the breaches of social decorum that they might have been twenty years earlier.

Sometimes in those 'roaring twenties' Claremont was visited by unwelcome excitements. On the night of 22 September 1922 the Roses' fine house, 'The Grange', was gutted by fire when the wooden top storey was set alight by an electrical fault during a charity ball. Old George Rose, who was rather deaf, was playing cards with friends in another part of the house and for a long time ignored his wife's pleas that the house was on fire and the brigade slow in arriving. There was no pressure in the hoses, and the guests were reduced to throwing buckets of water while others carted furniture and valuables on to the lawn. News of the fire was flashed on the screen at the local cinema, enticing pilferers to come and take belongings scattered on the lawns. It was a poor reflection on neighbourly behaviour in Claremont.[26]

More sensations followed. On the Australia Day weekend of 1923 a Scotch College boy, Charlie Robinson, was fatally mauled by a shark in the river not far from the Devil's Elbow. The Mayor of Claremont led the search for the beast, but it was never caught, and for years afterwards the story taught caution to many

LEFT: The Claremont Baths played an important part in the life of the community in the inter-war years and beyond. Here a photographer from the *Western Mail* captures the start of a race. (*Western Mail*, 10 March 1921.)

BELOW: A team from the Claremont Amateur Swimming Club won the Royal Life Saving Championship in 1925. L–R rear A. E. Middleton and E. T. Cosson, front L. Braddock and G. Smith.

young swimmers.[27] The following year a young man named George Auburn was accused of bashing a taxi driver to death at an isolated spot on Westana Road, south of Claremont, and dumping the body in Crawley Bay. After a dramatic trial he was found guilty, but because the absence of a convincing motive aroused suspicions that Auburn was taking the blame for somebody else he was not hanged, instead serving about twenty years in prison. The case was a boon to the local scandal-sheet, the *Mirror*, but its historian Ron Davidson comments that 'real estate agents attempting to sell land in "Desirable Dalkeith, the Cream of Claremont," were not so happy' and had Westana Road renamed Waratah Avenue.[28]

The 1920s were perceived as a time of change, and a mature suburb such as Claremont was challenged as first Nedlands, then Dalkeith, became the growth points of the locality. Claremont still possessed the advantages of longer establishment, so that many who did not actually live within the town boundaries still identified Claremont as their centre. The section south of the Perth–Fremantle Road between Doonan and Rockton Roads, marketed in 1896 as Claremont's 'Prinsep Vale' estate, continued to identify with Claremont in the 1930s.

Gwyn, Joan and Bid
Middleton and Mabel
Clough at the
Claremont Baths in the
1930s.

To the south, those living along Victoria Avenue as far as the Old Men's Home thought of themselves as residents of Claremont, especially after the provision of a tramline from Claremont station to the intersection of Victoria Avenue and Westana Road. In 1929 a body lobbying for the establishment of a school in the area called itself the South Claremont Progress Association.[29] Some families nevertheless felt that by moving to the newer districts of Nedlands and Dalkeith they had a fresh chance of creating a uniformly modern middle-class environment, whereas Claremont had a mixed character formed by accident and compromise.

A manufacturer's son, Jack Rowe, who lived in Claremont between 1913 and 1930, thought that Claremont suffered by comparison because the most desirable parts of the suburb had already been built out as an upper middle-class precinct:

The waterfront was a very desirable residential area... The lowlands near the school were not as desirable as the heights were, nor was the hinter-land... It was probably more predominant then because there was so much vacant land. Today the districts are so built up, you don't notice those things much because there's a house, a house, a house...

Nedlands was a different kettle of fish. Nedlands is predominantly residential, whereas Claremont, if you think about it, had all the churches, the ovals, the parks, the Showground, Butler's Swamp, all unrateable land. So Claremont was smaller and more compact in those days, whereas Nedlands was developed all of a sudden...[30]

The son of a farmer who grew up in the 1920s said the people who lived in Claremont were 'all working people, ordinary jobs for those times—not uppity-uppity or anything like that', but admitted that he had no contact with the families who lived in the big houses of the suburb. On the other hand the daughter of a surveyor thought that, in class terms, Claremont of the 1920s was 'very much where it is today…it wasn't quite in the same league as Peppermint Grove'. Although she admitted that a different sort of person lived in the small dwellings of Claremont as opposed to its large houses, when asked about the former she suggested that 'tradesmen lived there' but refused to elaborate: 'Oh, I wouldn't like to say'.[31] The same woman recalled that in the 1920s Nedlands was 'very new, it was going to be one of the better suburbs'.

The impression spread that Claremont was past its prime. The son of a manager who moved to Nedlands during World War I, although recalling that Claremont 'was always a superior address…with big blocks of land and big old houses', reflected that 'then again they had an awful lot of scungy parts of Claremont, so it's a bit difficult to tell'. The daughter of a merchant who bought a house in Nedlands just after the war confirmed this view, stating that even then:

> Claremont was very old… Very old families and big homes that had been there since the year dot… It's funny but there always seemed to be a few cripples about in Claremont—odd, really odd people about, I don't know why… There was more of a mixture in Claremont…[32]

The daughter of a journalist who moved to Nedlands in the 1920s did not even agree that Claremont was a good address:

> The fact that it was near the river didn't mean a thing… There were some odd people in Claremont… Claremont had the Lunatic Asylum over there; if you were going mad you were 'going to Claremont'… No, it wasn't a prestigious address in those days.[33]

As against this, a working-class Claremont child of the 1890s, who returned as a young man after serving in the war, recalled that people who came to live in Nedlands then were 'all hoodahs, you know: a bit flash, all motor cars'.[34]

These impressions are only partly borne out by the statistics. In 1920, 50 per cent of the men in Nedlands and 51 per cent of those in Claremont could be classified as lower middle-class; 28 per cent of Claremont and 35 per cent of Nedlands men were of various levels of working-class status, from unskilled to highly qualified. But in 1920 the number of upper middle-class residents in Claremont stood at only 21 per cent, whereas it had been 30 per cent in 1904.

It is worth exploring a little further the subjective impressions that people formed of Claremont and Nedlands. To some extent they may have resulted from the accidents of urban geography. Until—and even after—the development of Hollywood in the 1920s the core of Nedlands was defined as the area south of the Perth–Fremantle Road. It was thus a self-contained enclave, the highway on its northern edge carrying all the through traffic. It was also largely a product of post-war architecture, with tiled red-brick houses, neat gardens and small patios rather than verandahs—more homogenous than Claremont, with its mix of sprawling Federation villas, corner shops and weatherboard workers' cottages. On the other hand Claremont had always had passing traffic, from those years in the 1890s when Constable Huxtable had taken note of the foreigners, strangers and other passers-by moving between Fremantle and Perth through the heart of Claremont's central business district. Every year the Royal Show brought hordes of rural people to Claremont, as well as the showmen, Aboriginal boxing troupes and other itinerants who followed the agricultural shows. The Showgrounds were also used for other activities, like motorcycle racing, which drew crowds from all over the metropolitan area. Claremont's inhabitants grew used to the presence of unfamiliar faces in their streets. Throughout the year there were the stragglers from the Old Men's Home and perhaps outpatients from the Hospital for the Insane, students from the Teachers College and teenagers from the private

The residents of Claremont came from a variety of backgrounds. 'An old identity', Mr A. Street, was photographed for a newspaper feature on Claremont in 1931. He was a pensioner who had lived in a small humpy near the foreshore for nearly thirty years. (*Western Mail*, 22 January 1931.)

schools. Claremont residents were accustomed to sharing their public spaces with a variety of strangers.

In addition Claremont during the 1920s supported a number of small industries, not concentrated in one complex as modern town planning would recommend, but scattered among the residential streets. In Reserve Street Naylor & Currie ran what was claimed to be Western Australia's largest bakery, founded in 1898 and by the 1920s employing ten bakers and three apprentices to produce two thousand loaves daily. Robert Naylor and his wife, Isobel, said to be 'a driving force' in her husband's business and investment success, lived in an imposing house, 'Pipiriki', which spanned two blocks in Vaucluse Street behind the bakery. In 1920 the Westralian Knitting Mills established themselves in Osborne Parade, where for more than a decade they produced 'Swan' brand hosiery, its trademark calculated to appeal to local patriotism. At the Claremont Furniture Factory C. G. Matthews employed eighteen hands manufacturing the oak and walnut dining-room suites and bedroom furniture that appealed to the taste of the 1920s.[35] Nobody at the time seems to have suggested that these industries compromised Claremont's character. Instead they added to its vitality as a working community. Nedlands had no factories.

And Nedlands had no football team. In its formative years Claremont had not shown itself especially interested in Australian rules football. It was rather a working-class game, and certainly an imported Victorian game, and until World War I the name of Claremont was more notable in cricket and soccer than Australian rules. After the war a group of enthusiasts in Claremont approached the Western Australian Football League for admission, stating that they had secured the use of the Claremont Showgrounds as a home ground. Lacking a team with experience, they were rejected, but in March 1921 they negotiated a merger with a revived Cottesloe Football Club, which had enjoyed success in minor league football in the decade before the war. The Claremont–Cottesloe team was admitted to the 'B' grade competition when it was reconstituted in 1921. Its performance in five seasons was no better than moderate, but its advent was fortunately timed. In 1925 the

Motorcycle racing at Claremont Showgrounds in 1928.

'In the goal mouth': football match between Subiaco and Claremont–Cottesloe. (*Western Mail*, 13 July 1933.)

League was reorganized, with territories from the suburbs of Perth allocated to each team. The Claremont–Cottesloe area did not fall obviously within the ambit of any of the six established teams, so the club, having moved its home ground to Claremont Oval, was emboldened to renew its application. This time it was accepted.

Community support swung behind it. The Claremont Council found £5,000 to upgrade the oval and erect a wooden grandstand and changing rooms, although these were not ready for occupation until the beginning of the club's second season. Bay View Terrace businesses also helped. For instance in hard times the Hotel Claremont provided free board for members of the team who could not find work, and Drabbles employed a number of Claremont players in their large hardware store. (The manager, Horrie Mercer, later became Club President.)

Claremont–Cottesloe entered its first season in 1926 with plenty of enthusiasm. Unfortunately this was no substitute for experience: the team won only one game that year (by one point against South Fremantle) and one in 1927. Although they preferred to be known as the 'Riversiders' the press dubbed them the 'Babies' and speculated that they might be dropped from the League for their poor performance. They were also lampooned as 'college boys' because several members of the team were recruited from the local private schools rather than the more usual working-class milieu of the typical League footballer. Gradually new talent was recruited, including Maley Hayward, the first Aborigine to play League football in Western Australia, and George Moloney, who soon showed himself a mighty goal-kicker. Performance improved, though it would be ten years before Claremont reached a semi-final. By the end of the 1928 season the team were 'Babies' no longer, but were accepted as the 'Tigers'.[36] In a community that was in need of new interests the Tigers were to prove valuable in bonding many of the men—and some women—into a stronger sense of local identification.

It is worth considering a little further this elusive concept 'sense of local identification'. Claremont no longer possessed a resident elite giving leadership to the suburb and possessing time and leisure to devote full-time attention to community affairs in the manner of a Horace Stirling. Its middle-class householders were mainly commuters to the Perth central business district, a tendency probably increased after 1923 when a tramline was laid alongside the Perth–Fremantle Road with its terminus at Bay View Terrace. Part of a short-lived policy of suburban extension in the early 1920s, the Number 30 tram came too late. With the asphalting of roads in the 1920s private bus companies were entering into competition with government transport, and for Claremont residents the steam trains were still a good deal faster than the trams. In a study of the working-class Melbourne suburb of Footscray, John Lack has argued that the provision of commuter transport turned twentieth century suburbs into little more than dormitories. He concluded that the internal cohesion of the community broke down as the external workplace in the wider metropolis assumed greater significance.[37] An English writer has observed that the pattern of commuting 'gave physical expression to the social distance between the public male world of business and the private, feminine world of the household'.[38]

For Claremont in the 1920s such generalizations may be accepted only with considerable reservations: the workplace is not the only determinant of local identity. Australians have always enjoyed their leisure, and Claremont was still the scene of many shared activities at weekends. Attendance at football matches was only one such activity. Tennis parties were popular. Some well-off families had private grass courts, while a wider but still affluent public was attracted by the opening of the College Park Tennis Club in 1926. (Its fees were £1 1s 0d for ladies and £1 5s 0d for gentlemen. Interestingly, the Nedlands Tennis Club founded a year earlier charged twice as much.) River and ocean beaches were accessible to rich and poor alike, and it was thought neither a hardship nor unsafe for Claremont children to walk the two kilometres to the Indian Ocean in summer.[39] In addition, there were any number of unstructured social family activities: playing cards or dominos, working on home improvements or just going for Sunday walks. Old people who remember these times are insistent that neighbourliness bred a sense of security. 'Girls went out safely at night together', remembered Dorothy MacLeod, 'but not with young men.'[40] In this respect at least they believed themselves to enjoy the stability treasured by a generation that had survived World War I.

Leisure pursuits were one important factor in the persistence of local identity, but as Claremont gradually changed from separate village to commuter suburb another tendency emerged. It may be that the men who went as breadwinners to Perth each day were engaged in important aspects of public life, but in middle-class suburbs such as Claremont the absence of men made it possible for women to enlarge significantly their sphere of influence beyond the immediate confines of the home. Their role as guardians of the home extended to guardianship of the suburban environment and activity in a variety of organizations within that environment. To make time for these pursuits they planned and provisioned their domestic routines, using a combination of traditional domestic help and new technology. At the same time the schooling of the children of Claremont was undergoing changes. It is to this world of domestic Claremont that we should now turn.

Chapter VIII

Second Generation

WHEN ELDERLY PEOPLE record their memories for oral historians, those of their schooldays are often among the most vivid and illuminating, and yet until recently few historians paid much attention to the history of Australian education in the early twentieth century. Most educational histories emphasize narrative in their method and progress as their conclusion. Yet research on educational outcomes carried out in the late 1970s, based on over four hundred interviews with students, parents, teachers and school principals, found significant links between education and inequality in Australian society.

R. W. Connell, who headed the team conducting this research, argued that such links were even more pronounced in the past. Experience in Claremont tends to bear this out. Education had a profound influence in reinforcing and extending the values, beliefs, attitudes and social practices that upper- and middle-class children imbibed from their families. Parents welcomed, supported and encouraged education, for it provided a strategy by which they could ensure that their children maintained or improved their family's position. In the years between 1900 and 1950 such parents added education to yeoman values in order to pursue the gentry ideal put in place by the founders of Claremont in the nineteenth century.

If we stood in Goldsworthy Road, for instance, on a late summer morning in 1926 we would see, just as we see today, children setting off for school. There would not be many in sight, as the first generation of Goldsworthy Road children had already grown up. But there would still be a few, most of them in their teenage years. Among the first to emerge from his home would be twelve-year-old

Jack Rowe, from the corner of Princess Road. His years at a small private school, Glenara, and at Claremont Central were over, and he was now a student at Hale School in Parliament Place, West Perth. He might be rushing towards the main road to catch up with the Nathan boys from the corner of Hammond Road. They all caught the 8.23 train to West Perth together, conspicuous in their Hale School uniforms: a navy blue blazer with fine light blue stripes and a school coat of arms on the pocket over a white shirt and grey trousers, topped off by a straw boater. In 1929 such boys were even more conspicuous, for in that year the headmaster replaced the straw boater with a pith helmet.

A little later fifteen-year-old Frances Tupper would be seen walking down the gravel driveway of 'Laane-coori'. After a year as a boarder at Miss Parnell's

Marjorie and Dorothy Hagen with John Clark at the foreshore near the Claremont Jetty after school, *c.* 1929–31. John attended Glenara, a small private primary school on the corner of Scott Street and Thomson Road, and the girls are thought to have attended Loreto Convent.

Claremont Girls High School, she was now a student at Presbyterian Ladies College. She would be dressed in her PLC uniform: a navy blue box-pleated tunic over a white blouse, black stockings and gloves. On her head she would be wearing a panama hat with a striped band in the school colours (then dark brown, blue and gold) and a school badge pinned to the front. She was also making for the railway station.

Later still, in the same section of Goldsworthy Road, Jim Joyner, an eight-year-old, would be seen heading in a different direction. He would be walking along the dusty footpath towards Princess Road, where he would turn right towards Claremont Central. He did not wear a uniform, but was dressed in a serviceable grey shirt and short trousers. His feet would probably be bare and over his shoulders would be strapped a leather school bag, although there would not be much in it because he came home for lunch and rarely had homework.

At the other end of Goldsworthy Road we would see little Norma North, who might have just crossed the road. She could be turning back to wave to her mother, who had a baby girl on her hip and a three-year-old boy tugging at her skirt as she stood in front of their rented brick house waving goodbye to her eldest daughter. Norma would then turn to walk along the dusty verge in the slatted shadow of the high white picket fence of the Teachers Training College. She would follow it until, crossing the driveway at the entrance to the college, she turned the corner towards the sound of the school bell coming from the East Claremont Practising School. Like Jim Joyner, she was not wearing a school uniform. Perhaps she wore a dropped-waist cotton dress with sailor collar, long socks and buttoned ankle boots. If it were a hot day she might also have been wearing a cotton sou'wester hat.[2]

Almost all the children of Claremont went to a State primary school for at least the early years of their education, most attending the school on the corner of Bay View Terrace and Princess Road. After an early period of rapid growth in response to population pressure—from 217 pupils in 1897 to nearly double that number in 1909—Claremont Primary School had become one of six schools in Western Australia designated a 'central' school. This meant that it acted as a feeder school for children in surrounding districts in the upper levels of their primary schooling. As a central school Claremont also provided three two-year post-primary courses: commercial (for boys and girls), industrial (for boys only) and domestic (for girls). From 1915 a three-year professional course was also provided, at the end of which students could sit for the University Junior Certificate examination. After 1903 there was as well an Infants School to cater for children up to Standard IV.

Second Generation

Barefoot and ready for mischief: the Muhling boys outside the family home in Stirling Highway, *c.* 1921–23.

This conglomerate of systems and buildings was the setting for a sorry tale of overcrowding and insanitary conditions until the late 1930s. Health was a major concern for at least fifty years, and outbreaks of disease were frequent. Those parents who could exercise some choice in the matter of their children's schooling had good grounds for looking for alternatives. For instance, in April 1929 a visiting School Medical Officer, Dr M. Holloway, was appalled by conditions at Claremont Primary. Her report echoed the many criticisms of her predecessors:

> This school has not been redecorated for thirty years and urgently needs attention. In the cloakroom there is an old fashioned system of drainage. The basins should be replaced and the waste water trough—which has rotted—abolished. The sanitary arrangements are most undesirable. The urinal is foul and full of sodden leaves. The ventilation is poor… It is hoped that alterations will soon be effected at this school, that these infants buildings will be abolished, and new ones built next to those of the central school.[3]

But then came the Depression of the 1930s.

East Claremont Practising School, in the grounds of the Teachers Training College, provided parents with an alternative to the unsatisfactory conditions at Claremont. Overcrowding was never a real problem, the average number of children per classroom being thirty-three, in stark contrast to the situation in

Claremont Infants School, where in 1912 the corresponding figure was about sixty, reducing to forty-three after a diphtheria scare promoted the building of an extra classroom. During the 1920s and 1930s successive head teachers of the Practising School guarded against overcrowding by enforcing a rule that children living west of Goldsworthy Road—at times of real crisis, such as the Depression year 1931, even children west of Bay Road—would not be admitted, but must go to Claremont Infants. At other times there was greater flexibility; otherwise Norma North, and later her brother and sister, would have been banished to the latter school because she lived in Goldsworthy Road.[4]

East Claremont benefited from its nexus with the Teachers Training College, since its principal made prompt and frequent complaints to the Director of Education about major or petty shortcomings, and these were acted on without delay. W. J. Rooney, most famous of Teachers College principals, sent his own son to 'Prac' and kept a vigilant and interfering eye on classroom sizes. From 1922 East Claremont had an active Parents and Citizens Association which for a decade enjoyed a close relationship with successive head teachers. It assisted in fundraising, facilitated minor repairs in the school grounds and in the late 1920s ran a tuckshop.

Such activities might have reflected the fact that about half the school population came from upper- and middle-class backgrounds. In the years before and during World War I most children at East Claremont were from the families of white-collar workers—civil servants, clerks, accountants and small businessmen—while about 9 per cent were from the higher stratum of society, including the children of the Commissioner of Railways and the Chief Inspector of Fisheries as well as leading businessmen and professionals. One-third of the pupils were from working-class families. During the 1920s and 1930s the middle-class presence increased somewhat, but never sufficiently to reflect the 70 per cent of Claremont's male population who could be classified as middle class. Many of the better off parents in Claremont sent their children to private schools, whereas working-class children were more likely to start at Claremont Infants. Jack Rowe, who was there in the early 1920s, remembered that at Claremont 'you met everyone…rough, good, a cross-section'.[5]

John Walton, a teacher at East Claremont 'Prac' between 1927 and 1930, remembered that parents were anxious to have their children admitted there because of its excellent reputation and its size 'which also protected children from the rigid streaming into "A", "B" and "C" levels in each grade which was commonplace at larger schools'.[6] In contrast to most primary schools at the time, there were no formal morning assemblies from which children would march to their rooms, and in class they were addressed by their first names and encouraged to join in discussions with the teacher. No wonder places at East Claremont were eagerly sought after. The only difficulty with parents that Walton remembered was that many tended to expect too much of their children and pushed them too hard.

The East Claremont School was never held responsible for any health problems among its pupils. Dr Roberta Jull, School Medical Officer in 1923, voiced some concern:

> … Six children were found showing evidence of great poverty and under-nourishment: they belonged to two families, three to each. From enquiries made it would appear the fathers were inefficient workmen, and so were constantly out of employment, the mothers were the mainstay of the house-holds, so it was not unnatural the children should appear neglected. The general standard of nutrition was however good… Cleanliness was not good. Of the 97 boys examined 7.2% had pediculosis [head lice]: of the 99 girls 45.4%. A short talk on pediculosis and general hygiene was given to the girls.

Dr Jull's attitudes may have been remarkable, but in 1926 her successor, Dr Eleanor Stacy, was much more complacent:

> Classrooms bright and ventilated, and most attractively decorated, and throughout the school it appeared that great attention had been given to hygiene and general cleanliness.[8]

This report may say as much about Dr Stacy as about the school. In 1929 Dr Holloway, who two days earlier had written a report on what she considered abysmal conditions at Claremont Infants School, also had her criticisms of East Claremont:

> The lighting arrangements are some of the worst to be seen in any school in the State… Everything was as tidy and clean as is possible in a school so badly needing renovation.[9]

In the same year, however, when deep sewerage was introduced to the suburb, East Claremont was immediately connected, whereas Claremont had to wait until after a child died of diphtheria in 1937.

In the 1920s 11 per cent of East Claremont pupils and a smaller proportion from Claremont went on to private schools, most of them to the estab-lished colleges in the neighbourhood: Methodist Ladies College, Miss Parnell's

Masters and boys at Christ Church Grammar School, 1917.

Claremont Girls High School, Loreto Convent, Scotch College and the Christ Church school. The last was a smaller enterprise than the rest at this stage of its existence. It had been founded at the beginning of 1911 by the vigorous and popular rector of Christ Church, Canon W. J. McClemans, as a preparatory school for boys too young or insufficiently advanced for higher schools, and in its first two decades it led a somewhat chequered existence, especially after McClemans left as a result of personal problems in 1925. In 1930 the Anglican Church took over full responsibility for Miss Parnell's school and for Christ Church. The former was re-christened St Hilda's and moved to new quarters based on a pastoralist's home in Mosman Park on the border of Peppermint Grove. Its Claremont premises were then transferred to Christ Church, which opened as a complete grammar school in 1931.[10] It was to be many years, however, before the Alcock Cup schools—Scotch, Hale, Aquinas and Guildford Grammar—deigned to admit the newcomer to equality as a participant in their major sporting events. But at least Christ Church survived. Glenara School, run

Claremont Girls High School, 1920, formerly J. M. Ferguson's home 'Dalnabrek', now Walters House, Christ Church Grammar School.

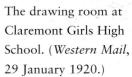

The drawing room at Claremont Girls High School. (*Western Mail*, 29 January 1920.)

by the Misses Collison at first on Claremont Avenue but later at the corner of Thomson Road and Scott Street, disappeared in 1930 after sixteen years of existence, presumably because of the Great Depression.

In her heyday at Claremont Girls High School Miss Parnell was a powerful influence on the social outlook of well-brought-up young Claremont women. Her elocution teacher was Lionel Logue, who later achieved fame by coaching King George VI to master his stammer. She owned a firm grasp of social distinctions, as one ex-pupil remembered:

> We were really sent to Girls' High School to learn to be ladies. Miss Parnell was terribly strict about manners… We were not even allowed to speak to the maids. In fact we were really quite snobbish. We considered ourselves superior to all other schools.[11]

Florence Broadhurst felt the edge of that snobbery:

> She was a snob you know, and after all my father was in business, and that's a thing you shouldn't be in, in those days… She thought the girls' parents should be either professionals or graziers and farmers…
>
> It was like a very private school. It was like a large home really… If anyone came to see you they came into the lounge. We were taught etiquette. We were taught to speak well, even how to walk. It is subtle. But it's those little things you learn that make the difference.

The girls wore a uniform: a navy tunic with three pleats falling from a yoke, over a white blouse. They wore stockings, but they were not black:

> Miss Parnell didn't like that sort of thing. She liked you to be a bit distinctive in a way… You had a school hat, panama with a brim. They didn't have to be all the same. Miss Parnell liked you to look nice… Our tennis uniforms (and I don't think the other schools had them) for going to matches were cream viyella. They were beautiful… When they left there the girls seemed to know how to dress.[12]

A kilometre along the road the Loreto nuns were impressing very similar values on their pupils and earning the same sort of reputation.[13]

At Scotch College the values instilled in their charges by P. C. Anderson and his staff were based less on conscious awareness of class—most boys shared the conservative ideas of their parents, but they liked to believe that at Scotch 'no

Archery lesson, Loreto
Convent, *c.* 1901.

Dancing lesson, Loreto
Convent, *c.* 1901.

Scotch College, 1910.

man was better than his neighbour'—than on standards of manly conduct of the sort that had been shown by the Anzacs at their best. A tragedy in 1928 exemplified these qualities when two boys, Oliver Hodgson and Neil Masters, took a dinghy out on Freshwater Bay. When an oar was lost from a rowlock Hodgson dived in after it, but was caught by the current and could not make his way back to the boat. Masters dived in to help him, but both were eventually exhausted. Hodgson drowned, and Masters was rescued only in the nick of time. At the coroner's inquest a lawyer commented:

> Both boys had shown even in this tragic crisis the splendid value of their school training, Masters by his heroic attempt to save his mate, and the deceased by the exhortation that came from his drowning lips, 'Leave me alone and get in yourself. I'll be all right'.[14]

There were more pragmatic reasons why parents who could afford private education for their children made the effort. The career prospects of young men were important, and at a superior school boys would make lifelong contacts that would assist them in their future careers. Florence Broadhurst's brother used to go up to stations in the North with friends from Scotch College during the holidays, and when he left school he was offered a job as jackeroo on one of them. Later he managed the station, and eventually he owned it. After his death it passed to his sons. During the 1930s and 1940s it was commonly believed that if there were two applicants for a job, the one with a private school background would get it.

Girls might later find marriage partners among the brothers of friends they made at a private school, or at least within the circle they met through attending such a school. Thus they would maintain, and perhaps improve on, their parents' social position. After she left school in the late 1920s Florence Broadhurst did not have to get a job:

> Well you see, you just *didn't* in those days. You came home and you led a terrifically social life… We had bridge parties and people calling in and out… We went to balls at Temple Court.[15]

And on one such occasion she met her future husband, son of a well-established North-West pastoral and pearling family. Dorothy MacLeod's reminiscences reinforce this picture. Girls did not work and never learned to cook, she said. But they did help with the housework and darn their brothers' socks. And their families had a housemaid—'whenever they could get one'.[16]

'Whenever they could get one…' It was a familiar plaint among the well-off in the early decades of the twentieth century. In Perth about 10 per cent of households in 1921 employed domestic servants, around the Australian average, but in Claremont the proportion was 12 per cent, having fallen from 20 per cent in 1901. Capacity to employ live-in help was not necessarily a sign of great wealth. Between 1904 and 1939 at least fourteen families in Goldsworthy Road employed a full-time live-in adult female domestic servant long enough for that person to figure on the electoral rolls as at least semi-permanent. One was employed as a housekeeper by two spinster typists and their brother, children of a pearler; another worked for a journalist/master printer, his wife and two adult sons. Another, described as a widow, kept house for a retired civil servant who was a widower; two others were employed in succession by a manager and his family.[17] Adolescent girls were also employed, but because they were under twenty-one years of age their presence left no trace in the electoral rolls. Some were Aboriginal girls whose employment was monitored by the Chief Protector, though not all came through this route. Daisy Corunna was brought down from a North-West station to work for her relations, the Drake-Brockmans, who now owned Sydney Stubbs's former residence, 'Ivanhoe'. Her memoirs indicate that the number of Aboriginal girls working in homes was sufficiently large for the Anglican rector of Christ Church to start a sewing circle for them.[18]

More usually the live-in maids would be daughters of working-class families within a radius of a few kilometres. One man recalled that his family lived in Langsford Street when they employed their first maid, and she later came with them to their new house in Goldsworthy Road. The house was designed with a room at the back adjacent to the kitchen for her accommodation. Following her resignation in order to get married they had two more maids in succession. Their duties were mainly cooking and cleaning:

That didn't mean that my mother was idle. She coordinated; there was not a great deal of ordering anyone to do anything. The instructions were all very clear as to the avenues that you worked in, and it was just done.

The maid also assisted with the children when they were small. She supervised meals, eating with the children in the kitchen, and occasionally joined in the children's games:

… they used to join in my boisterous cricket games, or kick a football with me occasionally on the tennis court.

As a result the children formed a close attachment to each maid and 'looked on them as part of the family'. Contact was maintained for a long time:

Believe it or not, when I got married and built my home, one of them—she was a grandmother then—asked if she could come down and do anything for us when our children were young… She didn't want me to remunerate her, but I insisted. That's the type of continuity we had with the girls who lived with us in those days.[19]

In other families the maid or domestic was sometimes a more shadowy figure. In the case of one family the employment of a casual live-in maid provided relief from the round of chores carried out by adolescent daughters.[20]

The domestic role of adolescent daughters has not generally been recognized, but it was an important feature of many middle-class homes in which the employment of domestic servants was not regular. One recalled that, during the 1920s and early 1930s,

I was maid of all work. We did have help at one stage: that made things easier. But those of us that were home all had to do chores… You set the table and washed the dishes or on Saturday morning you did things like cleaning the bathroom or doing your room—that sort of thing. As time went by, I fell for the family wash and at that stage my brother was living at home. I can remember on Saturday having six shirts to wash!...

After school you'd get home and there'd be the usual request to go up the street and get something from the shop, or there might be a note left— 'Would you get the vegetables on and ready for tea?'—that sort of thing...[21]

Outside work fell to the boys: chopping kindling wood, mowing the lawn and sometimes clipping the hedge. One man remembered cleaning the family car every week in the 1920s and 1930s. Another recalled mowing and marking the tennis court and barrowing loads of manure while his father dug the flower beds for the seasonal planting of annuals.

A few boys were useful inside the house. One recalled that in the 1920s he had to polish the brass door knobs and clean the silver. A few others helped with washing up, and one paragon would occasionally cook a roast dinner when he was in his late teens. More commonly, boys and girls followed the role models provided by their parents. Girls helped mother inside the home and boys helped father or —especially on weekdays when father was at work—took on what were seen as male responsibilities outside the immediate perimeter of the home. Where there were no sons, a daughter might take on a role that was ostensibly male:

If there weren't any men at home, we had to chop the wood. It's never been a hardship for me to go out and chop the wood. I used to be quite handy with the axe. I could chop the turkey's head off at Christmas if necessary.[22]

As in most of Perth during the 1920s and 1930s, one chore at least was spared the women of Claremont. They were not expected to buy food at the shops and then trudge home on dusty or muddy gravel footpaths with their load of parcels. In emergencies there were plenty of corner stores—during the 1920s and 1930s six were functioning within a half-kilometre radius of St Aidan's Church in Princess Road. More serious shopping expeditions were a major event, an outing for which one would wear a good dress and a hat and gloves. It was a pleasant experience during which one would meet friends, browse in a store or two and perhaps stop in a tearoom for refreshments. Any purchases too cumbersome to carry would be delivered.

Tradesmen delivered daily. The leading Claremont milkman came from Vivian's, a large dairy in the hollow near the corner of Bulimba Road on the eastern outskirts of Claremont. Usually families left a billy outside at night for the milkman to fill, skimming milk out of a bucket with his dipper. The baker's horse and cart also called daily. In summer another regular caller was the iceman. With a piece of hessian covering his hands, he would lift a block of ice out of his cart, heave it on to his shoulder and carry it down the side of the house to the back door. Once on the back verandah or in the kitchen, he would place it in the ice chest, an upright lead-lined wooden box on legs with a front opening.

Several grocers also delivered. Rogers Brothers, on the corner of Reserve Street and the Perth–Fremantle Road, 'sent a man round to take the order one day and deliver it the next'. Cordin's butchery called several times a week: 'Tommy Norton used to work for them. He used to come round with this cart. He'd just drop the back of the cart down, bring the meat out and he'd chop it on the block in the back.'[23] Most picturesque of all was the Chinese greengrocer, Hing Ware, whose big cart with a black hood had been a Claremont landmark since the 1890s:

> We used to raid the Chinaman's cart. We'd always know that the day 'Hing-haw' was there, 'Chop Suey' would be here. We'd be up into the cart and pinch a couple of oranges… They were good blokes, really good fellows.[24]

E. S. Rogers, provision merchant, outside his shop on the corner of Stirling Highway and Reserve Street, *c.* 1912.

With all this availability of home-delivery services, the women of Claremont did not have the chore of shopping that would be their daughters' responsibility. 'You did have a lot of service', a woman remembered sixty years later. 'It would be lovely to have that today'.[25]

Very old people who remember the Claremont of the 1920s before the Great Depression are apt to speak of it nostalgically as a time of simplicity and security, and there is a point beyond which it is difficult for their grandchildren to empathize with that era. The locality is discernibly the same, but how have attitudes changed? What does it mean that at the 1933 census 574 people, or nearly 10 per cent of Claremont's residents, habitually spent their nights in sleep-outs, presumably mostly on verandahs easily accessible from the street? Does this suggest a sense of security — that there was no danger to be feared from passing marauders?

If they were open to the world in some respects, in others the people of Claremont accepted well-defined conventions of privacy. As Sarah Shaw remembered it, her mother never visited a neighbour without a reason or an invitation. There was no casual 'dropping in', no sense that you could make free with somebody else's space. And the utmost privacy surrounded sexual matters. Again we have Sarah Shaw's testimony that there were few shotgun weddings, although couples might be engaged for years while they got together enough possessions to

TEL. F778 COTTESLOE.　　SEEDS, SHRUBS, FRUIT TREES
CUT FLOWERS, PALMS, &c.

GEORGE LUCAS,

High-Class Wholesale and Retail Fruiterer and Greengrocer.

SPECIAL ATTENTION TO 'PHONE ORDERS.　　BOQUETS, WREATHS, &c. AT SHORTEST NOTICE.

On request, orders will be REGULARLY called for and PROMPTLY delivered throughout the district.

Bay View Fruit and Vegetable Store,
CLAREMONT.

George Lucas, self-styled 'high-class' fruiterer and greengrocer, driving his dray laden with watermelons, c. 1916.

embark on marriage. She herself was engaged for four years, but decided that she preferred her independence.[26]

Most other accounts of the period bear out this impression. Among the few individuals privileged to breach privacy were the medical practitioners, and a trusted physician became part of the local folk memory. For years Claremont people spoke with respect of Dr Tregonning, who died a comparatively young man because he insisted on going out to attend a patient when himself suffering from pneumonia, or in a later era of Dr Mayrhofer. Nor is it easy to recapture the recreations of a generation with no television and only the most primitive of wireless receivers. They played cards, not only bridge but 500, whist, cribbage and rummy. They enjoyed sing-songs around a piano—possibly one of those new player pianos which beat out the tunes without human agency. They read a lot of fiction. In addition to the public library, they had access to the Wayfarers Library in Bay View Terrace, where books might be borrowed for threepence or sixpence a time.[27] The stock of 2,300 volumes ranged from Dickens to Edgar Wallace and Zane Grey, but it is a fair guess that in Claremont demand was strong for well-regarded middle-brow English novelists: Warwick Deeping, P. C. Wren with his tragic heroes of the Foreign Legion, Jeffrey Farnol with his historical romances, or for the more serious-minded the later volumes of John Galsworthy's *Forsyte Saga*.

We cannot judge how far these orderly routines built up a sense of security and stability among the people of Claremont. They had lived through World War I and through a period of industrial and social unrest in the early 1920s. Public men from time to time were given to alarming statements about the menace of Bolshevik Communism, but in a suburb such as Claremont, with many owner-occupied homes and a pleasant environment, with its river accessible even to the poorest, it must have seemed unpromising soil for political extremes of any kind. But if a sense of security and stability comforted the citizens of Claremont at the end of the 1920s it would soon be shaken. For 1929 was to be remembered as the last year before the Great Depression.

Chapter IX

The Thirties

IN THE LATE 1920s Australia gradually went into an economic recession which, between 1929 and 1933, deepened into the Great Depression and coloured Australian folk memories for two generations. It is remembered as a time of hardship in which one in every three trade unionists experienced unemployment, when out-of-work men tramped the country hopelessly, when morale was kept alive by sporting icons such as Don Bradman and Phar Lap, when mothers aged prematurely from the struggle of keeping their families fed and clothed. Yet, for the 70 per cent of Australian families that did not suffer unemployment, the 1930s might be seen as a time of modestly increasing prosperity since, although wages and salaries were cut as an economic expedient, the cost of living fell even more. This argument of course overlooks the fact that many of those who kept their jobs were constantly gnawed by uncertainty about their futures and could hardly be unaware of friends and relations worse off than themselves. Nevertheless Drew Cottle has suggested that in the affluent eastern suburbs of Sydney, 'the sunny side of the street', some families managed to weather the 1930s totally unaffected by the Depression.[1] In Western Australia Rob Pascoe found that, in Peppermint Grove, 'the mood of the locality remained bright through this period... In the village, trading continued as ever, with no bankruptcies and not much evidence of hard times.'[2] How was it then for Claremont, with its gentry origins and its prevailing middle-class ambience?

A snapshot of the Depression generation in Claremont is revealed by the census of 30 June 1933. At that time the population had still not recovered its pre-war figure, standing a little short of six thousand—2,666 males and 3,280 females. This imbalance of genders may reflect the lingering effect of wartime losses, but it is also likely that some young men had gone to the country attempting to find work. It was ethnically a most homogenous community, surpassing the traditional Australian boast of 98 per cent British origins: only 66 men and 42 women were born outside Australia and Britain, the rest being about three-quarters Australian in origin with the other quarter coming from the United Kingdom and Ireland.

Religious practice reflected these origins. Of those claiming allegiance to branches of the Christian faith over 52 per cent were Anglican, a higher proportion than in either Western Australia as a whole or the Australian Commonwealth. Presbyterians accounted for 13 per cent, Methodists 11 per cent and Catholics 12 per cent, this last figure being smaller than the State and national averages. Interestingly, more than three-fifths of the Catholics were women. The presence of Loreto sisters could account for some of this imbalance, but another factor might have been a substantial number of mixed couples in which a Protestant or agnostic householder married a Catholic wife and presumably agreed to bring up the children in the same faith. It remains an index of Claremont's character that the Catholic presence was comparatively inconspicuous, and that when St Thomas More's church was built in 1936 it was some distance from the central business district around which Claremont's other churches were clustered —though, true to the Catholic tradition of elevated sites, it stood on a hill overlooking the Showgrounds. And Australia's alternative religion, the digger tradition, was flourishing: 219 Claremont men were ex-servicemen who had served overseas, and the returned servicemen's organizations were well supported.

In 1933 the census returns of greatest concern to many would have been the unemployment figures. These of course excluded the women working full-time at home without wages as homemakers, as it was taken for granted they should. 'Wives didn't work', remembered the tailor Arthur Hardman. '[They were in employment] only if they needed the money or were greedy.' But it is instructive that such women were experiencing a change in self-concept. A sample taken from the 1930 State electoral role shows that 44 per cent in this category described their calling as 'home duties', implying that they saw themselves as exercising an independent role within the household. Back in 1904 every such woman had simply defined herself as 'married'.[3]

Of those in what was conventionally defined as the work force more than half of Claremont's males (1,358) and 20 per cent of the women (652) were in full-time paid employment; most were wage or salary earners, 176 were employers, 189 self-employed and 32 apprentices. Another 97 men and 20 women were in part-time employment, leaving 213 men and 76 women—about 13 per cent of the entire work force—unemployed. Of these, four out of five cited 'scarcity of work' as the reason for their plight. If these figures are typical of Claremont during the Depression years, it suggests that the area was not as badly off as other parts of Western Australia—in Bassendean, for example, the rate was estimated at over 40 per cent of the population[4]—but unemployment was serious enough to overshadow all other public concerns.

The Depression came later to Western Australia than to the rest of the Commonwealth, and it was not until the early months of 1930 that local authorities were called upon to address the problems of the unemployed. In May 1930 the Claremont Town Council, responding to a request from the local member of State Parliament, C. J. North, undertook to administer relief for the unemployed. The Mayor, Gus Mengler, and the Town Clerk, Walter Brockway, were competent and experienced, and they began by compiling a register of local workless and setting out to canvass for funds over and above the available government subsidies. No believers in the dole, the Claremont Council employed as many workers as possible at government-fixed rates designed to provide basic sustenance for a man and his family. In August twenty-nine men were placed on sustenance work projects administered by the Council, and by October the number had increased to forty out of the ninety registered unemployed.[5] All married men with two or more children were found sustenance work, though this sometimes told against experienced workers. Edward Shaw, for instance, though he came of a family of thirty years' residence in Claremont and had been a council worker for a considerable time, including service as acting foreman, was laid off because he was a bachelor without dependants.[6] The sustenance labourers were put to work on public improvements: College Park was upgraded at a cost of £75 and the sustenance workers' labour; the streets were cleaned; perhaps less agreeably, one party in the early summer was set to work raking up the algae that accumulated in the river east of the Chester Road baths even in those allegedly unpolluted years.

Private charity was also mobilized. In July 1930 the Council convened a meeting of churches and guilds to organize help. *The Claremont Courier and Swanbourne News*, a short-lived fortnightly issued in the latter months of 1930, chronicles a constant round of activities raising funds for the unemployed: a choral society concert in August, a sports meeting at the end of September, in October a Commercial Travellers Concert Party at the Princess Hall and a raffle for 'a superb oak bedroom suite' donated by the

Assist our LOCAL UNEMPLOYED!!

PARISH HALL - CLAREMONT

GRAND CONCERT

BY THE

...ercial Travel... ...ne...rt
Orche...

ON

THURSDAY, 29th SEPT. ...t 8 p.m.

Proceeds to be devoted to the Claremont Municipal

UNEMPLOYED RELIEF FUNDS

ADMISSION, 1/- (Seats may be Reserved 6d. extra)

Box Plan at Dean's Music Store, Bay View Terrace

The Claremont Printers, opposite Grand Chambers O'Bryan P 16232

CLAREMONT ROAD BOARD RELIEF COMMITTEE.

Old-Time Comedy Depression Dance

will be held in the

CLAREMONT ROAD BOARD HALL

on

THURSDAY, AUGUST 6, 1931, AT 8 P.M.

ADMISSION 1s.   First-Class Orchestra.

H. R McAUSLANE, HON. SEC SOCIAL COMMITTEE.

DIXON PRINT. 42 PROWSE-AV. CLAREMONT.

AT CITY PRICES!

Obtain your needs

in

FRUIT
VEGETABLES
GROCERIES
CONFECTIONERY
Etc. Etc.

from

C. J.

PRESTAGE

126 Perth-Fremantle Road,
Nedlands-Claremont.

The foreshore looking
west (*Western Mail*,
22 January 1931).

Claremont Furniture Factory. The relief committee set up in July estimated by the end of November that it had raised £270 towards helping the unemployed.[7]

As the hard times stretched on through 1931 and 1932, generous impulses flagged. The Council by October 1931 was insistent that sustenance workers who did not give a fair day's labour for their wages would be dismissed in favour of more productive labourers. Although it gave permission to an 'unemployed band' to play in the streets of Claremont, after nine months the council followed up complaints to find that the band consisted of only two players, with two other men as collectors, so its permit was cancelled. At the same time nine other groups playing without permission were ordered to desist.[8] (The public taste for band music may have been decreasing: the following year—1933—Council decided to remove the bandstand from Claremont Park and to sell its musical instruments. It proved difficult to find takers, although the Metropolitan Missionary Band offered to borrow the bass drum.) The Council gave priority to workers living in Claremont, and as late as 1935 was complaining to the water authorities for bringing in outsiders to work on their sewerage projects instead of hiring locals.[9]

Many showed ingenuity in keeping themselves fed and sheltered during the Depression without resorting to sustenance. 'Our family was never on the dole', recalled a woman from one long-established Claremont family. 'We sold and cleaned chickens and ducks, caught fish and grew vegetables.' Connie Efford, when first married in 1932, worked at setting traps for cobbler in Freshwater Bay, and with cobbler priced at a halfpenny each managed to earn up to ten shillings a day — which involved selling more than two hundred fish. She also polished crabs and sold them from door to door at fivepence each, and on a good night could expect to sell forty.[10] These stories remind us that Freshwater Bay and the country around it had been a source of nourishment for its people since Nyungar times, and for families such as the Effords and the Shaws, who knew the locality thoroughly, it continued to provide sustenance.

George Lucas with his son and daughter and Snowy the goat. On their Graylands Road property the family kept up to nine goats, which foraged in the bush.

The Depression greatly increased the number of hawkers who tried to make a living plying their wares around the streets of Claremont. Some were struggling local tradespeople: Bovell's, later to become one of Bay View Terrace's time-honoured institutions, began by vending pies and pasties around the streets in a pram. In 1932 the Health Inspector estimated that thirty or forty were marketing fruit, vegetables or fish. Some were memorable:

> A fellow that used to come round with his little knife-sharpening cart that he used to push — 'Jimmy Four-eyes' — he used to come up and down the street. Nice old chap, he was part Negro and part-Aboriginal I think.[11]

Oil painting of 'Jimmy Four-eyes' by K. M. Stephens.

The children enjoyed his arrival, and sometimes made posies of flowers to tie on his knife-grinder. Some of the Butler's Swamp Aboriginal community would appear in the streets from time to time, going from door to door selling clothes-props. Tommy Bropho's son recalled:

> My father used to walk miles to find straight trees which he'd pick and cut [for] clothesline props. He'd bark'em, and smoothe all the rough edges off. If he was strong enough and willing that day he'd take six, but four was his normal number — that's two on each shoulder. He'd tie these four railings at one end and put 'em on his shoulder and…walk down the street singing out 'Prop-oh, lady'.
>
> Some days it'd be good to him, some days he'd walk miles. These sticks would be sold for two and sixpence to three shillings. Some sympathetic white people then would take pity on him and give him five shillings…[12]

At other times he went caddying on the Swanbourne golf course and sometimes made cobweb brooms for sale. In wet weather there was sometimes money to be made as lookout for the East Fremantle two-up school. The children would gather smokebush for bouquets and collect empty bottles for refund after football matches. It was a hand-to-mouth existence for the poorest of the poor.

Twenty years after Tommy Pinbar's appeal for ten acres for a camping site, fifty years after Tommy Dower had asked for it, the Butler's Swamp Aboriginal community still had nowhere to call their own. The original descendants of Yellowgonga's clan had by now been supplemented and to some extent replaced by families from elsewhere. They owed more or less permanent quarters to the goodwill of two of the pioneering Claremont families. 'Granny' Briggs, widow of T. J. Briggs, allowed the Brophos and Leylands to reside on a corner of her property. A policeman who inspected the site in November 1933 found the children clean and healthy and the iron-and-canvas camp structures tidy and well kept, with a small vegetable garden. 'I could find no cause for complaint or any need to recommend any removals.'[13] Another group's camp is variously described as being on a Mr Neal's property or on the north-west corner of the Atkinsons' pensioner guard allotment. Although a police report of 1931 described the camp as 'untidy and neglected looking' Anne Kidd, member of a settler family at Butler's Swamp, remembered the humpy as 'spotless'.[14] In her memories there was no bitterness between the Aborigines and the settler families, some of whom went to the same school. But in Robert Bropho's recollection 'The barriers were always there, such as "nigger, nigger pull a trigger, bang bang bang" from the white kids. My brother Tom and my sister Ruth and I didn't last long at the school.' And it was a source of shame that on some days they had no midday meal or playlunch. Visitors from country districts would be sent back by the police to their place of origin; troublemakers were likely to be dispatched to the Moore River settlement.[15] Always liable to inspection by the police, constantly scratching for a living, the fringe dwellers were the oldest element in Claremont and the most constantly overlooked.

Not that the children in Claremont's State schools could expect much from a State Government that believed the economic crisis called for the utmost parsimony in government spending. Nothing was done about the substandard conditions in the Claremont Central School for several years. Perhaps there was insufficient pressure from the parents: the school catered for the less well-off sections of the community, and they might have lacked the time or the skills to challenge the status quo. In the 1930s the financial impact of the Depression compelled head teachers to insist that children could be admitted only from within the boundaries of their catchment area, and this may have had two effects:

families who had sought an alternative to Claremont within the State system were forced to send their children to the school nearest their home address; and some who might otherwise have chosen private education were brought back into the ambit of the government system. Thus Claremont School witnessed the appearance of a number of highly articulate parents who could voice their discontent and mobilize other parents in the same cause. In July 1933 a Parents' and Citizens' Association was formed, and its demands for a gymnasium for Claremont Infants might have been a factor in securing some long overdue renovations in 1935.[16] Even then the Infants School remained in an appalling condition, moving the Director of Education to strong words in a memo to the Under-Treasurer in 1936: 'The parents are keeping the children away from the school because they are afraid the building will fall down'.[17]

Matters came to a head in 1937 with an outbreak of diphtheria at Claremont Infants and the death of one of the five children diagnosed as having the disease. The press took up the issue of the school's condition, and the Minister for Education, Frank Wise, was besieged by letters from the Town Council, the Roads Board and residents. A hundred and twenty parents attended a highly charged meeting of the Parents' and Citizens' Association.[18] The government responded quickly to this prodding. In July 1938 two new entrance gates (sure sign of upper- and middle-class involvement) were opened by the Acting Minister for Education, and the president of the Parents' and Citizens' Association took the opportunity to invite the Minister to inspect the school and see the problems that still existed. Within a year new classrooms had been built. The *West Australian* sent a reporter to the opening ceremony, and he noted that in the previous twelve months the Parents' and Citizens' Association:

> ... had raised and spent about £120 on the school by the purchase of a piano, pictures on the classroom walls and other requirements... It was hoped by the efforts of parents...to construct a number of seats around trees in the grounds and to establish rose gardens.[19]

Self-help had achieved much, but there were still dropouts. Shortly after this effort seedlings in the rose beds were pulled out and a window broken at the school.

East Claremont Practising School felt the effects of the Great Depression profoundly. Although all schools suffered from lack of money, East Claremont lost status when the Teachers Training College was closed as an economy measure from 1931 to 1934. During this period the head teacher was E. A. Charlton, who came from a country school to take up the appointment. As the school's biographer observed, 'His predecessors were established and respected figures in the community…and parental expectations of Headmasters at Prac were very high… He set out to show that this was, after all, a quite ordinary little school.'[20] Probably Charlton had been radicalized by his war experiences. He is said to have lectured his classes on the evils of capitalism and on government failure to provide 'homes fit for heroes'. His feelings about this rather special little school, where the majority of children came from comfortable homes, can be imagined. Notably he sacked the committee of the Parents' and Citizens' Association in 1932, and it was not re-established until after the Teachers College re-opened in 1934. Once reinstated with a cultured and sympathetic head teacher, the art critic C. G. Hamilton, the association was as active as before, securing the construction of new brick latrines and writing to the Minister for Education when paintwork was required.[21]

The Mayor and Mayoress, Mr and Mrs Gustav Mengler, outside their home, 'Lumeah', on the corner of Agett and Goldsworthy Roads (*Western Mail*, 22 January 1931).

Charlton's radicalism was not a usual response in Claremont to the pressures of the Depression. Charles North, the local member, was intrigued—as were several other public men of the time, such as Walter Murdoch—by the Douglas theory of social credit, but this failed to grip the imagination of his electors. They were much more attracted by the movement for Western Australia to secede from the rest of the Commonwealth, and formed one of the strongholds of the movement. One of the first branches of the Dominion League, the body formed to propagate the cause of secession, was established at Claremont in September 1930. At a meeting in the Christ Church parish hall attended by Henry Gregory, MHR, Edith Cowan and the indefatigable Dominion League secretary, H. K. Watson, that old warhorse of Claremont civic politics, the architect Edwin Summerhayes, was elected president and the League's ideas were vigorously propagated.[22] In April 1931 the Claremont Council voted in favour of a referendum on secession, and eventually the State Government agreed to conduct it on the day of the 1933 general election.

Claremont was seen as sufficiently important for the Commonwealth Prime Minister, Joseph Lyons, to make the Princess Hall one of the three venues where he was to speak in March 1933 while campaigning for a 'No' vote. The other two speeches were scheduled for Perth and Fremantle, and at both meetings he was howled down by hostile audiences. When he came to Claremont he and his colleagues were heard in peace. But Watson pointed out that the meeting was chaired by the Mayor of Claremont, Gus Mengler, who was a secessionist, whereas the other meetings had been chaired by supporters of the Federal cause. From this he argued that the secessionists were better at running meetings even when they were giving a hearing to their opponents.

Their good manners spoke well for the voters of Claremont, who declared in favour of secession by 3,509 votes to 1,961, almost exactly the same average margin as the whole of Western Australia. It is interesting that the more affluent western suburbs such as Claremont were less strongly secessionist than populist working-class places such as Fremantle and Midland. Yet voting followed no obvious pattern. The newly married Alexandra Hasluck voted 'Yes' while her husband, Paul, voted 'No'. They reflected that they might have saved themselves the chore of going to the polls.[23]

The dying down of the secession campaign reflected the gradual improvement in the Western Australian economy. Recovery generated by the Kalgoorlie and Murchison gold industry brought about financial convalescence, and by the later 1930s unemployment had dropped below 10 per cent—an achievement that would command greater respect in the 1990s than it did in the prosperous years between.

It might have been expected that these improving conditions would have been reflected in the domestic technology of Claremont households. The Depression came just as a number of new amenities were coming to the suburb. Deep sewerage entered Claremont by stages from 1929— not before time, as the Town Council was still having trouble with pollution of the river from poorly constructed septic systems. During the summer of 1928–29 a gasometer was constructed in Alice Road (now Melvista Avenue) on the corner of Doonan Road to serve Nedlands and Claremont, but, probably for financial reasons, its benefits were not widely felt for some years. As late as 1936 the instructor at the Claremont Home Management Centre attached to the Claremont Primary School was requesting connection with the gas which 'has been laid on in the district for some time'.[24] Also in 1936 the formation of the State Electricity Commission encouraged the promotion of refrigerators, vacuum cleaners and other electrically powered household equipment.

Architects certainly expected that householders would respond to these opportunities. In 1929 the young architect Reg Summerhayes wrote:

> The equipment of a house has considerable bearing on the convenience and efficiency of the modern house. The electrical layout should be planned for convenience and utility, and for the use of the numerous labour-saving devices so popular in the house today...[25]

It may be that Perth architects, like other expert professionals, 'were aiming at altering women's lives and placing them under professional dominance',[26] as Kerryn Reiger has suggested, but if so their success was far from overwhelming.

W. St Clair Brockway, Town Clerk 1899–1907, Councillor 1909–11, Mayor 1911–12, Town Clerk 1915–22 and 1929–35 (*Western Mail*, 22 January 1931).

Although the evidence is scanty it seems that only a few of the new labour-saving devices were widely used in Claremont until after World War II, despite prolific advertising. Perhaps the continuing presence of servants, whether live-in or casual, made the new technology irrelevant to families that could afford it.

Again Goldsworthy Road may serve as an example. Until the mid-1930s labour-saving devices were apparently few. Cooking was still done on a wood stove, though in some homes a larger than average stove was used. The Tupper family in the late 1920s and 1930s had 'an excellent stove, an Instone, with an oven on each side and a firebox in the centre'. In other households a kerosene stove, 'a blue flame burner', was used. Even after gas came, in the early 1930s, a number of families purchased a gas stove but continued to use the wood stove in winter. At that time a Metters gas stove at £11 10s 0d was actually cheaper than a wood stove at £15, but installation cost around £60, so the family that replaced its wood stove with a gas appliance was making a substantial commitment.[27]

To keep food cold most Goldsworthy Road families at one time used a Coolgardie safe, although by the 1920s most had graduated to ice chests. Until the late 1930s refrigerators were regarded as luxury items. One household purchased a square Kelvinator refrigerator on legs in 1934, but another family observed that '...to run a refrigerator we would have had to rewire the house'.[28] Vacuum cleaners also seem to have been rare until the mid-1930s, partly because they were expensive but also because few homes had carpets. Most families relied on broom, mop, rag and 'elbow grease' to clean and polish linoleum, with a revolving carpet sweeper to clean rugs, these appliances often being wielded by a domestic servant. Subterfuge sometimes surrounded the purchase of a vacuum cleaner:

> I can remember our first vacuum cleaner. Never was anything bought on the 'never-never' system, but it was one of those upright vacuum cleaners and my stepmother took the plunge. In those days there were a lot of door-to-door salesmen, and she bought this vacuum cleaner from one. We think that Dad never knew that that was how it was acquired... But other than that, well nobody thought of appliances.[29]

It seems that electric irons were used in most Goldsworthy Road homes by the 1920s. They had been widely available in Perth since 1913 and were comparatively inexpensive. A number of other electric appliances were also available in the 1920s, but they tended to be 'crude, heavy and ungainly'. Most of them disappeared from the shops during the Depression, and in the late 1930s much more sophisticated versions became available. One change that did occur was that gas and electric radiators began to replace the wood fire in the sitting room from the mid-1930s.

In the 'washhouse' or laundry the pre-war wooden troughs were replaced by concrete troughs and a wood-fuelled copper, which in most Goldsworthy Road houses was replaced by a gas copper in the mid-1930s. Sarah Shaw remembered that at her Stirling Road home their practice was to soak dirty clothes overnight and soap them at the washboard on Monday mornings right up till the 1940s, when they acquired some gas appliances.[30] A few homes graduated to a round electric washing machine with a mangle or wringer in the 1930s, but this did not come for most Goldsworthy Road homes until after World War II. It was still possible to send out laundry commercially: Wing Hai's establishment continued to operate in Bay View Terrace and there were a number of less durable competitors.

Increased leisure might have allowed some women more time for tennis or bridge, but others involved themselves in philanthropic activities. Some members of the Women's Service Guild volunteered help in the Social Service department of the Perth Hospital; others went one day a week to assist elderly and other patients at a private hospital. Claremont women were also active in the infant health movement. Reiger's comments seem appropriate here:

> Some evidence does suggest that middle class women were more likely to respond favourably to the new style of infant care, partly because they had much in common in terms of attitudes and values with the scientific, professionally orientated experts... It was far more likely that the new precepts of infant care...could be carried out in a secure and comfortable home environment.[31]

Curiously, the neighbouring suburb of Nedlands was very tardy in taking up the infant health movement: it did not acquire a centre until 1937, whereas Claremont's was built in 1929. When its finances reached a low point in 1932, the committee virtuously refused to accept funding from the lotteries and instead managed to finance the centre's activities from bridge parties and other local efforts. Claremont even held functions to raise money for the annual State-wide Baby Week Appeal during the 1930s. Perhaps in Claremont, which had felt the effects of the epidemics of the 1890s, and which had a larger working-class population than Nedlands, the need for an Infant Health Centre was more apparent. Perhaps too the philanthropic gentry ideal followed by those late nineteenth century citizens who made their homes on the clifftops overlooking Freshwater Bay survived among the well-to-do women of Claremont even in the inter-war years. No less than their husbands, they provided leadership within the wider and the local community.

For women and men alike there remained the problems, in the face of limited finances, of maintaining Claremont's image as a more than ordinarily pleasant environment. 'No other suburb can boast such modern and up-to-date buildings as Claremont', trumpeted a local editor in 1930,[32] but in fact many of the shops in Bay View Terrace were past their first youth. A note of modernity was struck later in the year, when on 26 November the talkies came to the local cinema with a locally manufactured sound system. The first major feature show was *Acquitted*, starring Lloyd Hughes and Margaret Livingstone. In 1934 the cinema brightened the evenings along Bay View Terrace by displaying a neon sign—Cordin the butcher had applied for one three months earlier—and the example was soon followed.[33] By the summer of 1935–36 the street was ablaze in the evenings with the flash of red, blue and green neon advertisements along its length. No doubt the shopkeepers were encouraged by salesmen from Claude Neon, who had established their premises on the corner of Stirling Highway and Bay Road.

Claremont Council often reflected conservative middle-class values in deciding what sort of people were wanted in Bay View Terrace and its neighbourhood. Drunks, beggars and unlicensed hawkers could be dealt with by the police, but the Depression seemed to have stirred up a number of fringe religious elements, and in September 1934 the Council found itself obliged to take action against unauthorized street preachers, though it raised no objection a few weeks later when the Apostolic Church asked permission to pitch a marquee in Claremont Park from which it could conduct a tent mission.[34] Council also adhered to a moralistic view of young people's behaviour, in 1929 upholding a complaint from old Joseph Langsford and nine other citizens against Sunday tennis and in 1937 resolving that youths playing cricket in Claremont Park on Sundays were a nuisance and should be stopped.[35] Some carousing went on nevertheless. In September 1934 Walter Howson, proprietor of the Claremont baths, complained of damage by vandals, 'A number of young fellows had drifted down Bay View Terrace to the Bank corner where they had created a disturbance. They then went on through the Park towards the river.'[36] Councillors grumbled that the police had been lax.

When it came to the long-term future of the built environment, Council's touch was a shade less certain. Once the sustenance workers were back in regular employment Council paid little attention to the care and maintenance of the river beyond ineffectually deploring the occasional outbreaks of summer algae.

If Butler's Swamp appeared more frequently on the Council's agenda, this was largely because it was a breeding-place for the mosquitoes that brought troubled nights to residents north of the railway. Early in the century it had been 'teeming with wildlife', and Fred Doepel remembered it as 'a boys' paradise'.

('Girls didn't go there', he added.)[37] With the clearing of the original timber, the watertable of the swamp had risen much beyond its nineteenth century level to the extent that the high-level water mark was up by nearly a metre and a half after twenty years and the waters had spread over fences and paperbarks. The problem was increased by the diversion of stormwater outlets into the swamp.

After the war a plan had been floated for draining Butler's Swamp to provide allotments for ex-servicemen with interests in market gardening, but the idea was not pursued far. In 1914 Scotch College bought one of the original pensioner allotments from the Efford family, and during the 1920s worked to convert it into a memorial sports ground. A series of rainy seasons, notably 1926 and 1928, saw the swamp spread further, so that the grounds were regularly flooded in winter. 'Surely the powers that be will do something …', complained P. C. Anderson at the 1928 Scotch speech night. 'At present there are some 300 acres of the richest soil in WA under water—a breeding place for snails and mosquitoes… The sooner this area is drained and converted into botanical gardens the better.'[38] One or two enterprising individuals had endeavoured to counter-attack the mosquitoes by stocking the swamp with fish. Desmond Abraham claimed that his father had brought carp from Lake Monger, but this attracted thousands of shags which ate the fish faster than the fish could eat the mosquitoes. By 1933 the Council was looking at a proposal to pull out the remaining paperbarks so that the birds had nowhere to roost, but then concentrated on examining the

Harvesting at Butler's Swamp, 1931: L–R Aeneas Leonard, Henry Briggs, George Briggs, James (Dick) Leonard, great-grandchildren of John Atkinson, pensioner guard.

possibility of introducing gambusia fish, as they were said to prey on mosquitoes, but the problem remained unsolved for many years.[39]

In many ways Butler's Swamp was still redolent of the district's colonial origins. Descendants of the Atkinson family continued to live in the limestone house with its rammed earth kitchen floor and a tankstand and fowl run in the back yard. The house was lit by hurricane lamps and candles, and the children bathed in a tin tub in front of a wood fire. Wandering goats were a nuisance in the vicinity, despite a reward of five shillings for each one delivered to the local pound, and complaints about stray cattle and horses were made from time to time throughout the 1930s. Pankhurst, the dairyman, still found it necessary as late as 1938 to request permission to drove cattle through Claremont streets.[40] (Shrewd businessman that he was, he secured the contract to provide the Karrakatta Cemetery with manure for its rose bushes, an arrangement that lasted until the dairy closed in 1965.)

In counterpoint to these survivals from a rural past, Claremont was well to the fore in modernizing its traffic system as the automobile came to dominance. When the Perth–Fremantle Road was renamed Stirling Highway in 1931, it heralded the start of major upgrading along its length. Much of the time sustenance workers were used as a cheap work force, not unlike the convicts of the previous century. Some already foresaw that even the improved Stirling Highway might not be able to cope with future demands, and in 1935 a prominent citizen urged the Claremont Council to reclaim the Swan River foreshore for road-building. Fortunately either inertia or want of funds prevented the idea from going forward.[41]

Better roads encouraged the appearance of a number of private bus companies. The United Bus Company, established in 1931, plied from Claremont to Perth via Dalkeith and Nedlands, and in the late 1930s implanted itself on the memories of a generation by possessing Perth's one and only double-decker. Other lines operating through Claremont included the dark green Metro bus service from Fremantle to Perth and the rather less formal Pioneer company, whose services to the beach in summer were so crowded that men were sometimes seen standing precariously on the back bumper as the bus laboured beachwards.[42] There was also a certain raffishness about the Alpine Parlour Cars, whose passengers sat abreast in four benches across the body of the vehicle and which, because of their smaller size, always smelt strongly of tobacco smoke.

All this competition told on the popularity of the trams. In 1930 the service from Claremont railway station to

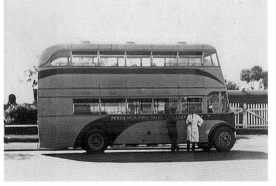

Bay View Terrace in 1927. Note the Hotel Claremont on the right, then known as McManus' Hotel.

Waratah Avenue was cut to six journeys daily, and the line was scrapped entirely four years later. The service along Stirling Highway to the city was also losing patronage. Trams did well in the inner suburbs or in shifting large crowds of passengers from football matches or race meetings, but on the nine-kilometre run from Claremont they were uncompetitively slow as against the buses or even the train. In 1936 the decision was taken to replace the tram with modern trolley-buses and to extend the service to the intersection of Congdon Street in Swanbourne, and by 1938 the trolley-buses were in operation.[43]

The new service traversed a Stirling Highway where new building was symbolizing the retreat of the Depression. Some entrepreneurs were beginning to erect modest blocks of flats, usually no more than four grouped around a central stair. In 1933 no more than sixty-two residents of Claremont lived in flats, but the Council was not sure if it approved of this trend. From 1936 Councillor Eric Gillett (later Mayor) steadily advocated the zoning of areas where flats might be built, mostly in the vicinity of Bay View Terrace and Stirling Highway.[44] A variety of public buildings also appeared. In 1934 the Lucknow private hospital, established around Alpin Thomson's former residence, moved to larger premises in

Stirling Highway, somewhat confusingly taking the name 'Lucknow' with it. In 1935 the Claremont Council chambers were enlarged and provided with a new façade. Two years later Loreto acquired a handsome Italianate chapel, complete with campanile. In 1938 Christ Church was enlarged, its rector, John Bell, proving sufficiently energetic and popular to win the necessary financial support despite the handicap of a reputation as a pacifist and social activist.

In the same year a new private school was established in Albert Street north of the Highway—St Louis, established by the Jesuit order—and work began on two substantial hotels in the art deco style favoured by architects Marshall Clifton and Reg Summerhayes: the Swanbourne in Claremont Crescent and the elegant Highway on the corner of Bay Road and Stirling Highway, which in its first two decades of existence was to achieve modest note as a smart—and for Perth even sophisticated—venue for dining out. This left the Hotel Claremont to settle more comfortably into its role as favoured pub for the working class and the sporting types.

The late 1930s were, as it happened, a time of reviving fortunes in the sporting world. The Claremont–Cottesloe Cricket Club was enjoying a successful run, winning the premiership in 1939, and the Claremont Football Club was undergoing a miraculous transformation after ten years as underdog. The recovery began in 1936 when the great George Moloney returned from five years in Victoria to serve as captain. Now a centreman rather than a full-forward as in earlier years, Moloney was not without a larrikin streak. The tale was often told of how, when Claremont visited Bunbury in 1936, he attempted to introduce a cow into the hotel bedroom of a drunken colleague, with disastrous consequences to the carpeted staircase. Under his captaincy Claremont's fortunes improved wonderfully. In 1936 the team finished the year at the top of the ladder, but was defeated in the grand final by East Perth; in 1937 they were again runners-up. With Johnny Leonard as coach, and with new recruits such as Jim Reid from

Perspective drawing of the Highway Hotel, designed by Marshall Clifton and Reginald Summerhayes and erected for the Swan Brewery (*The Architect*, vol. 1, no. 4, March 1940).

Melbourne and Johnny Compton, who 'would rather have a fight than a feed', Claremont was third time lucky in 1938. After a dead-heat grand final against East Fremantle, Claremont won the premiership in a replay and then went on to make it a hat-trick with wins in 1939 and 1940. No longer the perpetual losers, the Tigers became a source of pride and a focus of admiration even to many Claremont residents who were not normally much interested in Australian rules.[45]

Even the most meritorious of sporting achievements and even the most up-to-date improvement in building and transport around Claremont could not disguise a growing pessimism about trends in international politics. The generation that had lived through one world war uneasily read headlines in the *West Australian* and the *Daily News,* and heard news bulletins and commentaries on their new radio sets which reminded them that peace hung by a frail thread in a Europe where dictators increasingly ruled. Reactions voiced in Claremont were sometimes ambiguous. Although in 1934 the Mayor of Claremont was congratulated for an Anzac Day speech in which he spoke of the dangers of the international situation, there was considerable controversy in 1936 when the army proposed to upgrade and extend the forts at Swanbourne beach. Nervous citizens complained that the presence of the forts would depreciate property values and endanger the security of residents in time of war, and Council had to sponsor the officer commanding, Brigadier Macfarlane, to enlighten the public.[46] As the 1930s drew to a close the international horizon continued to darken. The preacher at the consecration of the new tower at Christ Church in November 1938 spoke of the need for 'substantial symbols of Christian Faith' at a time when, 'before long, perhaps, Christians might be asked to suffer persecution for the Faith'.[47] It came as no surprise when, on an evening in September 1939, in common with householders all over Australia, families in Claremont switched on their radios to hear the new Prime Minister, Robert Menzies, inform them in sombre tones that Britain and France were at war with Nazi Germany, and consequently once again Australia too was at war.

One young man whose life would be changed as a result of this war was the journalist Paul Hasluck, who, although he lived with his wife, Alexandra, in the locality now known as Dalkeith, identified with Claremont. He was to enter Australia's infant diplomatic service before graduating to politics as a supporter of Menzies, to become cabinet minister, governor general and a fine historian. To his recollections we may now turn for insight into the Claremont of the 1930s.

Claremont in the 1920s and 1930s — Paul Hasluck's View

IN 1920 THE NAME Claremont meant two things to the people who did not live there. One was the mental hospital and the other was the Royal Show.

The mental hospital stood remote from the town on the edge of the bush somewhere at the far end of a gravelled road, and I do not remember having seen even a distant view of it until I was doing my military training at the Karrakatta Camp from 1923 onwards. But, long before that, any schoolboy might hear the taunt 'If you don't look out they'll put you in Claremont'. It was generally known as the 'lunatic asylum', an expression that expressed the contemporary view of mental illness.

The Royal Show was the main reason why any boy who did not live in Claremont ever visited the place. The first show I remember was in 1917, and for years afterwards I never missed one. In those days most people went there by train, and the Claremont Railway Station was remarkable for having a big overhead footbridge, for use once a year for show traffic, in addition to the normal bridge connecting the two platforms. The crowd streamed to and from the showground along a dusty road that still had a few old jarrah trees on either side of it and never saw the town. In fact there seemed to be nothing but the showground on the north side of the line, although presumably there were some scattered houses alongside the road that led out to the 'asylum'.

My continuous knowledge of the Town of Claremont starts from about 1920, when we used to come from Perth Modern School to the Claremont Baths for weekly swimming training. In 1920 also, I sat for the Junior Examination in the Claremont Drill Hall. In 1923, when I commenced my Citizen Forces training in the 44th Battalion, I used to come regularly to the Drill Hall for night parades and, when I became an NCO, saw it even more often, for a small galvanized iron room at the rear of the Drill Hall, backing onto St Quentin Avenue, was made available as a club room for the Sergeants' Mess. In 1923, 1924 and 1925 I attended the annual camps and a number of special voluntary camps at the Karrakatta military reserve. We did our rifle shooting at the Swanbourne Rifle Range and always had to go there and back on foot, carrying our rifles and equipment. Sometimes we had to make this a formal 'route march', and went along the railway and Servetus Street; but mostly we took a short cut from Karrakatta, on the north side of Butler's Swamp, along the line of what is now Alfred Road but in those days was only a sandy track through the bush. We never passed any houses on this section of the journey.

At that time Butler's Swamp was, as I remember it, truly a swamp—one overgrown with trees. Perry Lakes and the lakes at Shenton Park and Jolimont were much the same—just patches of swampy ground. Somewhere about this time there was a rise in the watertable in the Perth region and the waters rose to form 'lakes'. Then the trees in Butler's Swamp died and it changed from a verdant place into a rather ghostly region of white dead tree trunks rising from the water.

At the same period I was seeing Claremont fairly frequently as I rode through it along the Perth–Fremantle Road—by bicycle from about 1921, by motorcycle from about 1924 and by car from about 1927. My memory is that the visible built-up area of Claremont began somewhere near the junction with Goldsworthy Road and ended on top of the Swanbourne Hill. A gap opened out when one descended into Cottesloe. There was another gap—a very marked one predominantly of virgin bush—between Broadway in Nedlands and Claremont.

In the interpretation of the history of the western suburbs it may be well to remember that, in the thinking of those days, certain institutions and services were always put in remote places. Hence we had the Infectious Diseases Hospital, the cemetery, the Hospital for the Insane and the Old Men's Home purposely out 'in the bush' away from built-up areas. Similarly the Salvation Army had what was called a 'prison-gate home' for the rehabilitation of recently discharged prisoners in the bush at the corner of Louise Street and the Perth–Fremantle Road (where the Nedlands rose garden is now) because that was an isolated spot.

In a somewhat similar way, there was a 'sanitary tip' (for the disposal of nightsoil from the pan system) located in the sandhills beyond Allen Park at Swanbourne because that also was a place where residential development was not expected to take place.

So long as the railway was the main public transport system, suburban development took place mostly within walking distance of railway stations. The cheapest land and hence the smallest houses were in the areas further from them. Throughout the 1920s and early 1930s the life of Claremont was centred on the railway station and the section of Bay View Terrace from the railway down to the Perth–Fremantle Road. The post office and the hotel were opposite the railway station. Most of the shops, two banks, the Princess Theatre (used as a picture theatre but also available for hire for other public gatherings), the Council Chambers, the undertaker's 'parlour' and various tradesmen were all in this general area.

In later years some people have wondered why the War Memorial was erected on such an awkward site as the corner of Bay View Terrace and Stirling Highway. When it was built this was the obvious place for it—in the centre of 'the village'. It was not a very busy intersection at that time because most traffic between Perth and Fremantle still went by rail.

The park behind the War Memorial and Council Chambers was always well kept and, in days when people went up to the shops or to the trains on foot, it was traversed daily by many residents and visitors. It was one of the distinctive features of Claremont. The two principal built-up residential areas of Claremont were south and east of this park around the north shore of Freshwater Bay and westward from the railway station towards Swanbourne.

I saw the eastern fringe of the Freshwater Bay area for the first time about 1918. The circumstances were that an old man was being transferred from Guildford to the Old Men's Home (afterwards called Sunset) and I had a chance of going along for a free ride with the taxi driver. We turned left from the Perth–Fremantle Road down Bay Road and then left into Victoria Avenue. The top part of Bay Road had scattered houses on the western side but the most remarkable sight was the avenue of gum trees, the predecessors of the present trees, alongside the Teachers College. I remember, too, the little day school at the corner of Princess Road, looking very much like a country school under the native trees. When we turned left into Victoria Avenue there were houses on both sides of the road but after a couple of hundred yards there was only the occasional house on the river side and virgin bush on the inland side. The road was a narrow ribbon of gravel in bad condition, with a very bad patch to negotiate at the Point Resolution corner. I cannot remember any houses being visible along what is now called Jutland Parade. I assume that there was no road fit for a motor car leading into Nedlands along the line of Birdwood Parade because we returned to Guildford the way we had come. The Old Men's Home was, incidentally, always referred to as being in Claremont.

East of the railway station and north of the Perth–Fremantle Road in the 1920s there were scattered houses, but my recollection is that there were very few east of Reserve Street. Certainly, travelling by road to Perth along the Perth–Fremantle Road there was, after one passed Loch Street, bush on both sides of the road until one came over the hill leading down to Broadway, Nedlands. On top of that hill, among gum trees, was a large iron water tank on an iron stand about twenty feet high. It was part of the metropolitan water supply scheme.

In 1921 and 1922 I was in a team from Perth Modern School that won a relay race from Fremantle to Perth that used to be conducted for senior cadets in the Citizen Military Forces. My 'lap' was from the Claremont Drill Hall, along the Perth–Fremantle Road and up Bay View Terrace to the railway station. My recollection is that after turning the post office corner at Claremont and passing about half-a-dozen houses there was nothing more to be seen until one reached the cemetery. I think the houses petered out near the showgrounds subway.

My continuous association with Claremont began in 1933 when we came to live there, first in Victoria Avenue (near the jetty) and from late in 1934 at Adams Road. At that time we still looked to the railway station as the centre of the town and the shopping area near the railway station was known as 'the village'. A tramcar ran backwards and forwards regularly between the railway station and Waratah Avenue. There was also a horse-drawn cab at the station which we used if we had something bulky to carry. The post office, the grocer, the chemist, the iceworks, the wood-yard, the hardware shop, the newsagent, the plumber, the electrician and the picture show were all up in 'the village'.

The grocery was Walkers—a family concern. They were efficient grocers who knew their trade and did their own buying of goods such as cheese, coffee, dried fruits and flour. Only a few lines were packaged in those days—tea, self-raising flour and the canned goods such as jam, preserved fruit, sardines. Most standard lines were weighed up and bagged by the grocer for each customer and hence grocery shops could vary a good deal from one another in the quality of the stock they kept. The Walker men all served in shirt sleeves and waistcoat, with an ankle-length white apron wrapped around the middle. On Monday mornings, similarly dressed, one of them called at the customer's door to take the weekly order for deliveries. Whether at the doorstep or behind the counter they would make suggestions: 'We've just cut a very good cheese' or 'the bacon is especially good—some very choice streaky'. They bought their cheddar cheese in eleven-pound loaves and stored them on the premises. It was a matter of pride that they never cut a loaf of cheese until they had let it mature in their own store for eleven months.

The butcher's shop was Cordin's, another family business, which also ran the iceworks. Most houses depended on an ice chest, and ice was delivered daily at sixpence a block. With good management a housewife could keep her ice chest cold with five blocks a week, the small residue from each day building up a large enough stock of ice to carry through the weekend. For special occasions (or for camping or parties or picnics) the householder could drive up to the back of the iceworks and load up huge blocks at eighteen pence each. There were two sorts of delivery carts used by butchers. One was a light cart for delivering orders and the other a 'cutting-up' cart—a box-like vehicle with joints and quarters hanging inside and a chopping block inside the rear door.

The chemists (Waldby's) was also a family business, run by father and son. Drabble's hardware shop was a rendezvous of all the handymen of the suburb. The shop assistants were knowledgeable tradesmen who would discuss a problem with a customer and give advice about the best way of doing a job and the best materials to use. It was a friendly place and, if occasion arose, a customer might be taken into the back of the store to be shown various materials or appliances. Mr Drabble himself was always about the place, and any customers who went there more than two or three times would be recognized and treated as a 'regular'. Another reason why it was a rendezvous was that when the Claremont Football Club was first formed, and a promising recruit had to be found a job, he often turned up behind the counter in Drabble's. George Moloney, captain of Claremont, was there for years.

On the south-west corner of the intersection of the Perth–Fremantle Road and Bay View Terrace was a branch yard of Millar's Timber Company, and this was also a common resort of suburban handymen. It had its own saw-bench and planing bench, and one could wander around, select some timber and have it lopped and dressed to one's own specifications. Below Millar's in Bay View Terrace was the local wood-yard, a one-man show. Most of the warming of houses was still done with wood fires—although the wood stove was being replaced in most kitchens by a gas or electric unit—and so almost every house in the suburb was a customer for one or two tons of firewood every winter. The rather musical whine of the circular saw, lopping the six-foot lengths of bush blocks for home delivery by a heavy horse and cart, was a characteristic sound of 'the village'. The newsagent for

practically the whole of Claremont was also in Bay View Terrace, in the same premises as the present one. I forget the name of the original owner, but somewhere about this time it was taken over by a young man named Kent, who in later years ran Albert's bookshop in Forrest Place.

The bicycle shop was notable for the 'tin man' over the front verandah. The shop itself was a jumbled sort of place with bits and pieces on the shelves as well as displays of the locally built bicycles, from racing models to the sturdy utility. There always seemed to be youngsters about there and I believe that Furniss, the owner, was regarded as something of an expert on various mechanical things. I am not sure but I think he also sold some fishing tackle, ammunition and other sporting requirements. He was certainly sought out by handymen in search of odd bits and pieces.

Going westward along the Perth–Fremantle Road from the corner of Bay View Terrace, the most notable buildings were the Drill Hall on the north side and the parish hall on the south. The parish hall was used for most social functions, being for hire both for private and public use. I can remember seeing some plays there and have a faint recollection that it was also used in the daytime for some sort of kindergarten or children's dancing lessons, but I am a bit hazy about this. At one time various bodies used to hold their weekly or monthly meetings in it.

Christ Church did not yet have its tower. At the corner of the Perth–Fremantle Road and Stirling Road was Underdown's service station. They had a very good reputation as automobile engineers, and the chief mechanic was supposed to be one of the best men in Perth at diagnosing and curing the faults in a car.

Although the population was not heavy, Claremont was a rather compact suburb compared with some of the others and, being among the older ones, its services were also relatively better developed. Water, electricity and gas were laid on. There was still a pan system of sanitation, but most houses had established their own septic tank systems. Deep sewerage was extended about 1936 and a dispensation was given to the householders who had septic systems already installed: they did not have to bear the expense of connecting with the main until after the lapse of two or three years.

We had two postal deliveries daily, one in the morning and one in the afternoon, and the staff at the post office counter were polite and attentive. There was no difficulty about getting telephones and telephone rentals were low.

Besides ice, meat and groceries, bread and milk were delivered daily. The milk round was done in the early hours of the morning by horse and cart, the horse plodding along on his familiar round while the milkman, carrying his pail, darted in and out of the houses, sometimes taking short cuts from one backyard to another. For bread delivery the baker's man came to the back door with a big basket on his arm containing a variety of five or six loaves so that the housewife could choose whether she wanted a tin loaf, twist, cottage loaf, brown or something else. None of the bread was wrapped. It was produced in local suburban bakeries, and one of the experiences of anyone coming home on a still night in the 'wee small hours' would be the fragrance of newly baked bread coming out of a bakery oven.

With this pattern of life, the coming and going of tradesmen's delivery carts was a feature of suburban road traffic. As I remember it, the conversion to motor delivery vans in the suburbs was coming in slowly about the mid-1930s. Consequently, in and around the suburbs there were still a few stables for tradesmen's turnouts. In some of the older large houses will be seen the buildings once used as a stable and coach-house for the family conveyance, but I cannot recall that any of these were still in use in the 1930s. Those who had been able to afford a horse and buggy presumably had also been among the first to acquire a motor car. By 1934 most people, like ourselves, would already have regarded a car as a necessity.

In a similar way, whereas in the 1920s one still occasionally saw windmills over a water well in the back yard, the improved reticulation of the water supply meant that by the 1930s most of those had disappeared.

Much of the life of Claremont was focused on the river. The Claremont Yacht Club was busy. There was a boathouse at the jetty where dinghies for rowing could be hired cheaply and where there was much coming and going of small craft. The jetty always seemed to be thronged with youngsters fishing also. The swimming baths were in constant use, and people came for picnics along the foreshore. One feature of summer nights was the coming and going of gaily lit pleasure boats on a 'river cruise'. There was usually music on board—nothing raucous, perhaps a piano and a mandolin and people singing. There were regular excursions run commercially, and schools, clubs and other organizations often arranged for their annual outing to take the form of hiring a large pleasure launch for a 'midnight cruise'—an expression that meant the river trip started in the evening and ended at midnight. Thus Claremont was something of a resort for people coming from other suburbs in those days, as well as affording recreation to its own residents.

There was still good crabbing and fishing in the river. A small group (perhaps three or four) of professional fishermen, who lived in huts in the little quarry at Point Resolution, used two rowboats and the usual six-foot net, and usually brought their catch in straight away after hauling the nets to the nearest beach, where a van would come down to take the catch to market. If they were fishing at the Claremont end of Freshwater Bay we could see them from our front verandah heading for the beach below the Old Depot, and often I would stroll down to watch them packing their catch. Usually three or four other householders from the neighbourhood would do the same. The fishermen counted the fish in dozens, after which they would have some odd ones left over—perhaps seven or eight mullet, some cobblers, three or four tailor, a flounder or two, some flathead. They kept some for themselves and sold the rest for a shilling or two to the bystanders.

In my experience of it, Claremont was not a separate community in any marked way but rather part of the entire suburban area. Most of us probably regarded ourselves as belonging to the whole of Perth rather than to Claremont in any distinctive way. You asked a question: Was it a divided community socially? I cannot remember that it was any different from the whole Perth community or that there was any local 'clique' or group of prominent citizens who made some sort of claim to be the leaders of local society. There was still a certain formality: when we moved into our own house in Adams Road four or five ladies from neighbouring houses left visiting cards.

Claremont was a good address but it was not a snobbish place. In later years we rather resented it when we were told that our postal address had been changed to 'Dalkeith', for we were a bit sniffy about the vulgar pretensions of the new Dalkeith housing and would have preferred to identify ourselves with the solid worth of Claremont.

Although Claremont was a mixture of small houses and bigger riverside dwellings, in the early 1930s it was essentially a place where the same families had lived in the same houses for some time and were not setting out to impress each other. It was a fairly stable place, and in our own particular neighbourhood there were very few changes of residence from year to year. It was also an orderly and quiet suburb: I cannot remember any vandalism or any worries about disorderliness or petty theft. We never thought of locking our cars.

Most houses had fences and gates and hedges behind them, but that was just the fashion of the day. The idea of removing fences started to come in shortly before the war as a new vogue. As compared with gardens today perhaps the chief difference was that more of the houses, especially the older houses, would have had a few fruit trees—lemons, figs, grapes and oranges. The change came when the Agriculture Department administered strictly the registration of 'orchards' and their inspection as part of a scheme for pest control, and it became a burden to the householder to have fruit trees. Many of us had vegetable patches in the back yard, and in our case there was some concentration on plants that were not common in greengrocers' shops, such as sweet corn, capsicum, globe artichokes, the November crop of 'new' potatoes and 'baby' carrots (i.e. those pulled when young), but we also grew tomatoes, beans, peas, passionfruit and cape gooseberries. The pattern of flower gardening was much the same as now, with rose beds, annuals and flowering shrubs.

The changes in our neighbourhood became marked from about 1934 onwards in the post-depression recovery of the building industry. Associated with this building on land previously vacant there was a marked change in transport.

Road passenger traffic between Perth and Fremantle began to increase about 1934. Vehicles called parlour cars, carrying about nine passengers each, ran frequently but as far as I remember they did not have a regular timetable. About this time a tramline was built from Broadway, Nedlands, to Bay View Terrace and, to protect tramway traffic from competition, the parlour cars were prohibited from picking up passengers along the tramway route. The same ban applied to buses when they started to run a few years later. The Dalkeith bus service, which was inaugurated by Colonel Margolin about this time, was not subject to this restriction on its roundabout run to Perth. It eventually operated three routes, all starting from the Claremont railway station and going down Bay View Terrace and along Victoria Avenue. One route was around Jutland Parade and Birdwood Parade into Bruce Street; the second along Waratah Avenue and into Bruce Street; the third along Alice Road (later Melvista Avenue), also terminating in Bruce Street. Like the parlour cars, these buses were prohibited from picking up passengers. The headquarters of Margolin's enterprise was a petrol station on the Perth–Fremantle Road at the corner of Leura Street, Nedlands, which he had run before he started the bus service.

The provision of this bus service was consequential on the housing development in the inland parts of Dalkeith and Nedlands during the 1930s. Another significant date in this connection was the opening of Edmiston's service station in Waratah Avenue towards the end of 1936. Previously there had been no through traffic along Waratah Avenue (previously called Westana Road), and residents from Freshwater Bay who drove themselves usually went to Perth either by going along Bay Road to the Perth–Fremantle Road or taking a rather tangled route along Watkins Road and the small cross streets into Princess Road and then down Vincent Street to the Perth–Fremantle Road.

The shopping centres in Waratah Avenue did not really develop to any extent until after World War II. Before this there had been since 1934 Millar's small mixed business at the western end, and at the corner of Robert Street another mixed store kept by Ellies. Somewhere about 1936 a chemist named Bodkin opened alongside Ellies.

From around 1934 I used to go horse-riding regularly by hiring horses from stables in Smith Street kept by Mr and Mrs Graham Hicks. They also had another stable in Johnston Street, Cottesloe. After mounting the horse in the Smith Street stables I would ride up Brown Street between the houses, which were much the same as they are now, but once I crossed Melville Street I was in open country. This was university endowment land and was not subdivided until the end of the 1930s. I crossed the railway by the overhead bridge (generally known as the Loch Street bridge, although it was not on the alignment of Loch Street) and rode down at the back of the showgrounds towards the asylum. There was then a choice of two routes. If I turned left, I skirted behind half-a-dozen or so houses at the end of Davies Road and was immediately in the bush between the asylum and the ocean. It was open bush all the way to City Beach, which in those days was approached only by a road continuing westward from Cambridge Street, Leederville. What is now West Coast Highway did not exist until it was constructed, mainly as a defence measure, shortly before the war. If I turned right at the asylum I rode through bush again at the back of its farm paddocks and came to Perry Lakes, which was just a swamp in the bush, teeming with wildlife, or to Reabold Hill. One remarkable feature of this unspoiled bush country was the abundance of Geraldton wax plants growing wild.

Chapter X

An Old Suburb
1940–1965

THE WAR OF 1939–45 differed in its impact on Claremont from the 1914–18 conflict. During World War I more families had a son or brother killed or wounded at the front, but there was no real sense of peril among the civilian population. World War II produced relatively fewer casualties, but as families were smaller in size it may be that the sense of bereavement was not much less widespread. In addition some families underwent the trauma of knowing that one of their number was a prisoner-of-war under the Japanese in Southeast Asia, his life at risk from privation and hardship.

What was very different about World War II was that for several months in 1942 West Australians had a lively fear of Japanese invasion. In this time of emergency considerable responsibility was thrust onto local initiative and organization by local authorities. Claremont, with army camps at the Showgrounds and Graylands, and with its location halfway between the Perth central business district and the port of Fremantle, shared to the full in these experiences.

Cathie May has written about Claremont's response to the war.[1] In its early stages, when the main threat seemed to lie with the German advance to the English Channel, it might have seemed that the second world war would be a repeat of the first, with civilian effort concentrated on giving the troops a good send-off and ensuring that they were well supplied with comforts and Red Cross parcels. But things were obviously very different when, some time later, Claremont mustered a strong local unit of the Volunteer Defence Corps, the home guard of older men, many of them members of returned servicemen's organizations with

The Returned Services
League Volunteer
Defence Force,
Claremont, September
1940.

experience in World War I, who might need to form an ultimate line of defence. By 1941, profiting from the example of British civilians during the Battle for Britain, preparations were in hand for a system of air-raid precautions, and with the entry of Japan into the war in December 1941 the situation took on urgency.

Many householders dug slit trenches in their backyards, and, although their amateurish excavation often left much to be desired, the Claremont Council did not inspect them, having more urgent priorities and serious shortages of staff. Better constructed shelters with timber lining were provided in Claremont Park and other open spaces, but a ratepayer who found himself in the less densely built-up part of Claremont north of the railway complained that during a practice air-raid warning there was nowhere to shelter. Happily, despite a brief alarm one night when an aircraft went unidentified for a time, the suburbs of Perth were not raided. Perhaps Claremont's most alarming moment came in 1941 when an earth tremor was felt, damaging one or two buildings on the Cottesloe waterfront but otherwise doing little harm.

In February 1942 local authorities were given wide powers over civil defence, evacuation and other crises which seemed all too likely in the month when the Japanese occupied Singapore and swept through Indonesia. At the same time staff and resources were much depleted. The Claremont Council attempted in April 1942 to have its accountant 'manpowered' (and thus not liable for call-up) because, as the Town Clerk explained with the unconscious male chauvinism of his generation, 'the two assistants…are female clerks and require constant supervision'.[2] He was more persuasive in saving the Council's Chevrolet truck from being commandeered, pointing out that it was in use for the collection of night-soil from the remaining unsewered parts of Claremont. Most of the businesses in Bay View Terrace were understaffed, older men, women and teenagers coping with wartime shortages. Shop windows were replaced by timber slats as a precaution against flying glass in air raids, and several businesses reverted to the horse and cart for deliveries in response to petrol rationing. Despite beer shortages, the Hotel Claremont did a roaring trade in these years, with Australian and American servicemen adding their thirsts to the normal civilian traffic. In Claremont, as everywhere in Australia, 1942 and 1943 were stressed and abnormal years.

By 1944 the Japanese and their allies were beyond doubt on the retreat, and thoughts began to turn towards planning the postwar world. In Claremont there does not seem to have been any grand concept to guide the remodelling of the suburb for the second half of the twentieth century; instead it seemed sufficient to attend to the problems of maintenance and upkeep that inevitably followed six years of wartime shortages succeeding a decade of depression. If Claremont was taking any fresh initiatives it was in the direction of providing new hospitals. In 1944 the Seventh Day Adventists acquired the old 'Lucknow' site, overlooking the river, and there established 'Bethesda', which over the next half-century was to grow into one of the State's leading private hospitals. In the same year the Silver Chain Association stretched its resources in order to purchase William George's house and land in Bay Road, converting it into the Alfred Carson Hospital for people who, through advanced age or illness, were in need of institutionalized care. Later a smaller private hospital, 'Jalon', was established on the corner of Princess and Goldsworthy Roads. Many who lived in Claremont were no longer young, and no doubt it was reassuring to have these hospitals close to hand—as also the new public hospital, the Sir Charles Gairdner in nearby Hollywood, when it followed in the late 1950s.

The end of the war in August 1945 came somewhat unexpectedly. It had been only three months since Germany and Italy had surrendered, and most commentators believed that the Japanese would resist long and stubbornly. Two atomic bombs, their awesome potential as yet barely appreciated, prompted a quick Japanese bid for peace, and on 15 August 1945 Australians everywhere poured from their homes, shops and offices to celebrate the end of the war. Many

During World War II
the old Sandover
property 'Knutsford'
was taken over for the
training of army
nurses.

joined the rejoicing crowds that surged through the main streets of Perth's city centre, but in Claremont the end of the war was celebrated with a moving and more understated ceremony. For on that day 260 former prisoners-of-war released from captivity in Europe were brought to Claremont railway station for reunion with their families. It had been one of Perth's wettest winters, but after twelve days of rain 15 August was mild and sunlit. The Western Command Band lined up on the station platform with appropriate music, and shortly after 1p.m. the train steamed into the station, where Major-General Boase, the officer commanding Western Area, stood ready to welcome the servicemen. After the formalities, scenes of quiet emotion followed. Some families such as the McAuliffes, Hausteds and Cliffords welcomed back two brothers.[3] It is not clear why Claremont was selected as the venue for this ceremony rather than Perth central station or Fremantle, but it may be that with its ample railway yards and its suburban ambience Claremont seemed preferable, especially if the authorities foresaw that access to the city might be choked by victory celebrations. Whatever the reason, this ceremony, rather than the more extrovert rejoicing elsewhere in Perth, was the highlight of V-J Day in Claremont.

Where World War I on the whole seemed to have left the residents of Claremont with a more positive self-concept, if only as a community that had done its bit in supporting the British Empire and the Anzac achievement, the social impact of World War II was rather more ambiguous. It was harder to feel enthusiastic about the presence of military camps in the area after a night in August 1944 when the Claremont Football Club's grandstand and clubrooms went up in flames. At first it was surmised that the fire was started by a casual vagrant, but as two wooden structures at the Showgrounds were set on fire on the same night, suspicion pointed to bored absentees from the military camp.[4] The exigencies of wartime had also brought some dubious elements into Claremont. It was not good for Claremont's reputation when in October 1946 a police sergeant was shot dead at the corner of Bay View Terrace and Victoria Avenue by a petty criminal arrested in a Bay View Terrace flat.[5] This was not the stable and law-abiding neighbourhood Claremont imagined itself to be.

Perhaps the aftermath of wartime told most harshly on the Butler's Swamp Aboriginal community. In the years during and after the war complaints about their brawling and misconduct increased, even among families who had formerly been sympathetic towards them. Blame for the deterioration was placed on American servicemen in search of cheap sex, who brought liquor into the community and encouraged gambling. Eventually, as a result of repeated complaints, the Nedlands Council, on whose land the community was now located, sent in a bulldozer without warning and razed the Aborigines' homes. The inhabitants were offered transport to the Bassendean Aboriginal settlement, but refused. The officials of the Department of Native Affairs thought the Council had behaved brutally and insensitively, but was within its legal rights.[6]

About the same time the old name of Butler's Swamp was discarded in favour of 'Lake Claremont', perhaps marking a recognition that postwar growth in the Claremont municipality would largely occur in the area north of the railway. Just as seventy years previously 'Butler's Swamp' had seemed too plebeian a name for the railway station serving Claremont, so it was now to be swept away entirely. Better drained and less hospitable to mosquitoes, Lake Claremont bore a name of greater promise. However the Claremont Council's attempts to induce the State Government to take over the lake as a site for botanical gardens was eventually rejected in 1962.

Graylands, the area to the north and east of the lake, developed rapidly after the war. One stimulus to growth north of the railway was the Education Department's takeover of the army camp for the establishment of a second teachers training college. Whereas only fifteen years previously the State Government had seen fit to close the original Teachers Training College at Claremont for three years because Western Australia could not afford education, it was an index of the changed conditions of the baby-booming postwar years that the demand for schoolteachers suddenly became urgent. The State Housing Commission constructed several streets of housing on land that had previously been deemed unfashionable because of its proximity to the mental hospital, and there was some private building. The hospital itself underwent a change of name, becoming divided into two sections: Graylands and Swanbourne. Thus after nearly half a century Claremont rid itself of the burden of being a byword for insanity, but only at the expense of its newer and less fashionable neighbours.

Graylands was to symbolize more than schoolteachers and mental illness. In the late 1940s the Commonwealth Government set out, with no great fanfare, to revolutionize Australian immigration policy by drawing migrants from other than the traditional sources, Great Britain and Ireland. Thousands of refugees from the power politics of Nazi Germany and Soviet Russia, the original 'displaced persons', would be admitted with an obligation to work for two years wherever labour shortages made them essential. Later, reassuringly for those who feared the dilution of the British connection, migrants from the United Kingdom were encouraged between 1951 and 1971 by the offer of passages to Australia for £10, provided they remained for at least two years. Later still, during the 1950s, even more migrants would be admitted from every part of Europe and eventually, belatedly, the White Australia Policy would crumble and new Australians would be recruited from all over the world. In the first years of assisted immigration accommodation had to be found for the new arrivals, and in 1947 an area of 7.2 hectares of former army land was set aside for the Graylands Migrant Hostel.

About 350 people could be housed in the camp, the accommodation consisting at first of makeshift structures from army disposals. Conditions were spartan, as Nonja Peters describes them:

> The floors were bare boards. Being unlined, without ceilings, and open at the eaves, these wooden, tin-roofed corrugated iron huts were unbearably hot in the summer and freezing cold in the winter. There were no heating appliances…canvas screens separated each bay and loose hessian flaps covered the front and acted as doors. A hessian flap was also hung in front of the female latrines…[7]

With the advent of the £10 British migrants in 1951, Graylands graduated to prefabricated hemispherical Nissan huts. These lasted until 1967, when they were replaced by more substantial brick and tile buildings.

Although poorly served by public transport in its early years, the Graylands Migrant Hostel contributed new elements to the shopping population that frequented Bay View Terrace. At first there were 'Balts', displaced persons from Eastern Europe whose presence was fairly inconspicuous. Then came the English

Nissen huts under
construction at the
Graylands Migrant
Hostel, 1951.

migrants, many of them probably looking in vain for the kind of small cosy pubs they had left behind in their former High Streets. For continental Europeans the Australian streetscape seemed even less familiar. Then, in the later 1970s and 1980s, Chileans and other Latin Americans, Taiwanese and Vietnamese made Graylands their first staging-post in Australia.

Most of the migrants stayed only a few months, though one English family is believed to have lived at Graylands for seven years. Very few settled in Claremont. Even as late as 1971 Claremont's population was overwhelmingly Anglo-Celtic in ethnicity, with a handful of Dutch-born and hardly any southern Europeans. The Graylands migrants were transients who were, for the time they were around, absorbed easily enough into the Bay View Terrace streetscape, which until the 1960s had changed very little from its pre-war appearance.

In the 1950s Bay View Terrace seemed a suitable main street for a comfortably ageing community, the one concession to modernity being the installation of traffic lights at the Stirling Highway corner in 1956. Many of the businesses were long established: pharmacists Edith Jacobson and Doug Waldby, Whittle's newsagency at the corner of Stirling Highway and Bovell's pie and cake shop all served their customers long and well. Many valued these continuities. 'We have had the same chemist, same bootmaker, same greengrocer, same grocer for fifteen years', wrote one satisfied commentator as late as 1972.[8] Yet this comfortable

conservatism may have masked a certain stagnation. Arthur Hardman, who was tailoring on Bay View Terrace for forty years from 1934, thought when he arrived that 'Claremont was a poor little town, wouldn't keep a tailor',[9] and the shops and houses were ramshackle. Business was brisker after the war, but he still considered Claremont a sleepy old town, and very provincial, its shops tacky with rotten wood and falling apart. In his recollection there was not much social contact between businessmen, and this implied that they seldom bestirred themselves to act as a civic pressure group.

Many still found their social centre in the corner shops. These were enjoying their Indian summer in the late 1940s and 1950s before the competition of chain stores and modern shopping centres drove them out of business. Most notable of all was the one run by John Hedges, an ex-serviceman who in 1947 put his deferred pay into a shop in Princess Road opposite St Aidan's Church, where for nearly thirty years he became, as one customer put it, 'locally famous: he presides over the entire neighbourhood with paternal care'.[10] Open for twelve hours daily, his shop stocked everything from lollipops to lawnmowers. There was no Mrs Hedges, and he apparently devoted his life to the service of his customers despite the affliction of damaged vocal chords which reduced his conversation to a hoarse whisper. He always delivered to the elderly, and even gave them unsold goods rather than have them go to waste. He visited many of them regularly to ensure that they were well, helped with their gardening and did odd jobs such as plumbing. On one occasion he came out at midnight to repair a fuse wire for an elderly customer who would otherwise have passed the night in darkness.[11] But he was not a soft touch. When a young fellow came into the shop one evening and demanded money with menaces John Hedges simply picked up his broomstick and pursued the miscreant down Princess Road.

It will be noted that many of Hedges' customers were elderly people in need of a handyman. Claremont in those years gave the impression of an ageing suburb. After the immediate postwar burst of growth in Graylands and elsewhere had taken the town's population beyond 8,500, numbers became static, fluctuating during the next forty years between eight and nine thousand while the rest of Perth trebled in size. Nor was it simply that the last of the founding generation of Claremont identities was passing away. (Sydney Stubbs died in 1953 and J. W. Langsford in 1957; the builder Samuel Rowe survived until 1974, but by then he was the oldest man in Western Australia.) Reflecting this ebbing of civic dynamism, Claremont was deprived of its own seat in the Legislative Assembly in 1968 and has since been divided between Cottesloe and Nedlands. It could be observed also that Claremont's increasingly staid image in those years was reflected in a lack of the sporting success that marks a youthful community. The Claremont–Cottesloe cricket team went without a premiership between 1939 and 1965; the Football

1898   1948

HIS WORSHIP THE MAYOR AND COUNCILLORS
OF THE MUNICIPALITY OF CLAREMONT

request the pleasure of the company of

at an

Official Dinner Party

TO BE HELD AT THE HIGHWAY HOTEL, CLAREMONT
ON TUESDAY, 12TH OCTOBER, 1948, AT 8 P.M.

IN CELEBRATION OF THE 50TH ANNIVERSARY OF THE FOUNDING OF THE MUNICIPALITY

R.S.V.P. BY 28TH SEPTEMBER
TO TOWN CLERK, CLAREMONT   DRESS OPTIONAL

Club, disheartened by the destruction of its clubrooms, experienced twenty years from 1944 in which it never managed even to reach a semi-final. Perhaps all this contributed to the impression of Claremont as something of a backwater.

This is not to say that it was a malfunctioning suburb, or that it had lost its capacity to provide many of its residents with a sure sense of belonging and well-being. These were years of full employment and modestly but consistently growing affluence. As elsewhere in Australia, Claremont residents acquired their first cars or traded them in for newer and larger models, purchased their black-and-white television sets when these came on the market in 1958, took the opportunity of holidays in the eastern States or overseas on retirement and crossed their fingers whenever they thought of an international situation where the Cold War was only gradually giving way to the more sensational and less lethal competitiveness of the exploration of the moon and beyond. The benefits of life in an established suburb such as Claremont were often underestimated. In 1946 an English scholar wrote with deplorable gender bias but considerable insight: 'In the suburb each man can see his own handiwork... To some extent he can feel responsible for his own environment and thus get a sense of controlling his destiny.'[12] These words might have been written of the Claremont of the 1950s, as might Douglas Stewart's poem 'Fence', written about the same time:

Fence must be looked at; fence is too much neglected;
Most ancient indeed is fence; but it is not merely
White ants' and weather's ravage must be inspected,
The broken paling where we can see too clearly
The neighbours at their affairs, that larger hole
Where Hogan's terrier ate it, or very nearly;
But fence most quintessential, fence in its soul.

For fence is *defensa*, Latin; fence is old Roman
And heaven knows what wild tribes, rude and unknown,
It sprang from first, when man took shelter with his woman;
Fence is no simple screen where Hogan may prune
His roses decently hidden by paling or lattice
Or sporting together some sunny afternoon
Be noticed with Mrs Hogan at nymphs and satyrs;

But fence is earthwork, *defensa*; connected no doubt
With *fossa*, a moat; straight from the verb to defend;
Therefore ward off, repel, stand guard on the moat;
None climbs this fence but cat or Hogan's friend.
Fence is of spears and brambles; fence is defiance
To sabre-toothed tigers, to all the world in the end,
And there behind it the Hogans stand like lions.

It is not wise to meet the Hogans in quarrel,
They have a lawyer and he will issue writs;
Thieves and trespassers enter at deadly peril,
The brave dog bites the postman where he sits.
Just as they turn the hose against the summer's
Glare on the garden, so in far fiercer jets
Here they unleash the Hogans against all comers.

True it is not very often the need arises
And they are peaceable people behind their barrier;
But something is here that must be saved in a crisis,
They know it well and so does the sharp-toothed terrier.
They bring him bones, he worships them deeply and dankly,
He thinks Mrs Hogan a queen and Hogan a warrior,
Most excellent people, and they agree with him, frankly.

The world, they feel, needs Hogans; they can contribute
To its dull pattern all their rich singularity;
And if, as is true, it pays them no proper tribute,
Hogans from Hogans at least shall not lack charity.
Shielded by fences are they not free to cherish
Each bud, each shoot, each fine particularity
Which in the Hogans burgeons and must not perish?

It is not just that their mighty motor mower
Roars loudest for miles and chops up the insolent grass,
Nor that the Iceland poppies are dancing in flower,
Nor the new car all shiny with chromium and glass,
Nor the fridge and TV, nor that, the bloom of their totem,
Their freckled children always come first in the class
Or sometimes at least, and never are seen at the bottom;

It is all this and so much beside
Of Hogans down the ages in their proud carriage
And Hogan young and Mrs Hogan a bride
And napkins washed and babies fumbling their porridge,
Things which no prying stranger can know or feel —
All locked in the strange intimacy of marriage,
Which by all means let decent fences conceal.

So let us work, good neighbour, this Saturday morning,
Nail up the paling so Hogans are free to be Hogans
And Stewarts be Stewarts and no one shall watch us scorning
And no one break in with bullets and bombs and slogans
Or we will stand guard at the fence and fight as we can.
World is against us, but world had had its warning;
Deep out of time is fence and deep is man.

But the 1950s passed, and then in 1962 the Cuba crisis, without a third world war to threaten the security of the suburbs. By the early 1960s the Claremont community was ready to take its first steps towards modernization.

At a distance of more than thirty years it is difficult to identify the turning-point, but a hint of change could be detected in the early 1960s. One portent could be seen in the initiative of Claremont Rotarians, who in 1962 organized a fair in Claremont Park for charitable purposes. It was so successful that the

Rotary Fair soon became an annual event in the local calendar. It was usually held in summer at the end of March. Over twenty local service organizations came to participate, and thousands of dollars were raised for such causes as cancer relief, the heart appeal and the local hospitals. The long dearth of sporting achievements came to an end. In 1964 the Tigers surprised themselves and their supporters by winning the premiership, and in 1965 the Claremont–Cottesloe Cricket Club followed this example, aided by a new coach in the English bowler Tony Lock and promising youngsters such as Graham MacKenzie, Laurie Mayne and Barry Shepherd, who all went on to represent Australia internationally in test cricket.

Cultural activities flourished along with sport. Although the Claremont High School (as the old primary, then central, school had become) was closed in 1958 to make way for a larger successor at Hollywood, it was replaced in 1964 by the Claremont Technical College, initially a centre for commercial studies but soon to specialize in another direction with a Diploma of Fine Art course. With lecturers including Robin Phillips, David Gregson, Hans Arkeveld and Leon Pericles, the College for more than thirty years proved 'a spirited place', stimulating not only the work of many West Australian artists but also the foundation of several local commercial galleries.[13] Surviving the onslaught of economic rationalists through the establishment of the Claremont School of Art Foundation in 1981, the institution at last succumbed in the late 1990s, though its traditions of creative energy were still diffused throughout the community.

Claremont during the 1960s also attracted a number of creative writers, to the extent that the suburb attained the dignity of an entry of its own in the *Oxford Companion to Australian Literature*. 'Lucy Walker' (Dorothy Lucie Sanders) wrote a number of popular novels based at 'Pepper Tree Bay', a thinly disguised picture of the Claremont – Peppermint Grove area where she had grown up—in the rectory at Christ Church.[14] The poetry and novels of Nicholas Hasluck drew partly on experiences of boyhood around Freshwater Bay, whereas Elizabeth Jolley's novels *The Newspaper of Claremont Street* and *Mr Scobie's Riddle* were set around the older streets of the suburb. The *Oxford Companion* quoted Jolley's elegy on the large old gentry houses 'now divided into tiny flats and risking demolition':

> Some day, they too would be pulled down and the big old trees, Norfolk Island pines, Moreton Bay fig trees and the gigantic mulberries in the old gardens, would all be bulldozed and burnt and cleared away. New houses in Spanish or Mediterranean style would take their place, together with the two-storey town houses with white walls and red tiles, built in squares around car parks...[15]

Other notable writers living in Claremont included Fay Zwicky and Peter Cowan.

Young abilities were encouraged through the initiative of Joan Pope, who in 1965 organized a Festival for Children, from which developed the Children's Activity Times Society (CATS), a boon to parents during school holidays when youthful energies needed diversion into creative outlets. Originally supported by Claremont families, CATS expanded to draw in children from the entire Perth metropolitan area. Children interested in drama could also spend Saturday mornings at the Rectangle Theatre created by Peter Parkinson, architect of The University of Western Australia's Octagon Theatre, and his wife, Helen. A rejuvenated Claremont was becoming an enlivening environment.

Young professional families—academics, lawyers, scientists—began to move into the suburb. The conventional wisdom, as expressed by the veteran manager of The University of Western Australia's bank, held that no house with a corrugated iron roof would fetch more than $15,000, and that ruled out many of Claremont's late Victorian and Edwardian survivals. Those who had witnessed the revival of old suburbs in Sydney or Melbourne, and those who valued an

New residents moving into Claremont in the 1970s valued the remnants of Claremont's past, this store being at 29 Bay Road. Photograph by Michal Lewi.

environment less stereotyped than the conventional brick-and-tile of postwar suburbia, were not easily persuaded.

New blood began to find its way into the ranks of the Claremont Council. In 1963 Victor Garland, soon to become local federal member and then cabinet minister, and 'Jock' Morrison, great-grandson of Claremont's founding godfather, became councillors, neither of them out of his twenties. In 1969 they were followed by an even younger Bob French, later to become first Chief Justice of the National Native Title Tribunal, and in 1971 Thelma Strauss became the first woman elected to Council. 'Claremont', editorialized a local paper in 1963, 'is recovering its prestige as the one-time model residential suburb of the Capital.'[16] In the heady decades of expansion and development that awaited Western Australia and its capital, Perth, it was not easy to foretell the impact of this growth on Claremont or the collective wisdom with which these challenges would be met. Some of the feel of Claremont at this time is communicated by George Seddon, a scholar with a rare discerning eye for the physical and human environment, who bought into Victoria Avenue in 1963.

Claremont in the 1960s — George Seddon's View

In the early 1960s we bought a house in Claremont near the river for £10,000. We didn't have ten thousand pounds, so we borrowed nine thousand as a mortgage with the Colonial Mutual Life, and somehow managed to persuade our bank manager to lend us the deposit. He was not at all keen, not because we should have saved up the deposit first, but because it was an old house, built in 1896, and the banks did not like to lend money on old houses. That it was near the river was its only good point in his eyes. Our university colleagues also thought it was odd, mainly on the grounds that it was so far out. Most of them lived in Myers Street, just south of the University, or Monash Avenue, just to the north, in university housing let at very low rentals. There was no *need* to own a house, and anyway they were all too busy reading Grantley Dick-Read and doing the exercises for natural childbirth. The area was known as Fertility Row.

But we found the Nedlands environs of the University bleak, as was most of that suburb. Nearly all the houses were built shortly after the war, and they looked raw. So did the gardens: in the 1960s few had wells, and almost no-one was reticulated. There were no deliveries of trailer-loads of peat and all the soil improvers, and trees came in small pots, so gardens were slow to establish in the sand. Now parts of Dalkeith, full of mature trees, are gracious with greenery generous enough to hide generally mediocre architecture. Those houses now appearing that look like stage sets straying from *Gone With The Wind* were quite unthought of: red-brick Californian bungalows with Wunderlich tile roofs were the mode.

Claremont, by contrast, looked settled. We felt comfortable in Claremont. There was an abundance of mature trees, for which there is no substitute, including the great avenue of sugar gums down Bay Road—still there—and those in College Park and the generous grounds of the Teachers Training College. My son went to primary school there, in a little one-man, one-room schoolhouse that was a component of the Claremont Practising School. It was called the Rural School, run by Mr Mews, who knew his job and taught it to trainees who would go to small country schools. There were six classes together, and they got on splendidly and happily.

There was what is now called 'a good social mix' in Claremont: people of different ages, different occupations and economic standing, young and old, well-to-do and struggling, professionals and tradesmen and clerical workers. There was a corner store within a short walk of every house in the neighbourhood, and one of them, Mr Hedges' in Princess Road, was a community focus. I celebrated him in my book *Sense of Place*. People left messages with Mr Hedges: 'If my wife comes in later, tell her…' or 'Ask around to see if anyone wants some almonds' and so on, whenever fruit trees you had in your back yard produced more than you could use yourself.

Claremont was a very safe place. No-one we knew was robbed or mugged or ram-raided. We had a Yale lock in the front door, and we generally left the key in the lock in case friends called while we were out—they might like to come in and have a beer or use the phone. But it was also a very simple place. We went to the Re Store 'over the Horseshoe Bridge' in town to get fresh-ground coffee if we were having a dinner party ('Northbridge' is a recent invention). They also had exotic things like olives in big jars.

The fruit and vegetables in Perth in the 1960s were mostly tough and fibrous— it seemed to me that the carrots and parsnips were converging towards the character of the grass trees, banksias and woody pears. One of the quantum leaps of the last thirty years is the appearance of the superb produce that now pours into 'Claremont Fresh' daily. Dependence on imported manufactured goods was total, and if anything broke down you often had to wait months to get a replacement part from 'the eastern States'. The secession movement seems to have peaked when dependence, both economic and for the supply of goods, was at its highest.

But none of this worried us in Claremont. We knew many of the people within our quarter, from Stirling Highway to the river, and we had several good friends within a block or two. We walked a good deal: to school; to the shops in Bay View Terrace up through the park; to Mr Hedges' and the deli and the Conti and the doctor's and the quiz nights in the Teachers Training College. On one occasion, Geoffrey Bolton doggedly insisted that the answer the quizmaster gave was wrong: it was about the first appointment as the governor-general of Australia. Lord Hopetoun was the GG of the *Commonwealth* of Australia, but it seems that both Fitzroy and his successor, Denison, Governors of New South Wales, had been given the titles of Governor General of *Australia* at the urging of the Colonial Secretary, although the new title was not used. Bolton would not give up. He was in our team. We were mortified. The rest of the audience became hostile. In fairness, it must be said that Bolton's concern was not that *he* be right, but that the *answer* be right. He was a lovely, unyielding witness to historical accuracy. [NOTE: Bolton's recollection is that George Seddon was quizmaster. Oral history *is* hazardous.]

We had no television in the 1960s but ABC radio was outstanding. Catherine King, Walter Murdoch's daughter, ran the best womens' program in Australia, with good speakers on major topics. We had dinner parties. Everyone had dinner parties, and every new staff member went the rounds.

Leonard and Elizabeth Jolley were among our near neighbours. The first time Elizabeth invited us to dinner she expressed the hope that we would appreciate her hand-embroidered vegetables. She was an indifferent cook, but a charming and hilarious hostess. At that time she was in the early stages of inventing herself as her best comic character. She buried our cat once: he was a very distinctive cat, all black but for a patch of white under his neck, and on the paws. We called him Oliver. Oliver used to wander, and the Jolleys knew him well as he turned up in their back yard from time to time (suburban culture at that time was at the very beginning of the move from back yards to back gardens). After Oliver had been missing from our place for a couple of days, Elizabeth came around with a long face. She had found Oliver, dead, under their back verandah. She gave him a decent burial, and showed us the grave, on which she had put some geraniums, which were the only flowers they had. She had not invited us to the burial service, however, as Oliver was a bit high, and she put him under with some alacrity. We grieved together briefly for Oliver and had a cup of coffee. That night he walked in the back door, presumably down to eight lives. We changed his name from Oliver Seddon to Oliver Sudden.

A neighbour over the back fence was another academic colleague. We had received a coveted present from Rose Skinner, who had opened the first private art gallery of any significance in Perth. There was an avocado tree at her premises in Mount Street, a rarity in the Perth of those days, and she gave us three of the stones, which we germinated. We planted one and gave the others to the two neighbours over the back fence. Ours grew vigorously and was soon fruiting prolifically. The other two were not doing so well. Then we went on sabbatical leave. When we came back we asked the tenants if they had enjoyed the avocados. 'Well, no', they said. 'A man came in one day and said "I'm the avocado man", picked them all and went away.' They described him. It was our neighbour, our enterprising academic colleague.

The neighbours on each side were colourful. To the west there was a fairly young couple, he an Australian, she Italian. They had two delightful olive-skinned shiny small boys. What was new to us was the Italian way of conducting a relationship, which was generally at full blast—screaming and yelling. Yet they seemed to get on together as well as most people.

On the eastern side there was a man in his early fifties who lived with his mother and their dog. He seemed in the pink to us, but he had retired from some modest employment—I think he had been a clerk. They spent most of their time sitting on the sunny back verandah. There was not much conversation, and what there was was conducted, very audibly, through the dog. About five o'clock most evenings, he would get up 'to go down and buy the evening paper' (we still had one in those days—The *Daily News,* with brilliant cartoons by Paul Rigby and a good column by Kirwan Ward). He would say, to the dog, 'Well, Bozo, I think we might pick up some steak for tea tonight'. There would be a short silence: Bozo would make no reply. Then mother would address the dog in plaintive tones: 'Bozo, you know I can't eat steak with my teeth'. Bozo again made no reply, but presumably negotiation had taken place: the man and dog went off to the corner store, two blocks away. After a couple of years of this, the dog died. Six weeks later, mother died and after a few more months the man sold up and left.

The store he went to was the deli next to the Conti. The Conti was 'The Continental', a two-storey pub from the turn of the century. It had a beer garden, well furnished with sixty-year-old trees and dilapidated tin chairs and tables that looked to be of much the same age. The Conti is long gone: now it is a high-rise and chic town houses. The deli was a delicatessen-cum-neighbourhood-store run by a cheery English woman from the Midlands. She had a rotisserie, which was quite the latest thing in the 1960s, and she would do a roast chicken, but you had to order it ahead. If you went down to do this, she would say 'Wait a sec till I put it in the chook book'. The deli has long gone also, replaced by an up-market restaurant, the *San Lorenzo.* My recollection is that the deli did a better roast chicken, but memory is not always reliable. A decade or so ago Alan Bond and Eileen, the lady he was married to at the time, built a house two blocks around the corner from where we used to live. The story goes that Eileen started up the restaurant because she preferred to have the kitchen separate from the house, a common custom in early Fremantle, her birthplace.

New neighbours moved into the house next door, a woman with two very small children and a globular chap who looked like the Michelin Man. Our children called him Bubbles. One day I caught my daughter, aged four, with her face pressed to a gap in the pickets of the front fence, looking at him. She said 'You're FAT'. He got his face down to her level, returned her beady gaze, and said 'And you're rude', which was quite correct. Bubbles didn't always get on well with his wife. He often had a few beers after work and would roll in about six o'clock to a household of two screaming children and a near-hysterical woman, demanding dinner. One chilly winter night at half past six he arrived home to find that she had locked the doors and windows. He banged around for a while yelling, but she didn't open up. So he took the fuses out of the fuse box on the verandah and drove off. The house, like many others at the time, was all-electric —lights, heaters, stove. Later they split up, but the house is still there.

Across the road in a big old house with river views and a verandah all around lived the McCauslands, who had been there for a long time. A rather smart young couple, Doug and Judy Thompson, moved in next door and the older residents had a few of the neighbours in for drinks one evening. Judy Thompson was complaining of the smell of decomposing algae in Freshwater Bay, which was much worse then than it is now. It was especially pungent if you had a high-priced riverside block. Mrs McCausland consoled Judy with the voice of experience: 'My dear, think of it as the smell of money'.

The smell of money permeates most of Claremont now. Not much of the old Claremont is left: just a few pockets like parts of Riley and Goldsmith Roads. The population density must have risen substantially along and near Victoria Avenue, which is full of apartments, town houses and even a couple of tower blocks. The apartments and the new housing subdivisions north of the railway have managed to balance the loss in population due to decreasing family size: according to the Australian Bureau of Statistics, there were 8,939 people in Claremont at the 1966 census, 8,885 in 1991 and 9,325 on 30 June 1994.

The shabby-genteel days we knew have long since gone. Claremont is smart; even Bay View Terrace, incredibly, is smart—a kind of suburban Via Veneto, the aroma of fresh-brewed coffee curling around the queue at the automatic teller outside the bank next door. The car parks behind it are full of Landcruisers, driven by women in their late thirties with long blonde hair and sunglasses permanently pushed up into it. Even the swamp north of the rail is now Lake Claremont, the dump is a golf course and the sand dunes around it are Mount Claremont.

Chapter XI

Modern Claremont

GEORGE SEDDON'S NEIGHBOURLY Claremont encountered new pressures as the mineral boom of the late 1960s injected a new dynamism into Western Australia's society and economy. It was not just that the demand for real estate was stimulated as newly moneyed families looked for up-market residences with views of the river in an attractively mellowed suburb. Demand also arose for forms of housing more versatile and glamorous than the homes on quarter-acre plots and the modest blocks of flats that had hitherto sufficed for suburbs such as Claremont.

As it began to look kindly on proposals for high-rise developments, the Claremont Town Council was simply following a trend already apparent in Sydney, not to mention the major cities of the United States and Canada; but it was new thinking in Perth where, until a few years previously, the tallest building in the central business district had been the ten-storey CML building, and where even a two-storey structure stood out in the suburbs.

In circumstances of some controversy, permission was granted for the erection of a ten-storey block of flats in Davies Road, east of Lake Claremont. Plain and functional in its architecture, the Davies Road block fitted a little incongruously into what was still in some respects a semi-rural environment. Concerns were raised about its social impact, but before long residents of the locality grew habituated to the presence of the flats. The long-established general store in Davies Road took on a new sophistication as a well-stocked liquor outlet. Flat-dwellers united with other householders from time to time in resisting suggestions that the authorities widen and upgrade Davies Road to form a major supplementary highway linking Claremont to the northern suburbs. Davies Road survived as a neighbourhood.

More ambitious plans for high-rise development soon followed. An eleven-storey hotel, the Sundowner, was built in Stirling Highway near the Cottesloe border. Despite its views over ocean and river it was a little before its time in hoping to attract a large tourist clientele, and it was not close enough to the sea for convenient beachgoing. The building was taken over by Anglican Homes Incorporated and in October 1975 converted into an aged-care facility with eighty-seven independent units and a hostel accommodating forty-one. The appropriate name 'Sundowner' was retained.

In 1969 the Hotel Continental, long past its glory days as a riverside resort and in latter years a little notorious for the decibels of its Saturday rock concerts, was purchased. As a preferable alternative to a new and potentially even noisier hotel, permission was given for intensive residential development, and during 1970 there arose on the site Continental Court, an eighteen-storey block of flats whose river views were planned to appeal to retirees and childless couples among the professional classes. It was flanked by Freshwater Close, a more modest grouping of town houses. Further proposals for high-rise development included an eleven-storey complex on the corner of Stirling Highway and Leura Avenue, where long ago the Hunt Club had taken afternoon tea in the grounds of Horace Stirling's 'Norfolk'. Now, under the town plan of 1970, it would become the site of a motel with shops on the ground floor, substantial convention facilities, two steakhouses and, above the eight floors of motel units, a fashionable restaurant with commanding views.

Then in 1971–72 the mineral boom subsided. This provided a breathing-space in which the Claremont Council had second thoughts. Perhaps it would not add to the amenity of the suburb if it were too much dominated by high-rise buildings; possibly the character of Victoria Avenue would be spoiled if it became a canyon of vertical residential developments vying for river glimpses. Owners of neighbouring properties had reacted critically even to the well-planned Continental Court development, and they feared more and worse high-rise. At any rate the Council almost entirely ceased to welcome proposals for such developments, leaving the Continental and the Sundowner as isolated landmarks of the late 1960s. Instead the councillors and planners began to realize that Claremont had a past worth preserving and that its present character lay in part in its mixture of the new with an old going back to the nineteenth century.

It was not possible to save many of the turn-of-the-century gentlemen's residences along the waterfront of Freshwater Bay: rating policy meant that private residents could no longer afford, in an era without servants, the maintenance and repair of these large houses. One by one they were demolished and replaced by apartments, home units and town houses planned on a scale tolerably in keeping with the surroundings. Alexander Matheson's maisonettes at the foot of Bay View Terrace were refurbished and survived, but few neighbouring buildings matched them in celebrating a hundredth anniversary.

As the number of apartment blocks and town houses increased, Claremont's population began to rise once more, to a maximum of nine thousand. This growth partly reflected the increased numbers that could be accommodated as quarter-acre blocks were utilized so as to take advantage of modern plot ratios. On those rare occasions when new land came on the market it was usually subdivided into small blocks, resulting in developments with a fairly high population density. Thus John XXIII College, formed in 1977 by the amalgamation of Loreto and St Louis, decided in 1984 to move to new quarters in North Claremont near the Graylands Hospital. This meant that the St Louis playing fields, on the south side of Lake Claremont, could become the site of an up-market retirement village, as did the grounds of the school itself. Loreto was similarly subdivided, in this case with the consequence that the last remnants of the Osborne Hotel and the 1937 school chapel were demolished—outcomes that the Council and many members of the community deplored but were powerless to prevent.[1]

Such projects, together with the release of seventy-one blocks from the Graylands and Swanbourne Hospital grounds to form St John's Wood, brought to the district newcomers who tended to gravitate to central Claremont's shops. This new population further strengthened the already strongly professional and middle-class character of Claremont, whereas working-class families, even in the Graylands area, tended during the 1980s and 1990s to sell their old weatherboard or postwar State Housing Commission residences and move elsewhere. Modern Claremont may not have replicated exactly the gentry ideals of its founder Alpin Thomson, but the middle-class values dominant since the turn of the century still flourished. Morrison's prophecy of the 1880s, that Claremont would become as South Yarra was to Melbourne and Kensington was to London, had at last been fulfilled.

Changing residential patterns were paralleled by changing retail trading. One by one the corner shops in the older parts of the suburb shut their doors, since a car-owning community no longer needed its shopping within walking distance. Even John Hedges closed down in 1975, though ahead of him lay another fifteen years of community service as councillor and eminently useful citizen. Claremont's shopping continued to be centred on Bay View Terrace, though the days had long gone by when that street was by itself enough to satisfy local needs. Most of the small shopkeepers and tradespeople yielded place to bigger competitors or new services, though a very few survived on their old sites. The Claremont Newsagency was coming close to notching up a hundred years on the same site, and the Claremont Drapery made a virtue of retaining the atmosphere of a long-established linen and manchester shop. Bovell's pie shop and bakery seemed likely to prove a third survivor, but in 1987 it was forced out by increasing rents. A few others migrated to one of the new arcades that from 1966 were opening off Bay View Terrace. One such, the neat and forthright Arthur Hardman, who had been tailoring on the Terrace since 1934, took upstairs premises in Claremont Arcade and in due course handed on a business that has survived to the late 1990s. He was an exception. The bootmaker Harry Gisnet hung up his apron and closed his shop after operating in the same premises for thirty-three years. The grocers and greengrocers went after the 1960s, when first Tom the Cheap Grocer and then Coles brought their supermarkets into the Claremont shopping area, shaping the thrust of expansion down St Quentin Avenue. The last remaining Bay View Terrace grocery, Mathesons, graduated from possession of a 'gallon licence'—which permitted the sale of liquor in bulk, but not in small quantities—into specialization as a liquor store. Where once Claremont shoppers placed their orders with a grocer who delivered, they now wielded shopping trolleys and met their acquaintances in the densely stacked corridors of a supermarket.

When Tom the Cheap Grocer succumbed to price wars in the early 1970s, the premises were taken over by Aherns, the last of the locally owned department stores. Cautious about expanding beyond its original city emporium, Aherns was establishing one of its first suburban branches in Claremont, where members of the family lived. During the next twenty-five years St Quentin Avenue expanded as part of the shopping complex. Five terrace houses surviving from the nineteenth century were demolished to make way for shops during the 1970s, and copious parking was provided. In 1983 the establishment of the Claremont Growers' Market, specializing in fresh produce, pioneered the seven-day shopping week in the suburb. The RAAF Air Training Corps moved out of its premises in the old Lucknow Hospital in 1986, taking with it the Vampire trainer conspicuously mounted on the Stirling Highway frontage, because there were not enough young men in the vicinity of Claremont interested in its activities. The property became part of Alan Bond's empire, but his fall from fortune left his plans unrealized, and in the 1990s the site saw the Times Square development.

Balancing this growth to the west of Bay View Terrace came the development of the block between the Terrace and Leura Street, though an acceptable outcome was reached only after years of controversy. The site on the corner of Stirling Highway and Leura Avenue reserved under the 1970 Town Plan for an eleven-storey motel passed to a new owner in 1979, who wished instead to build a supermarket and shopping complex. This plan was supported by the Claremont Council, which had definitely turned its face against high-rise building. (Even with an existing high-rise, the Sundowner, the Council in 1982 refused to accede to the Anglican organization's application for a six-storey annexe.) Unfortunately the motel was the only use stipulated by the plan, and the Metropolitan Regional Planning Authority was unwilling to alter the zoning because it considered that Claremont was already close to its allocated maximum of shopping space.

The Council favoured the change because it would allow the re-alignment of Leura Avenue so that it could function more efficiently as a relief road for Bay View Terrace. If this were done it would fend off an alternative plan, favoured by the Main Roads Department, to widen Stirling Highway to the east of Bay View Terrace. This proposal would have entailed the demolition of the police station and the ambulance depot, as well as the excision of a strip of Claremont Park very close to the site of the original convict depot. Main Roads argued that such an expedient would avoid the cost of relocating underground services, including a major Telecom line. The Council was not persuaded by this reasoning.[2]

From another side the Council was beset by some of the Bay View Terrace traders, who feared that the realignment of Leura Avenue would increase pressure to turn the Terrace into a mall, with consequent loss of custom. This notion had been aired from time to time ever since the completion of Claremont Arcade in 1966, but had always been rejected because it created too many problems with flow of traffic. The critics also believed that Claremont would be overprovided with shops, to the detriment of its character. One businessman predicted that the heart of Claremont would become a concrete jungle.[3] Another, however, argued that demand was increasing in Claremont. The local community, which provided two-thirds of the shopping area's customers, was increasing in size and the number of shoppers from outside Claremont was also growing. Support for this view came in a 1986 survey, which showed that 43 per cent of Nedlands residents went to Claremont for their grocery shopping.

Amid all the controversy the Council remained consistently opposed to high-rise and in favour of the Leura Avenue re-alignment. Eventually the Metropolitan Regional Planning Authority relented, and in April 1986 plans were announced for the new shopping centre. Contrary to the owner's original intentions, it contained only a small supermarket, the remainder being tenanted by a central café surrounded by two layers of speciality shops. Generous underground parking helped to alleviate the constant problem of insufficient parking space in the town centre. By balancing the development along St Quentin Avenue, the Leura Avenue complex left Bay View Terrace in its role as Claremont's 'Main

Street'. Such growth invited the criticism that central Claremont was at risk of becoming one great emporium which died outside shopping hours.

The churches that clustered within a few hundred metres of Bay View Terrace no longer loomed so prominently in the public eye. The Anglicans' Christ Church kept up a presence as church of the faith to which the largest number of Claremont citizens at least nominally belonged, and remained a favoured venue for weddings. But the Methodist and Congregational churches in Stirling Highway were found surplus to requirements when these denominations joined with the Presbyterians to form the Uniting Church. Seizing the opportunity, the Town of Claremont acquired the Wesleyan church and converted it into the Town Hall that the municipality had never previously boasted. It was officially opened by the Governor, Sir Richard Trowbridge, in October 1983.

Claremont's central business district was further enlivened in the spring of 1984 by a street parade to celebrate the opening of the Royal Agricultural Show but, although the first parade was considered successful, it failed to establish itself as an annual event. Claremont citizens seem to have been a little shy of organized merrymaking. It is probable that more togetherness was promoted by chance encounters of householders during weekends at the Brockway Road tip, until the decision was taken to close it in 1987.

It was no coincidence that at this period of accelerating change there was an upsurge of concern to preserve the historical character of Claremont. The oldest surviving building, and by now one of the oldest in the entire metropolitan area, was Mrs Herbert's schoolhouse of 1862. Its origins had so much been forgotten that many believed it to be the original convict depot. When a group of citizens persuaded the Claremont Council that the building had potential as a museum and craft centre, it secured the grant of the property from the State Government. This was in 1972, and on 12 April 1975 the restored building was ready for opening by Sir Paul Hasluck. The museum soon generated further activity such as the beginnings of a collection of historic photographs and the research in which this history has its origins, and during the 1980s oral histories of a number of veteran Claremont residents were recorded. But it was perhaps in its core capacity as a museum that the old school house made its most striking contribution to the preservation of Claremont's past.

As Claremont's small tradespeople and shopkeepers retired, the museum provided a home for their tools of trade. Early on it acquired Cordin's butcher's cart as well as the stock-in-trade of a Stirling Highway bootmaker. In 1984, when Knight the barber retired, the contents of his shop were transferred to the museum and re-assembled as a memento of those years when men went to the barber as much for the conversation and the racing tips as for their fortnightly clip and trim. In the following year, helped by contributions from three veteran Claremont families—the Efforts of Chester Road, the Abrahams of Davies Road and the Shaws of Stirling Road—the museum assembled a kitchen depicting the working environment of many Claremont women between 1900 and 1945. Its contents included a carefully restored wood stove, flat irons for use on the kitchen table, baking dishes, dinner and tea services, even a kerosene tin for the stove kindling. More than many communities, Claremont was looking after the inheritance from its working life as well as those relics conventionally classed as 'historic'. This was a useful corrective to any interpretations of Claremont's past that might stress gentility and Edwardian elegance.

The museum's supporters, particularly the first curator, Sally-Anne Hasluck, were instrumental in preserving several of old Claremont's most notable buildings. When Australia Post embarked on a policy of closing old post offices in favour of more commercially oriented sales centres, the museum's workers ensured that Claremont's Temple Poole post office was saved from destruction and adapted for contemporary use.

This group was also well to the fore in the move to save Claremont's railway station after Sir Charles Court's Government shut down passenger services on the Perth–Fremantle line in 1979. The Government justified its action on the basis that patronage of the railway had fallen steadily during the 1960s and 1970s. Ern Sladden, the last stationmaster before the closure, recalled that when he came to work at Claremont it was the heavy forklift depot for the metropolitan area before the building of the Kewdale yards, and its signal box was manned twenty-four hours a day. When the nearly century-old station was closed in 1979, Sladden was aware that 'some of the Westrail officials would have liked to put a bulldozer through it'.[4] By this time, however, enough historical consciousness had been generated in Claremont for a lively preservation movement to arise. The buildings, and with some difficulty the signal box, were scheduled for preservation. The station buildings were refurbished at a cost of $153,000, with Ron Bodycoat as consulting architect and the National Trust assisting. The stationmaster's house became offices for a local real estate firm. In 1983 approval was also given for a commercial garden centre to operate in the main station precinct, but in that year a new government came into office and pledged to reopen and upgrade the passenger rail service. Claremont station, one of the few remaining survivors from the age of steam, was once more open for commuters. This was not a usual outcome in Perth's suburbs, and suggests that by the early 1980s Claremont was developing a collective sense of itself as valuing past heritage. Bodycoat also instigated the compilation of a municipal heritage inventory, the second in Western Australia after Swan Shire and well ahead of the relevant State legislation.

Some relics of the past were beyond preserving. The Claremont baths at the foot of Chester Road had given good service for many years as a venue for school competitions and even international swimming events. But as early as 1935 there had been talk of replacing the facility with a modern one in Claremont Park. Because of cost this came to nothing, but by the 1960s the baths were no longer nearly adequate for aquatic sports, and their jellyfish-infested waters held no great charm for a generation with easy access to the ocean beaches. Trevor Nicholas, who in 1956 began more than three decades of service on the Claremont Council, made it his personal crusade to campaign for a modern aquatic centre. He later recalled that it took fourteen years of lobbying to achieve his objective. Originally the centre was envisaged as a joint venture among the western suburbs, and a site was set aside in Davies Road a little to the south of the high-rise flats. In the upshot the brunt of the cost was borne by Claremont, with smaller contributions from the State Government and neighbouring municipalities. Having been opened in November 1972, by 1984, when renovations were undertaken, the aquatic centre claimed 124,000 users. At its twenty-fifth anniversary in 1996, in a warmly appreciated compliment, the main swimming pool was named after Trevor Nicholas.[5]

The aquatic centre's success reflected changing recreational tastes. Claremont's two inheritances from the 1920s, the Claremont Football Club and the Speedway, still had their loyal following, but their days of dynamic growth were over. When the Tigers went through a period of poor performance in the mid-1970s, gate receipts fell and the Council was losing money on the maintenance of the oval. Recovery came as the team built up again with such players as Steve Malaxos and Warren Ralph, and a premiership in 1981 promised a brighter financial future. But when the Club's lease expired in 1985 the Council hesitated. Whereas it was spending $57,000 a year on upkeep, the Club had been contributing little more than half that amount. There were difficult negotiations, and at one point there seemed a serious likelihood that the Tigers might quit Claremont altogether and migrate to Floreat or even some new suburb.

Eventually the difficulties were composed, but it was not long before a fresh challenge arose with the creation of the nationwide Australian Football League and the resulting strong publicity push in favour of the new national teams—the Eagles and the Dockers. The old suburban-based clubs such as Claremont found themselves relegated to secondary status, and although the Tigers won premierships in 1987, 1991 and 1993, the crowds that found their way to Claremont Oval in the 1990s were well down on those of earlier years.

The Claremont Speedway, located in the Showgrounds, was also commanding a smaller share of the market after more than sixty years of popularity with

Friday night spectators. And increasingly it was the target of complaints from nearby householders, particularly on summer nights when a warm north-easterly wafted the roar of the motorbikes and supercharged cars across quiet suburban streets. After years of trying to enforce a strict closing time of 10.30 p.m., the Council threw its weight behind a scheme to shift the speedway to the less built up Rockingham district, south of Fremantle, whose working-class ratepayers were thought less likely to object to its presence. Traditionalists were dismayed, but by 1998 the date had been set for the move. In place of such old spectator sports, up-to-date Claremont residents were more likely to be found putting themselves through strenuous contortions at one of the generously equipped gymnasiums that set up on two or three street corners along their stretch of Stirling Highway. Nevertheless a study conducted in 1986 revealed that 62 per cent of Claremont interviewees claimed to watch or participate in some sport, the highest proportion in any of the suburbs surveyed.

'Claremont' wrote a journalist in 1983, 'is renowned for its shady avenues whose variety of trees give the neighbourhood much of its character and charm.'[6] Until a few years previously mature trees had not always been thought an asset by councillors and householders, whose highest environmental priority was tidiness. In 1966 it had taken persuasive lobbying by the Tree Society to ensure that the avenue of sugar gums flanking the Teachers College on Bay Road was scheduled for preservation. By 1983 John Oldham, a leading landscape architect, had compiled a survey which referred to that section of Bay Road as 'the finest avenue of mature eucalypts in the State, and should be treasured'. Other precincts praised for their garden-like ambience included Parker and Loton Roads in the old Glebe estate, Hammond Street and George Avenue off Bay Road, and Queenslea Drive, where one of the suburb's rare deciduous avenues bordered Christ Church Grammar School. Only Bay View Terrace, with its two rows of monotonous and unhealthy box trees, fell short of community expectations, and even this area was redeemed by the big Norfolk Island pines and lemon-scented gums of Claremont Park. In the following fifteen years civic landscaping was to build on this report.

Alertness to the aesthetic quality of Claremont's environment often surfaced on the Claremont Council during the successive mayoralties of Henry Milner (1966–72), R. E. Partington (1972–78), Bruce Houston (1978–85) and Peter Weygers (1985–97). When the State Electricity Commission attempted to prolong the life of the jarrah trunks that supported Claremont's streetlights by encasing them with unsightly steel cladding, the Council protested immediately and pressed for alternatives such as concrete. When Macdonalds sought to establish its presence on the corner of Bay Road and Stirling Highway, at a point where

East Claremont schoolchildren had to cross the busy Stirling Highway, the Council decisively knocked back the application. It was, they said, a matter of juvenile safety, but they would have known that many residents deemed Big Mac too garish to be quite a suitable neighbour. Hungry Jack's was tolerable because it was in the centre of the main shopping area. Later, when Timezone wanted to establish an electronic games parlour in a shopping arcade, strong public reaction discouraged the Council from giving approval. Again, the stated objection was that teenagers from Claremont's schools might be tempted to spend too much time and money at Timezone, but there was also an underlying sense that such establishments might be all very well in working-class or commercial precincts such as Fremantle or Innaloo, but they were somehow out of keeping in the main Claremont shopping area.

It was not always easy to defend environmental amenity. The Council vigilantly restricted the proliferation of hoardings along the railway verge, to the dissatisfaction of advertisers who complained that their billboards were obscured by trees and shrubs planted by the Claremont Council. On Stirling Highway businessmen grumbled that Claremont's by-laws were too restrictive in the matter of pylon signs, being stricter than the normal local government code. To this the Town Clerk, David Tindale, commented: 'The lack of a clutter of signs is what has prevented Stirling Highway from becoming like Scarborough Beach Road'...[7] Again it was implied that Claremont consciously sought to maintain a better-looking suburban environment than was evident in the more industrial suburbs. In 1985 Council was incensed when the Minister for Town Planning upheld an appeal by a property owner who had conducted unauthorized renovations to a Stirling Highway showroom without securing a building licence, providing enough parking or conforming with the fire regulations. Claremont disapproved of a government policy allowing developers wishing to depart from the town planning scheme to appeal to the Minister. Their anger was futile, as later ministers for planning, whether Labor or Liberal, had at best a very uneven record in supporting Claremont's attempts at good environmental management.

Stewardship of Claremont's built and planted environment had its reward in satisfied citizens. In 1986 Chris Berry, a postgraduate in The University of Western Australia's Department of Geography, released the results of a survey of attitudes in Perth's western suburbs. He reported that 54 per cent of Claremont interviewees stated that they were very contented in their suburb and 76 per cent would be 'very sorry to leave', higher figures than those returned in any other suburb. More contentiously he suggested that there existed a strong community of interest between Claremont and Nedlands (as against Claremont and Cottesloe, for instance, or Nedlands and Subiaco).[8] This gave rise to speculation that the two local authorities might consider amalgamation, restoring the old Claremont Roads Board boundaries of the 1890s, but neither side showed much enthusiasm. Their jocular rivalry went back a long way, perhaps to the beginning when the two municipalities had separated. In 1984, when Governor Gordon Reid attended his first official ceremony in Claremont, Mayor Houston commiserated with him for living in Nedlands, which had no town hall, no railway station and no football team.[9] And of course Claremont was the senior suburb.

Outside pressures continued during the 1980s and 1990s to keep the issue of amalgamation alive. To an administrative rationalist the boundaries of the western suburbs must have seemed an irritating anomaly. Six units of varying sizes and illogical shapes—Claremont, Nedlands, Subiaco, Peppermint Grove, Mosman Park and Cottesloe—covered an area no bigger than one of the fast-expanding outer suburban municipalities such as Wanneroo or Cockburn. Separated, they could not practise the economies of scale or employ the diversity of staff that a single large local government authority might encompass, but the residents of the western suburbs were comfortable with their small and accessible local authorities. They did not want to be lumped into an amorphous mass and obliged to travel several kilometres into strange territory to consult their council.

As early as 1932 a minister in Sir James Mitchell's Government had written: 'I am definitely of the opinion that there are too many districts...between Subiaco and North Fremantle'.[10] Claremont helpfully expressed willingness to take over Mount Claremont and Swanbourne, but nothing had been done when the Government lost office at the April 1933 elections. The incoming Labor Government spoke of imposing total amalgamation on the western suburbs councils, but the project soon went into the 'too hard' basket.

The matter resurfaced at intervals of about twenty years. In 1955 Claremont ratepayers were polled about a merger with Nedlands, but decisively rejected it. In 1971–72 the State Government appointed a judge to conduct an inquiry into local government boundaries, to which Nedlands made a strong submission in favour of rationalized boundaries and proposed to take over the Crawley precinct of Subiaco and the whole of Claremont. Learning that Claremont would then become merely one ward among five parts of Nedlands, the Claremont Council and ratepayers were unimpressed with the scheme, and no action was taken on the inquiry's report.

In its turn, the Liberal–National coalition that came to office under Richard Court in 1993 made an effort to rationalize local government boundaries through-out the Perth metropolitan area. Large councils were set the task of subdivision; small ones were pressured to amalgamate. Some had hoped that as Court was the local member of parliament he would be especially alert to feeling in Nedlands and Claremont. As Claremont neared its centenary in 1998 the idea emerged that a new City of Freshwater Bay might come into being, to include Nedlands, Claremont and that smallest but toughest of all municipal nuts to crack, Peppermint Grove.

What claims had Claremont to survive as an independent unit? It could not argue that it was one of the dynamic growth points in the Perth metropolitan area, although in the ten years between 1986 and 1996 its population had once more begun to grow modestly, from 8,101 to 8,805. Claremont was one of Western Australia's most elderly communities, with 18.5 per cent of the residents aged sixty-five or more, a figure exceeded only narrowly by Victoria Park in the metropolitan area and by the warm retirement communities of Exmouth and Shark Bay elsewhere in the State. These senior citizens ensured that Claremont retained its record as a community with more women than men, since the half of Claremont's citizens who were under forty were evenly balanced by gender. It was among the middle-aged and elderly that widows, female divorcees and single women predominated.

Perhaps it was for these reasons that Claremont did not figure as an out-standingly prosperous community. The median income of a household stood at $714 weekly, above the State and national average but no higher than thirty-fifth among Western Australia's 150 municipalities and little more than half the figure of $1,328 for frontrunner Peppermint Grove. In terms of home ownership Claremont stood only at fifty-seventh place, with 47.1 per cent of fully owned homes, but there were many more whose owners were paying off loans and mortgages. On the other hand Claremont's unemployment record put it among the top 20 per cent of the State. The level was no more than 5.6 per cent, and the figures for youth unemployment were consistently better than average, perhaps reflecting a high proportion completing secondary education and going on to tertiary qualifications of some kind. In short, the census revealed that Claremont remained a comfortable community whose residents were largely spared some of the social problems resulting from excess of either poverty or wealth.

Sense of community depends on more than statistics and the criteria of economic rationalism. Having begun as an independent settlement halfway between Fremantle and Perth, having been developed by civic leaders with a strong sense of the quality of community they wished to establish, and having grown into a suburb of character, Claremont tended to value its Town Council as a symbol of individuality. In recent years three trends could be discerned as perhaps posing some threat to the ambience of Claremont. One was the pressure of traffic. Another was architectural: to what extent could Claremont accom-modate changing styles and tastes in homebuilding without sacrificing its matured streetscapes and without denying all change so as to freeze into a heritage time warp? The third problem arose from the metamorphosis of Bay View Terrace and its environs from local shopping area to a sophisticated major centre attracting patronage from a wide radius.

Not that the growth of the Claremont shopping area was the main factor in traffic problems. Despite the restoration of the railway service, commuters used Stirling Highway in great numbers, and Claremont, the isthmus between Freshwater Bay and Lake Claremont, inevitably became the bottleneck where at peak hours cars slowed to a crawl and queued with more or less patience at a succession of traffic lights. At times, especially in the mornings, the problems were exacerbated by cars taking students to Methodist Ladies College, Christ Church Grammar School and Scotch College. All the obvious palliatives were tried, but the throttling of traffic flow on Claremont's major roads remained a concern, since it was caused not by increased pressure of numbers within Claremont itself but by the apparently limitless growth of through traffic.

Architecture was a more contentious issue. Whenever an old house was pulled down—and, although some were at the end of their useful lives, others might have responded to sympathetic restoration—it was a cause for regret and very occasionally for protest, but much depended on the calibre of the late twentieth century architecture that was put in its place. Some new houses were built in a pastiche of the Federation style. Others chose an idiom from a climate comparable to Western Australia's, such as Tuscan or Californian. One or two still followed the red-brick traditions of London's affluent suburbia, but they were a minority. It remained debatable whether the siting of houses and the choice of materials always showed that sensitivity to local geography and materials that George Seddon had commended more than twenty-five years previously in his *Sense of Place*.

As for Claremont's central shopping district, it was characterized in 1987 by the *Sunday Times* as a scene of 'badly parked Porsches and colour-coordinated toddlers',[11] but in practice Bay View Terrace managed for the most part to serve its role as the local village street as well as to cater for the affluent customers of restaurants, up-market gift shops and expensive boutiques. Kim's bar and outdoor–indoor cafe, supplanting an old-fashioned wine bar, pioneered a lifestyle appealing to a smart clientele. It was the scene of a legendary party on the night that *Australia II* won the America's Cup, at which Alan Bond and his crew were offered free drinks for the rest of their lives. On a later occasion Bond's fiftieth birthday party was celebrated there.

During the 1990s the built environment of the Bay View Terrace area stabilized, but at the end of the decade some controversy was aroused by a proposal to redevelop the area between Gugeri Street and St Quentin Avenue covered by Coles and Claremont Arcade. Ratepayers attracted to Claremont by its character were profoundly ambivalent about such a major change.

Probably the most contentious development of the late 1980s and the 1990s was the establishment of what became a popular nightclub in the precinct and the transformation of the Hotel Claremont from local pub to trendy meeting-place. Renamed the Continental, and more recently Redrock, its decor certainly contrasted with the late Victorian sobriety of the nearby post office and railway station. The development was accepted by those who considered that young people looking for a night out were safer walking home from Claremont than venturing into Northbridge. Unfortunately during 1996 and 1997 this argument was badly punctured by the murder of two young women, and the disappearance of a third, who had been patronizing one or other of these venues. It was not easy to exorcize the shock and dismay that these tragedies wrought in the Claremont community.

Yet, as so often in the past, Claremont's sense of identity was stamped by its environment. There were still continuities with the environment that the Nyungar had known and enjoyed, where the pensioners found themselves a living, where the professionals of late Victorian and Edwardian Claremont had tried to create a village community and where generations of children of every background had enjoyed the river and the back lanes and the trees and the sense of growing up in an established community.

So many of Claremont's pleasures were accessible to all residents that it is sometimes possible to forget the amount of good luck and good management that has gone into keeping it an agreeable environment. At the end of the Town of Claremont's first hundred years it is not possible to tell into whose hands the stewardship of its environment will pass. It is clear, however, that the managers and citizens of Claremont inherit a community in which they can continue to take pleasure and a modest pride—provided they look after it.

Notes

The following abbreviations are used in this list:

BL	Battye Library
CNP	*Claremont–Nedlands Post*
CSN	*Claremont Courier and Swanbourne News*
DN	*Daily News*
PG	*Perth Gazette*
RHSWA	Royal Historical Society of WA
ST	*Sunday Times*
WA	*West Australian*
WC	*Western Chronicle*
WM	*Western Mail*

Chapter I   Mooro and the Colonial Agitator

1 CSO 4/99, quoted R. Catomore, *Dan-Joo Together: Colonists, Convicts and Pensioner Guards* (Claremont, 1995) p. 31.
2 Butler to Colonial Secretary, 11 Feb. 1830 (SDUR/B1/19).
3 Lands and Surveys, Department of, Book 51, p. 31, 22 Feb. 1830.
4 Butler to Goderich, 28 April 1831 (SWRP/8/56).
5 *PG*, 23 Nov. and 14 Dec. 1833.
6 Jane Currie, diary 1829–1832 (BL).
7 Butler to Governor James Stirling, 18 Feb. 1832 (CSO 20/132).
8 Butler to Colonial Secretary, 16 Jan. 1833 (CSO 26/42).
9 *PG*, 1 March 1834.
10 *PG*, 18 Jan. 1835.

11 R. Pascoe, *Western Australia's Capital Suburb: Peppermint Grove* (Melbourne, 1983), p. 15.

12 Catomore, p. 53.

13 This material draws on the map 'Kau Nyungar boodjar gabbee gnarning Quobberup' (Len Collard, consultant) published by the Claremont Museum, 1997.

14 *WA*, 11 May 1912.

15 *PG*, 14 Jan. 1842.

16 *PG*, 24 July 1850.

17 Pascoe, pp. 18–19.

Chapter II   Pensioner Settlement

1 *PG*, 22 March 1850, p. 5.

2 Fitzgerald to Earl Grey, 18 July 1850 (*Convict System*, vol. 5, p. 224).

3 Gordon to Governor Charles Fitzgerald, 23 July 1850 (*Convict System* vol. 5, p. 224).

4 Bruce to Secretary at War, 14 June 1852 (*Convict System*, vol. 5, p. 224); see also F. H. Broomhall, *The Veterans: A History of the Enrolled Pensioner Force in Western Australia, 1850–1880* (East Perth, 2 vols, 1975–76) and G. C. Bolton, 'Who were the Pensioners?' in C. T. Stannage (ed.), *Convictism in Western Australia: Studies in Western Australian History*, IV (1981).

5 Bruce to Secretary at War

6 Bruce to Secretary at War

7 Comptroller General Return No. 3: General Remarks, September 1855: *Convict System*, vol. 7, quoted Catomore, p. 143.

8 Quoted Catomore, p. 152.

9 *Inquirer*, 4 Oct. 1854; Lt-Col. Hull to Commissariat, 18 Nov. 1881 (CSO 471).

10 H. C. Prinsep, *The Magistrate*, 31 Aug. 1918, p. 121.

11 Bishop of Perth (Mathew Hale) to Colonial Secretary (F. P. Barlee), 17 June 1867 (CSO Incoming Letters, Ecclesiastical, 1867, No. 3088); Catomore, pp. 171–3.

12 CO 18: Recl. No. 1664, Piece No. 165, Part II: Jan.–June dispatches, 187a.

13 Western Australia, *Votes and Proceedings of the Legislative Council*, 1877; Report of the Central Board of Education for the Year Ending 31 December 1876, Appendix III, p. 15.

14 T. Briggs, *Life and Experiences of a Successful West Australian* (Perth, 1917), p. 14.

15 M. Gibbs, 'Report on the Excavation of the Freshwater Bay Convict Depot, Claremont, July 3–14 1989 (Department of Archaeology, The University of Western Australia); *CNP*, 4 Sept. 1984.

16 G. P. Stevens, quoted in *WA*, 14 Oct. 1936.

Chapter III   The Coming of the Gentry

1 Perth Roads Board, Minutes, 26 Dec. 1872.

2 This and following details of land transactions, based on an extensive analysis of Certificates of Title, are from J. Gregory, 'The manufacture of middle class suburbia; the promontory of Claremont, Nedlands and Dalkeith within the City of Perth, Western Australia' (PhD thesis, The University of Western Australia, 1989, henceforth cited as 'Gregory'), chapter 4.

3 Western Australia, *Parliamentary Debates*, vol 2, pp. 44–50, 66.

4 This and the following response are from Governor's correspondence 3-97A, BL Acc. 392 Box 68.

5 *Herald,* 5 May 1883; *Votes and Proceedings,* 1882, p. 382.

6 *Inquirer,* 31 Dec. 1884.

7 *WA,* 2 Oct. 1885.

8 *Inquirer,* 13 Oct. 1886, also 29 Sept.; G. C. Bolton, 'Tommy Dower and the Perth newspapers', Aboriginal History, 12 (1988), pp. 79–83.

9 *Inquirer,* 5 April 1889.

10 Perth Roads Board, Minutes, 6 April 1889.

11 E. M. Goode, 'Some record of the Sandover family', 1989 (typescript held at Claremont Museum). Discussion of the original homes at the head of Freshwater Bay is from Gregory, pp. 121–2. Further information can be found in the 1996 conservation plan for Burnside's home undertaken by D. Erickson and P. Griffith for Methodist Ladies College.

12 Disraeli Bird, *WA,* 15 April 1955.

13 R. & J. Oldham, *George Temple-Poole: Architect of the Golden Years, 1885–1897* (Nedlands, 1980), pp. 87–90.

14 For a character sketch, 'Truthful Thomas', Through the Spy-Glass (Perth, 1905), p. 41.

15 *DN,* 1892, quoted in W. D. Richardson, 'The History of Claremont', 1958 (typescript held at RHSWA).

16 J. Lang, *A Living Tradition: A History of Methodist Ladies' College* (Perth, 1980), p. 35.

17 See Annual Reports of Postmaster General, Commissioner for Railways and Central Board of Education, *Votes and Proceedings.*

18 Gregory, p. 124.

19 P. Sharp & L. O'Hara, *A Goodly Heritage: Christ Church Claremont 1892–1992* (Claremont, 1992).

Chapter IV   Constable Huxtable's Village

1 Gregory, pp. 129–32.

2 Gregory, pp. 135–6. For further details see also F. W. Miller, 'A Brief History of the Claremont Congregational Church 1895–1956', pamphlet, c. 1956.

3 Gregory, p. 129.

4 Gregory, p. 132.

5 J. Carter, *Bassendean: A Social History 1829–1979* (Bassendean, 1986), chapter 4.

6 *WA,* 22 and 24 Dec. 1894. The story about Mrs Osborne was related by Theo Archdeacon, *WC,* 14 April 1923.

7 W. B. Kimberly, *History of West Australia: A Narrative of her Past together with Biographies of her Leading Men* (Ballarat, 1897), p. 201.

8 *WM,* 23 Dec. 1898; M. Vivienne, *Travels in Western Australia* (London, 1901), p. 71.

9 A. E. Williams, *Nedlands: From Campsite to City* (Nedlands, 1984), p. 65 and chapters 9–10 passim.

10 D. C. Napier, 'A Pioneer Remembers' (WA Council Week, 1981), p. 27 (copy held in Claremont Museum).

11 Goode.

12 Williams, pp. 63–4.

13 Claremont Police Occurrence Book 1896–97 (PROWA OB 1210), 14 Aug. 1897.

14 Napier, p. 29; also Claremont Council, Minutes, 24 Feb. 1903 [3388].

15 The material in the next seven paragraphs is drawn from the Claremont Police Occurrence Book 1896–97, summary by Sally-Anne Hasluck held at Claremont Museum; also Aborigines Department file 39/1898.
16 Caporn interview.
17 *WA*, 23 Nov. 1898.
18 *WA*, 15 Oct. 1898.

Chapter V Creating a Council 1897–1905

1 Western Australia, *Year Book* 1896–97, p. 43
2 *Pioneer*, 27 Feb. 1897
3 *WA*, 5 Oct. 1898
4 *Pioneer*, 27 Feb. 1897; J. McKenzie, 'The birth of Subiaco: a study of the economic, demographic, structural and behavioural development of the suburb during its formative years' (MA thesis, The University of Western Australia, 1981), p. 93.
5 *WA*, 19 Dec. 1896.
6 *WA*, 21 Dec. 1896.
7 Williams, pp. 68–9.
8 *DN*, 8 July 1898.
9 *DN*, 9 July 1898.
10 *WA*, 21 Dec 1897.
11 *DN*, 26 April 1898; also 30 April.
12 *DN*, 18 May 1898.
13 *DN* cutting *c*. 1950 held at Claremont Museum; *WA*, 15 Aug. 1899.
14 Claremont Council, Minutes, 12 Feb. 1901 [2258].
15 Claremont Council, Minutes, 29 June 1900 [1164].
16 Caporn interview.
17 Caporn interview.
18 See B. Moore, *From the Ground Up: Bristile, Whittakers and Metro Brick in Western Australian History* (Nedlands, 1987) for further discussion of this point.
19 Photograph in Claremont Museum Collection (75-24).
20 *WA*, 3 June 1899. See Gregory, chapter 6, for further discussion of real estate sales in Claremont at the turn of the century.
21 *Government Gazette*, 28 March 1899; C.-F. Swindells, 'The development of local government in the Claremont area between 1893 and 1910' (PGDipPubHist thesis, Murdoch University, 1990: copy held at Claremont Museum).
22 *Guardian*, 19 Jan 1907.
23 *WA*, 24 Feb. 1905.
24 District Inspector's Report, Jan. 1901 (Box 26).
25 Reports, 12 May and 20 Aug. 1898 (Public Health Department, unregistered correspondence 1897–1901, Box 26).
26 Alex Matheson to Claremont Board of Health, 16 Nov. 1898 (as above).
27 Constable Huxtable's report, 1 Dec. 1899, also 28 April 1900 (as above).
28 Dr W. J. Hodge, report, 27 March 1901 (Public Health Department, unregistered correspondence, Box 34, file 1475/01); Shaw interview.
29 Napier, p. 29.

30 Braddock interview.
31 *WA*, 3 Jan. 1898.
32 J. S. Battye, *Cyclopaedia of Western Australia*, vol. 1 (Perth, 1913), pp. 766–7.
33 *WA*, 19 Sept. 1898; *Guardian*, 9 May 1903.
34 *Guardian*, 9 May 1903; also, for tennis club, Claremont Council, Minutes, 12 April 1902 [2917].
35 *Guardian*, 20 June 1903.
36 J. Barnes, *The Order of Things* (Melbourne, 1990), p. 358, quoting Furphy to Miles Franklin 28 June 1905 (Mitchell Library MS 364); also p. 357.
37 National Trust of Australia, *Historical Places Assessment Form: Nyleeta* (Nov. 1992); also *CNP* 30 July 1985, 21 Jan. 1986; information supplied by Mrs Ray Oldham.
38 R. Virtue, 'Lunacy and social reform in Western Australia, 1886–1905', *Studies in Western Australian History*, I (1977), pp. 29–65; P. Best, 'A thesis on the history of Claremont Mental Hospital' (HS/PR/1314, BL).
39 *Guardian*, 6 June 1903; Claremont Council, Minutes, 26 June 1903 [32597].
40 Information Dame Rachel Cleland.
41 D. Mossenson, *A History of Teacher Training in Western Australia*, ACER Research Series No. 68 (Melbourne, 1955), pp. 8–11; Education Department file 2790/1897.
42 M. Berson, *Prac: East Claremont Practising School 1905–1985* (Claremont 1985); *CNP* 26 Feb. 1985.
43 Caporn interview.
44 *DN*, 31 August 1907; Doepel interview.
45 A. Carter, *Beyond All Telling: a History of Loreto in Western Australia* (Nedlands, 1997), chapters 8–9.
46 J. Gregory, *Building a Tradition: A History of Scotch College, Perth, 1897–1996* (Nedlands 1996) pp. 63–72. In subsequent references this book is cited as Gregory (Scotch).
47 Gregory, pp. 164–5.

Chapter VI Consolidation 1905–1914

1 Gregory, p. 191.
2 Gregory, p. 192.
3 Gregory, pp. 192–3; I. Molyneux, *Looking Around Perth* (Perth, 1981), pp. 40, 49.
4 Gregory, p. 193.
5 *WA*, 27 Feb. 1909.
6 *WA*, 13 Feb. 1909.
7 Gregory, p. 194.
8 *WA*, 31 Oct. 1908.
9 Braddock interview.
10 Gregory, pp. 299–301.
11 G. Davison, *The Rise and Fall of Marvellous Melbourne* (Melbourne, 1979), p. 138.
12 Aborigines and Fisheries Department file 1664/12; Claremont Town Council, Minutes, 1912–17 [146].
13 Battye, vol. 1, p. 563; *WA*, 1946.
14 Shaw interview.

15 Caporn interview.
16 Personal information, GCB.
17 P. Hasluck, *Mucking About* (Carlton, 1977), p. 118.
18 I. Conochie, 'Some Claremont Memories', Denmark, 1988 (typescript held at Claremont Museum), p. 1.
19 For Wilson and George, 'Truthful Thomas', *Through the Spy-Glass*.
20 Claremont Town Council, Minutes, 1912–17 [330].
21 Conochie, p. 1.
22 Doepel interview.

Chapter VII   War, Peace and the Search for Stability

1 Gregory, p. 173.
2 A. C. N. Olden, *Westralian Cavalry in the War* (Melbourne, 1921), p. 14 and pp. 12–18 generally; *WA*, 29 Oct. 1914; Sharp & O'Hara p. 41.
3 *WA*, 9 Oct. 1979.
4 C. Longmore, *'Eggs-a-Cook': the Story of the Forty-Fourth* (Perth, 1921), p. 2.
5 ibid., pp. 118, 123.
6 Banner in WA Museum (Ref. W.71/44).
7 *WA*, 17 Dec. 1916, 4 Jan. 1917.
8 Abraham, Coulter interviews.
9 Claremont Town Council, Minutes, 1912–17 [302-03]; 1917–23 [47, 53].
10 Claremont Town Council, Minutes, 1912–17 [759, 892–8]; *Western Women*, July 1917, p. 19, Sept. 1917, p. 1.
11 Claremont Town Council, Minutes, 1917–23 [36, 68, 127]; *CNP*, 28 Jan. 1981.
12 Gregory (Scotch); J. Lang, *A Living Tradition: A History of Methodist Ladies' College* (Nedlands, 1981), p. 28; A. Carnley, *Treading Lightly in Their Steps: A Pictorial History of St Hilda's 1896–1996* (Mosman Park, 1996), p. 22.
13 Claremont Town Council, Minutes, 1917–23 [155, 191, 216, 225].
14 G. C. Bolton, *A Fine Country to Starve In* (Nedlands, 1972), p. 36.
15 Walter Murdoch to A. W. Pike, 22 August 1922 (Claremont Council File No. 89, Acc. 900).
16 *WA*, 26 Sept. 1922.
17 Gregory, pp. 194–5.
18 Material in the above four paragraphs in Gregory pp. 197–200, 244.
19 Elsie Rooney, quoted Berson, p. 6.
20 Abraham, Braddock, MacLeod interviews.
21 Abraham interview.
22 *WC*, 3 March 1923.
23 Gregory, pp. 364–5.
24 Byatt, Shaw interviews.
25 Abraham interview.
26 Rose interview.
27 Gregory (Scotch), pp. 165, 202–3; *WA*, 29 Jan. 1923
28 R. Davidson, *High Jinks at the Hot Pool* (Fremantle, 1994), p. 69 and chapter V generally.

29 Analysis from Western Australia, Legislative Assembly rolls, 1930 and 1939; Gregory, pp. 444–5; Education Department, Buildings and Works file 1067/26 (Dalkeith Primary School).

30 Rowe interview.

31 Johnson interview.

32 Brommell, Male interviews.

33 Brommell interview.

34 Caporn interview.

35 *CSN*, 5 Sept., 17 Oct., 31 Oct. 1930; J. R. Rowe, 'From whence we came' (typescript held at Claremont Museum).

36 Material in these two paragraphs is taken from K. Casey, *The Tigers' Tale: the Origins and History of the Claremont Football Club* (Claremont, 1995), pp. 9–23.

37 J. Lack, 'Residence, workplace, community: local history in metropolitan Melbourne.' *Historical Studies*, 19, 74 (1980), p. 39.

38 C. Dyhouse, 'Mothers and daughters in middle class homes c. 1870–1944', in J. Lewis (ed.), *Women's Experience of Home and Family 1850–1940* (London, 1986), p. 31.

39 'College Park Tennis Club' (Claremont Roads Board file); Shaw interview.

40 Shaw interview.

Chapter VIII   Second Generation

1 R. W. Connell and others, *Making the Difference: Schools, Families and Social Division* (Sydney, 1982).

2 Gregory, pp. 385–6.

3 Report of Dr M. J. Holloway, Medical Officer of Schools, 27 April 1929, Education Department, Buildings and Works file 77/22 (Claremont Infants School).

4 Memo from Head Teacher to Director of Education, 4 Feb. 1931, Education Department, Buildings and Works file 207/25 (East Claremont Practising School).

5 Rowe interview.

6 Quoted Berson, pp. 54–5.

7 Report of Dr R. H. M. Jull, Medical Officer of Schools, 8 May 1923, Education Department, Buildings and Works file 207/25 (East Claremont Practising School)

8 Report of Dr E. M. Stacey, Medical Officer of Schools, 25 Oct. 1926, Education Department, Buildings and Works file 207/25.

9 Report of Dr M. J. Holloway, Medical Officer of Schools, 29 April 1929, Education Department, Building and Works file 207/25.

10 Carnley, pp. 22–3.

11 Interview with Mrs H. Howells, conducted by D. Deakin, *St Hilda's Bulletin*, Nov. 1987, p. 10.

12 Male interview.

13 Carter.

14 Gregory (Scotch), pp. 165, 202–3; *ST*, 4 Nov. 1928.

15 Male interview.

16 MacLeod interview.

17 Gregory, p. 335.

18 S. Morgan, *My Place* (Fremantle, 1987) p. 333.

19 Rowe interview.
20 Johnson interview.
21 Johnson interview.
22 Johnson interview; also Braddock, Joyner, Rowe interviews.
23 Rowe interview.
24 Braddock interview.
25 Johnson interview.
26 Shaw interview.
27 *CSN*, 31 Oct. 1930.

Chapter IX The Thirties

1 D. Cottle, 'The Sydney rich in the Great Depression', *Bowyang*, 1, 2 (1979).
2 Pascoe, p. 108.
3 Gregory, p. 369; Hardman interview.
4 J. Carter, *Bassendean: A Social History 1829–1979* (Bassendean, 1986), p. 173.
5 *CSN*, 21 Aug., 17 Oct. 1930.
6 Shaw interview.
7 *CSN*, 21 Aug., 3 Oct., 31 Oct., 28 Nov. 1930.
8 Claremont Town Council, Minutes, 14 Sept., 26 Oct. 1931, 13 June 1932.
9 Claremont Town Council, Minutes, 10 July, 28 Aug., 9 Oct. 1933; 24 June 1935.
10 Efford, Shaw interviews.
12 Rowe interview.
13 R. Bropho, *Fringedweller* (Sydney, 1980), p. 5.
14 Aborigines Department 283/31; Inspectors' reports, 9 June, 20 Sept. 1931, 12 Nov. 1932, 2 Nov. 1933.
15 Leonard interview.
16 Bropho, p. 9 and pp. 5–12 generally.
17 Claremont Town Council, Minutes, 14 July 1933, 27 May 1935.
18 Director of Education to Under Treasurer, 5 Dec. 1936 (Education Department, Buildings and Works file 1080/32).
19 *WA*, 15 April 1937.
10 *WA*, 26 May 1939.
20 Berson, pp. 73–4.
21 Education Department, Buildings and Works file 2162/35.
22 *CSN*, 19 Sept. 1930.
23 Bolton, *A Fine Country to Starve In*, p. 253.
24 *WA*, 24 Nov. 1928; Education Department, Buildings and Works file 139/29.
25 R. Summerhayes, 'The ideal small house: suggestions for designing', *Western Homes*, Dec. 1929, p. 10.
26 K. Reiger, *The Disenchantment of the Home: Modernizing the Australian Family 1880–1940* (Melbourne, 1985).
27 Gregory, p. 357.
28 Johnson, Rowe interviews.
29 Johnson interview.
30 Shaw interview.

31 Reiger, p. 149; Gregory, p. 367.
32 Gregory, p. 367.
33 *CSN*, 19 Sept. 1930.
34 Claremont Town Council, Minutes, 8 Jan., 26 March, 9 April 1934 and 1934–35 generally.
35 Claremont Town Council, Minutes, 24 Sept., 26 Nov. 1934.
36 Claremont Town Council, Minutes, 10 Sept. 1934.
37 Doepel interview.
38 Quoted in Gregory (Scotch), p. 152.
39 Abraham interview; Claremont Town Council, Minutes, 8 Oct. 1934.
40 Claremont Town Council, Minutes, 16 Dec. 1929, 26 July 1937, 26 April 1938; Kidd interview.
41 Claremont Town Council, Minutes, 11 Feb. 1935.
42 Shaw interview.
43 Claremont Town Council, Minutes, 6 April 1936, 12 June 1938.
44 Claremont Town Council, Minutes, 8 Oct. 1934, 18 May 1936.
45 Casey, chapter 3.
46 Claremont Town Council, Minutes, 14 May 1934, 27 April 1936.
47 *WA*, 21 Nov 1938.

Chapter X   An Old Suburb 1940–1965

1 C. May, 'The suburbs at war' in J. Gregory (ed.), *On The Homefront: Western Australia and World War II* (Nedlands, 1997), pp. 19–28.
2 May, pp. 24–5.
3 *WA*, 16 Aug. 1945.
4 Casey, pp. 56, 57.
5 *DN*, 30 Oct. 1946.
6 Aborigines Department file 283/31.
7 N. Peters, 'Arriving in the lucky country' in J. Gregory, *On the Homefront*, pp. 258–9; *ST*, 22 Nov. 1987.
8 G. Seddon, *Sense of Place* (Nedlands, 1972) p. 257.
9 Hardman interview.
10 Seddon, p. 257.
11 *CNP*, 29 Jan. 1985.
12 J. M. Richards, *The Castles on the Ground: the Anatomy of Suburbia*, 2nd ed. (London, 1973) p. 34.
13 J. Hugo, *A Spirited Place: 25 Years at the Claremont School of Art 1968–1993* (Claremont, 1993).
14 Pascoe, pp. 140–2.
15 P. Pierce (ed.), *Oxford Literary Guide to Australia* (Melbourne, 1990) pp. 453–4, citing E. Jolley, *The Newspaper of Claremont Street* (Fremantle, 1981) pp. 19–20.
16 *Claremont–Nedlands Observer*, 15 May 1963.

Chapter XI   Modern Claremont

1 The Loreto Chapel bell tower was later reconstructed in Northbridge in 1992, from the original architectural plans and, supposedly, from the original bricks.
2 *CNP*, 25 Sept. 1984, 29 April 1986.
3 *CNP*, 24 Feb. 1982
4 *CNP*, 25 Sept. 1984; also 28 June 1982, 18 Sept. 1984.
5 *News Chronicle* 10–13 Dec. 1996.
6 *CNP*, 9 Aug. 1983.
7 *CNP*, 28 Aug. 1984.
8 *CNP*, 22 April 1986.
9 *CNP*, 18 Sept. 1984.
10 J. Lindsay to Nedlands Roads Board, 18 July 1932 (copy in Claremont Town Council archives).
11 *ST*, 8 Nov. 1987.

Bibliographical Note

Most of the materials cited in this book are held in the collection of the Claremont Museum. Among other sources the undermentioned were of most use:

Books and Articles

BERSON, M. *Prac: The East Claremont Practising School 1905–1985* (Claremont, 1985)

BOLTON, G. C. 'Tommy Dower and the Perth newspapers', *Aboriginal History*, 12 (1988)

BRIGGS, T. J. *Life and Experiences of a Successful West Australian* (Perth, 1917)

HASLUCK, P. *Mucking About* (Carlton, 1977)

MOSSENSON, D. *A History of Teacher Training in Western Australia* (Melbourne, 1983)

PASCOE, R. *Peppermint Grove, Western Australia's Capital Suburb* (Melbourne, 1983)

SEDDON, G. *Swan River Landscapes* (Nedlands, 1972)
— *Sense of Place* (Nedlands, 1973)

WILLIAMS, A. E. *Nedlands: From Campsite to City* (Nedlands, 1984)

The following works of fiction reflect background and atmosphere:

JOLLEY, ELIZABETH *Mr Scobie's Riddle* (Ringwood 1983)
— *The Newspaper of Claremont Street* (Fremantle 1981)

Any of the works of Dorothy Lucie Sanders ('Lucy Walker'), particularly the Pepper Tree Bay series.

Newspapers and Periodicals

These files have been consulted selectively but not exhaustively:

Claremont Community News (current)
Claremont Courier 1930
Claremont–Nedlands Post (current)
Daily News 1882–1900
Herald (Fremantle) 1867–1886
Inquirer (Perth) 1840–1901
Morning Herald (Perth) 1896–1908
Perth Gazette 1833–1874
Sunday Times (Perth) 1897–current
West Australian 1885–current
Western Australian Parliamentary Debates, 1876–1889; new series 1890+
Western Australian Votes and Proceedings

Oral History Sources

The following oral history interviews by Denise Cook and Jenny Gregory were used as source material for this book:

(i) Battye Library, Oral History Collection

Denise Cook:
Desmond Abraham (OH 1774)
Esmee Byatt (OH 1777)
Arthur Hardman (OH 1778)
Anne Leonard, née Kidd (OH 1775)
Dorothy MacLeod (OH 1780)
Sarah Olive Shaw (OH 1776)
Gladys York (OH 1779)

(ii) Claremont Museum

Alex Doepel (9 March, 16 March 1988, 23 February 1989)

Jenny Gregory:
Lisle Braddock (July 1986)
Malcolm Brommell (April 1986)
Roy Caporn (July 1986)
Frances Johnson, née Tupper (July 1986)
Jim Joyner (July 1986)
Florence Male, née Broadhurst (April 1986)
Jack Rowe (July 1986)

Councillors and Mayors

Adam, K. A.	1975–1977	
Airey, D. C.	1974–1976	
Anthony, R. E.	1990–1993	
Balfe, M.	1997–	
Barrett, A.	1898–1899	
Barrie, N.	1984–1985	
Beart, E. J.	1905–1907	
Bennett, W. E.	1922–1926	
Bentley, R. J.	1995–1997	
Birkbeck, G. F.	1938–1951	
Boon, E. W.	1990–1991	
Breakey, N.	1999–	
Briggs, T. J.	1898–1899	
	1901–1902	
	1903–1907	
	Mayor 1907–1909	
Brockway, W. St C.	1909–1911	
	Mayor 1911–1912	
Bulloch, J. A.	1907–1910	
Burke, R. A.	1971–1975	
Butterly, V. S.	1979–1982	
Byrne, G. F.	1994–1997	
Caporn, W. H.	1947–1953	
Carter, P.	1994–1996	
Carter, T.	1932–1938	
	1939–1945	
Chambers, F. W.	1899–1900	
	1901–1907	
	1910–1913	

	1921–1922	
Chapman, R.	1904–1909	
	1914–1918	
Cherry, W.	1919–1923	
Clarke, D. P.	1982–1987	
Clarkson, M. W.	1932–1935	
	1936–1939	
	1939–1944	
	1945–1946	
Connett, A.	1956–1964	
Cooling, M. C	1919–1920	
Cox, A. E.	1922–1924	
Cox, R. J.	1919–1920	
Creswell, J. S.	1951–1968	
Crommelin, H. W.	1953–1963	
Crooks, A. W.	1930–1932	
	1933–1939	
	1941–1953	
	Mayor 1953–1966	
Daskein, J.	1899–1902	
de Castilla, J.	1898–1899	
Denny, M. P. M.	1989–1994	
Dethridge, W.	1911–1915	
Dewar, D. J.	1918–1920	
	1921–1922	
	1924–1927	
Deykin, S. C.	1996–1999	
Drabble, W.	1910–1913	
	1921–1923	

Drake-Brockman, A. B.		
	1916–1921	
Easton, R. A.	1985–1994	
Eaton, S. V.	1913–1916	
Edwards, C. J.	1986–1989	
	1999–	
Fitzpatrick, P. J.	1898–1901	
Foreman, H. J.	1927–1936	
	1948–1951	
Frank, C. A.	1936–1939	
	1952–1953	
French, R. S.	1971–1974	
French, S. S.	1981–1983	
Garland, R. V.	1963–1970	
Gardner, G. A.	1965–1970	
Giambazi, C. M.	1982–1988	
Gilham, F. A.	1934–1940	
	1940–1941	
Gillett, E. W.	1935–1940	
	Mayor 1940–1953	
Gralton, P.	1970–1973	
	1974–1986	
Grave, J.	1898–1899	
Hammond, J.	1907–1911	
Hankinson, F. W.	1913–1914	
	1915–1916	
Hardy, H. T.	1904–1911	
Harney, E. A.	1898–1899	
Harrison, C. E.	1916–1918	

Index

Pages listed in **bold type** indicate a photograph.